The Philosophical Basis
of Inter-religious Dialogue

The Philosophical Basis
of Inter-religious Dialogue:
The Process Perspective

Edited by

Mirosław Patalon

CAMBRIDGE
SCHOLARS
P U B L I S H I N G

The Philosophical Basis of Inter-religious Dialogue: The Process Perspective,
Edited by Mirosław Patalon

This book first published 2009

Cambridge Scholars Publishing

12 Back Chapman Street, Newcastle upon Tyne, NE6 2XX, UK

British Library Cataloguing in Publication Data
A catalogue record for this book is available from the British Library

ISBN (10): 1-4438-0164-X, ISBN (13): 978-1-4438-0164-5

TABLE OF CONTENTS

Introduction
Mirosław Patalon 1

Whitehead on Religion: A Philosophical Basis for Inter-religious
Dialogue?
Santiago Sia 5

Between Ecstasy and Eschatology: Immanence, Transcendence,
and the Metaphysics of Process
Jonathan Weidenbaum 22

Religious Experience in William James and Whitehead
and the Question of Truth
Helmut Maaßen 46

Inter-religious Dialogue: By Whom, For What Purpose or:
How to Overcome the Clash of Religions
Louwrens W. Hessel 60

Inter-religious Dialogue and Religious Pluralism: A Philosophical
Critique of Pope Benedict XVI and the Fall of Religious Absolutism
Matthew Lopresti 66

'The Contrasted Opposites' in Nishida and Whitehead
Hiromasa Mase 95

Buddhist 'Śunyata' and Christian 'Kenosis': An Attempt
of Comparison on the Ground of Whitehead's Metaphysics
Bogdan Ogrodnik 100

The Purpose of Human Existence and the Meaning of Immortality
in Daoism
Romualdas Dulskis 109

The Truth Propagated by Mahatma Gandhi as a Base of Strong
Dialogue between Religions
Mariola Paruzel.. 121

The Dialogue as a Precondition for the Freedom of Belief
and as Prerequistite for the Christian Inculturation: The Experience
of the Bulgarian Orthodox Priests after 1989
Petar Kanev.. 131

Discursive Construction of the Subject and Inter-religious Dialogue
from the Perspective of Process Theology
Mirosław Patalon 138

Confessions 2008
Minoru Inada.. 152

What New Insight Gives Us Wilber's Integral Philosophy/Psychology
in Understanding the World?
Przemysław Koberda and Urszula Stodolska-Koberda........................... 160

On Mystic Experiences of Saint Hildegard of Bingen
Magdalena Otlewska.. 169

The Meaning of Heart in Christian and Indian Mystics
in the Philosophy of Boris Vysheslavtsev
Marta Kuty 175

INTRODUCTION

MIROSŁAW PATALON

In the present epoch of tensions between civilizations, challenges being brought by globalization processes and the necessity of the coexistence of various cultures and traditions, the subject of inter-religious dialogue seems to be particularly significant. Can religions remain isolated islands? Are their claims of being the only source of theological truth justified? Or should it rather be understood as an effect of interaction between different points of view and common effort of looking for the answers to the questions about God and his relations to the world? What is the role of dialogue? Is it only a politically correct element or maybe something more essential – the basis of reasonable existence and development of religion? Should the direction traced by 20th century's partisans of ecumenical movements be widened in order to embrace also non Christian religions? What is the orthodoxy and where are its boundaries?

These are some topics discussed during the international conference that was held in Katowice, Poland in May 2008, organized by The Whitehead Metaphysical Society in Poland, Franciscan Seminary OFM in Katowice, The Pontifical Academy of Theology in Cracow, and the Institute of Philosophy at University of Silesia. The process philosophy creates a convenient and favorable atmosphere for this kind of considerations. The articles selected for this book represent different points of view of the discussed topic. At the conference we were honored to host scholars from Lithuania, Hungary, United Kingdom, The Netherlands, Japan, Bulgaria, USA, Germany, and Poland. We hope that the variety of approaches will be beneficial not only to the scientific discourse but also will influence the social relations in Poland. The book is addressed to all who deal with the inter-religious dialogue: both clergy and laymen as well as scholars and students interested in the subject.

In the first paper in the collection, *Whitehead on Religion. A Philosophical Basis for Inter-religious Dialogue?*, Santiago Sia considers the essence of religion in connection with culture, pointing out to the various definitions of religion. The author analyses this issue in light of the writings of Alfred North Whitehead whose broad understanding of religion, not confined to the sphere of dogmas and rituals, is particularly helpful in today's reality of the secularized Western world. A confrontation with the most important, the most profound and the ultimate is only possible when one decides to challenge the existing tradition and cultural paradigms. Thus achieved solitariness, according to Whitehead, is the foundation of religious experience, though it need not manifest itself in a *stricte* religious activity. In addition, Sia shows how Whitehead goes beyond Cant's understanding of religion (seen, in the first place, as the source of morality) by relating it closely to metaphysics – conceived of not as an irrational image of the non-material world but as knowledge of the general and, at the same time, a determinant of everything that happens in the world.

In his paper *Between Ecstasy and Eschatology. Immanence, Transcendence, and the Metaphysics of Process*, Jonathan Weidenbaum deals with the issue of diverse religious experience among various confessional groups, isolating two main types thereof: mysticism and faith. The former aims at uniting a human being with the Absolute while the latter at submitting in everyday life to a god conceived of in personal terms. In the perspective of interreligious dialogue, the author – following John B. Cobb and David Ray Griffin – considers a possible harmonization of both attitudes, which may become a significant step in achieving mutual understanding between the respective traditions. Does Whitehead's philosophy of organism enable harmonization of this kind by providing it with epistemological coherence? Do the rational and the irrational, the scholarly and the religious, the physical and the spiritual complement and stimulate one another within its confines? These are some of the basic questions posed by Weidenbaum.

In the article *Religious Experience in William James and Whitehead and the Question of Truth* Helmut Maaßen examines Jamesian concept of experience in relation to the epistemological assumptions of process philosophy. Louwrens W. Hessel in the article *Inter-religious Dialogue. By Whom, For What Purpose or: How To Overcome the Clash of Religions* argues that "there is no philosophical basis for inter-religious dialogue, but philosophy is indispensable for minimising derailments and for preventing stagnation". Accordingly Matthew Lopresti in his text *Inter-religious dialogue and Religious Pluralism. A Philosophical Critique of Pope Benedict XVI and the Fall of Religious Absolutism* deals with the incompatibility of different views of reality. He asks if it is "possible to hold an absolutist view of the truthfulness of one's own traditions and still engage in an open inter-religious dialogue with other religions?"

Hiromasa Mase in the paper *The Contrasted Opposites' in Nishida and Whitehead* juxtaposes the thought of the founder of the Buddhist Kyoto School with the views of Alfred North Whitehead regarding the relationship between transcendence and immanence. The meaning of the category of *emptiness* and *kenosis* is discussed in the context of the Christian-Buddhist dialogue. A similar purpose is pursued by Bogdan Ogrodnik, the author of *Buddhist 'Sunyata' and Christian 'Kenosis': An Attempt of Comparison on the Ground of Whitehead's Metaphysics.*

From a viewpoint of a Christian theologian, Romualdas Dulskis analyses selected doctrines of Daoism in his paper *The Purpose of Human Existence and the Meaning of Immortality in Daoism*, thus looking for stimulation for a deeper understanding of his own religion, particularly as regards salvation and immortality. Mariola Paruzel in her paper *The Truth Propagated by Mahatma Gandhi as a Base of Strong Dialogue Between Religions* deals with the problem of morality, considered as a very important platform of understanding between religions. In her view it is the quality of human life, rather than the set of accepted dogmas, that is a true determinant of dialogue. The author examines both the views and behaviour of Mahatma Gandhi, presenting specific suggestions regarding education in the spirit of mutual respect and development. That is because religion, with its open questions and hypotheses, is capable of dynamizing culture, as long as its adherents are willing to challenge the existing stereotypes and paradigms.

Petar Kanev in his paper *The Dialogue as a Precondition for the Freedom of Relief and as a Prerequisite for the Christian Enculturation. The Experience of the Bulgarian Orthodox Priests after 1989* presents a survey of an empirical study conducted among the clergy of the Eastern Orthodox Church in Bulgaria with respect to tolerance and openness to other religious traditions as well as research regarding the Christian-Muslim relations in Bulgaria. Likewise, Mirosław Patalon's *Discursive Construction of the Subject and Inter-religious Dialogue from the Perspective of Process Theology* presents a report from empirical research regarding openness to theological variance, conducted among religion teachers of various confessions in Gdańsk.

In *Confessions 2008*, Minoru Inada against the background of historical Christian creeds presents a specific view of religion from the perspective of contemporary scholarship, concluding that "the lamps are different, but the Light is the same." Przemysław Koberda and Urszula Stodolska-Koberda in their text *What New Insight Gives Us Wilber's Integral Philosophy/Psychology in Understanding the World?* present the basic thesis of Ken Wilber's thought trying to find it's application for the dialogical co-existence in today's world. The last two papers in the collection, *On Mystic Experiences of Saint Hildegard of Bingen* by Magdalena Otlewska and *The Meaning of Heart in Christian and Indian Mystics in the Philosophy of Boris Vysheslavtsev* by Marta Kuty, focus on the significance of mysticism as inspiration for contemporary ecumenical dialogue.

WHITEHEAD ON RELIGION: A PHILOSOPHICAL BASIS FOR INTER-RELIGIOUS DIALOGUE?

SANTIAGO SIA

Introduction

Although inter-religious dialogue has been occurring for some time and in various forms, in our times it has been precipitated by a number of events, not all of which can be described in positive terms. Nonetheless, it is something that we should welcome as a step in the right direction and work towards making it more fruitful.[1] At the same time, conscious of the sensitivity and complexity of the situation, we need to engage in the dialogue in a spirit of mutual respect.

Inasmuch as the theme of this conference of the Whitehead Metaphysical Society in Poland is "The Philosophical Basis of Inter-religious Dialogue", I should like to focus on Whitehead's philosophical notion of religion. My aim is to discuss selected insights in his philosophy with a view to showing how they can provide some kind of philosophical basis and incentive for inter-religious dialogue. In developing the topic of this paper, I will first discuss A.N. Whitehead's notion of religion. Since a fundamental concern in the dialogue among religious believers is the competing claims to the truth of the beliefs of the different religions I will then examine his understanding of the origin and status of religious beliefs.

---

[1] In his *Lights of the World: Buddha and Christ* (Dharmaram Publications, 1997), Ninian Smart shows how inter-religious dialogue between Mahayana Buddhism, Hinduism, Islam and Christianity is not only possible but also can bring about harmony to human civilization while preserving the distinctiveness of the religious traditions. As I see it, the purpose (or expected outcome) of such a dialogue—as I explained in response to Stanislaw Krajewski at the conference—can also simply be that engaging in dialogue is itself something beneficial for all parties concerned. As Martin Buber in his philosophy of dialogue shows, the reality of the "in-between" transforms both parties of the dialogue.

The Notion of Religion

Given the complexity of its meaning and use, the term "religion", requires some clarification first. It is not surprising that Wilfred Cantwell Smith would question the validity and the helpfulness of the concepts "religion" and "religions". Because the concept of religion in the West has evolved and because religion itself has been reified, he claims that these concepts are not only unnecessary but also much less serviceable and legitimate than they once seemed. [2]

A popular illustration of this complexity can be seen in discussions as to whether Buddhism should be regarded as a religion insofar—at least as generally understood—it does not believe in a transcendent god. Compounding that difficulty of classifying Buddhism as a religion is the fact that there are different kinds of Buddhism.[3] Again, as is well known, there has been some claim that Marxism, because of its demands on its followers, is a religion except in name. Additionally, the sophistication of the more established religions such as Christianity or Islam has led at times to the suspicion that native religions found in Africa or Asia are nothing more than superstitious beliefs—to the annoyance of those who regard them as genuine, if undeveloped, religions. More recently, we have been faced with the rise of what are labeled as "cults" rather than religions despite the fact that in some cases their present development appears to parallel the early stages in the growth of the more established religions.

The existence of many general interpretations of religion leads John Hick in his book, *An Interpretation of Religion*, to opt for dividing them into "naturalistic", i.e. religion as a purely human phenomenon, or "religious", i.e. confessional. In contrast to these two groups Hicks offers what he considers to be a theory of religion that is not confessional but one that acknowledges its plurality of forms. Focusing on belief in the transcendent, he bases his interpretation on "a family-resemblance understanding" of religion.[4] Likewise, the variety of competing definitions of religion and the difficulty of judging their correctness cause Peter Clarke and Peter Byrne to turn to the "family resemblance definition" of religion

---

[2] Wilfred Cantwell Smith, *The Meaning and End of Religion: A Revolutionary Approach to the Great Religious Traditions* (London: SPCK, 1978), 121.
[3] In his *Pure Land Buddhism: Historical Development and Contemporary Manifestation* (Dharmaram Publications: 2004) Kenneth K. Tanaka gives a historical and theological account of Pure Land Buddhism, a form of Buddhism that is less known outside Asia compared to Zen or Tibetan forms.
[4] John Hick, *An Interpretation of Religion: Human Responses to the Transcendent* (Basingstoke: Macmillan, 1989).

as a looser, more informal mode of definition. They believe that there can be no finality in the definition of religion because the phenomenon of religion keeps developing as illustrated by the New Religions, which have disclosed fresh insights into the relationship between religion and our present culture.[5] The "family-resemblance understanding or definition" of religion can be useful in stressing the commonality amidst the diversity of religions. At a time when inter-religious dialogue is particularly called for, such an understanding of religion can help set the appropriate context. It is also important in distilling what is essential in the different religions.

Whitehead's Understanding of Religion

Whitehead's account of religion is contained principally in his *Religion in the Making*. But this is complemented by shorter discussions in *Science in the Modern World, Adventures of Ideas* and other writings. Commenting on Whitehead's discussion of religion, John Cobb notes that Whitehead depended heavily on secondary sources with which he had limited familiarity. Nevertheless, he adds that Whitehead's discussion is valuable not only because it throws light on his philosophy but also because he develops his understanding of the relationship between philosophy and religion, a point that should be of particular interest to us at this conference.[6] Cobb also observes that Whitehead was not really preoccupied with religion, despite returning to this topic again and again. Whitehead's attention was more focused on what have become known as penultimate questions. But religion remains in the background, securing the importance of these questions; however, it is rarely itself at the centre of the stage.[7] Thus, it seems even more worthwhile to explore his conception of religion further.

A well-known definition of religion by Whitehead is "what the individual does with his own solitariness".[8] He states that the essence of religion is to be discovered, not in public dogmas, practices, or institutions, but in confrontation with "the awful ultimate fact, which is the

---

[5] Peter B. Clarke & Peter Byrne, *Religion Defined and Explained* (Basingstoke: Macmillan/N.Y.: St. Martin's Press, 1993).

[6] John Cobb, Jr., *A Christian Natural Theology: Based on the Thought of A.N. Whitehead* (London: Lutterworth Press 1966), 216.

[7] Cobb, *Christian Theology,* 223. Bogdan Ogrodnik had made a similar observation at the conference.

[8] Alfred North Whitehead, *Religion in the Making* (Cambridge University Press, 1926), 17; also, 47.

human being, consciously alone with itself, for its own sake."[9]   This association of religion with solitariness will no doubt strike many as highly suspect and therefore unlikely to be of much help to us after all. Indeed in an article developing this definition of religion, Donald Crosby observes that Whitehead's description of religion has been frequently quoted and usually disparaged. However, he argues—and I agree with him—that it is seldom understood in anything like the way Whitehead intended.[10]

One of the misconceptions of Whitehead's definition of religion is that he is championing an individualistic interpretation of religion, which seems to contradict the teaching of many an established religion. Admittedly, Whitehead does place great importance on individuality insofar as he maintains that religious consciousness does not arise until one has risen above what he calls "communal religion", that is, beyond the stage in one's development that is informed by the myths, collective rituals, emotions and beliefs of one's society. As Whitehead puts it, "The moment of religious consciousness starts from self-valuation."[11]   One becomes "religious" when one stands out as an individual, breaking out of the confines of the traditions and mores of inherited culture. One needs to loosen the strong grip of tradition upon oneself, thereby removing the sense of being at the mercy of arbitrary power.[12] Only then will that individual be confronted with the concerns which are of utmost importance and depth. Only then will he or she become aware of the inadequacy of social custom and authority to answer the most fundamental of questions and be forced to turn elsewhere. Stripped of one's sense of belongingness, experiencing solitariness, one begins to ask: "What, in the way of value, is the attainment of life?"[13]   One discovers then one's uniqueness rather than one's society as the focus and source of freedom and value. For Whitehead religiosity, it would seem, really stems from the exercise of one's individuality, particularly as experienced in solitariness.

It is important, however, to contextualise what Whitehead says regarding solitariness. Although Whitehead does stress that religion is primarily individual, the solitariness that one experiences is due to the detachment

---

[9] *Ibid.,* 16.
[10] Donald A. Crosby, "Religion and Solitariness," in: Lewis Ford & George Kline (eds.), *Explorations in Whitehead's Philosophy* (New York: Fordham University Press, 1983), 149.
[11] Whitehead, *Religion in the Making*, 59.
[12] *Ibid.,* 39-40.
[13] *Ibid.,* 60.

from one's immediate surroundings. This in turn leads one to search for something permanent and intelligible to throw light on one's immediate environment.[14] Religion expresses, according to Whitehead, "the longing of the spirit that the facts of existence should find their justification in the nature of existence."[15] The detachment or disconnection from immediate surroundings is thus a prerequisite for "the emergence of a religious consciousness which is universal, as distinguished from tribal, or even social."[16] Whitehead in fact sees a close connection between solitariness and universality. Although the moment of religious consciousness starts from self-valuations, as we have noted already, "it broadens into the concept of the world as a realm of adjusted values, mutually intensifying or mutually destructive."[17] Whitehead denies that there is such a thing as absolute solitariness: "Each entity requires its environment. Thus man cannot seclude himself from society… But further, what is known in secret must be enjoyed in common, and must be verified in common."[18]

Elsewhere Whitehead describes religion as "the reaction of human nature to its search for God."[19] Whitehead does not believe human nature to have a separate function which could be regarded as a special religious sense. Nor does he hold that religious truth is something other than the highest form of knowledge, which had been first acquired with our ordinary senses and then developed by our intellectual operations. As he puts it succinctly, "religion starts from the generalisation of final truths first perceived as exemplified in particular instances."[20] What follows then is the amplification of these truths into a coherent system and the amplification of them to the interpretation of life. This interpretation serves as the criterion for the success of these truths. Although in this manner religious truths can be judged like any other truth, they are peculiar in that they explicitly deal with values. By this claim Whitehead means that religious truths make us conscious of what he calls the "permanent side of the universe which we can care for". In this way

---

[14] *Ibid.,* 47.

[15] *Ibid.,* 85.

[16] *Ibid.,* 47.

[17] *Ibid.,* 59.

[18] *Ibid.,* 137-138. It should also be borne in mind that in Whitehead's metaphysics "relatedness" or "the social" is more fundamental and inclusive than individuality.

[19] Alfred North Whitehead, *Science in the Modern World* (Cambridge University Press, 1926), 266.

[20] Whitehead, *Religion in the Making,* 124.

religion enables us to discover meaning in our own existence against the
background of the meaning of the wider scheme of things.[21]

   Inasmuch as Whitehead's description of religion as "a human reaction"
involves knowledge, it invites comparison with Plato's. Plato, it will be re-
called, regarded religion as the culmination of the search for truth. Plato
differentiated and distanced his conception of religion from the more anthropomorphic versions, which were prevalent in his time. In contrast,
Whitehead, while regarding "communal religion" with its myths, practices
and beliefs as merely a stage in the development of religious consciousness,
nevertheless prefers to discuss religion in the context of what he refers to
as "the great rational religions". For him these religions are "the outcome
of religious consciousness which is universal, as distinguished from tribal,
or even social".[22] Furthermore, Whitehead's definition needs to be
qualified by what he says elsewhere; namely, that the immediate reaction
of human nature to God is worship.[23] In this sense it is much closer—and
further removed from Plato—to Charles Hartshorne's conception of
religion as essentially worship by which Hartshorne means "devoted love
for a being regarded as superlatively worthy of love". Hartshorne
maintains that what distinguishes true religion from primitive ones is the
worshipful attitude which it inspires.[24]

   Whitehead sees an intimate link between life and religion.[25] In fact,
Whitehead claims that "justification" is the basis of religion. By
justification he means that one's character is developed according to one's
faith. For him this is the preliminary inescapable truth. As he puts it,
"Religion is force of belief cleansing the inward parts."[26] Consequently, he
maintains that sincerity is the primary religious virtue. In terms
reminiscent of Kant, Whitehead holds that even the doctrinal side of religion, i.e. the system of general truths, will transform one's character so long
as these truths are sincerely held and vividly apprehended. Religion also

---

[21] *Ibid.*
[22] *Ibid.,* 47.
[23] Whitehead, *Science in the Modern World,* 192.
[24] See, among others, Charles Hartshorne, *A Natural Theology for Our Time* (La
Salle, III: Open Court, 1967). I have discussed this point in some detail in *God in
Process Thought: A Study in Charles Hartshorne's Concept of God* (Dordrecht:
Martinus Nijhoff, 1985), 9-18.
[25] At the conference, Louwrens Hessel asked whether the link between religion and
life in Whitehead's philosophy would include attention being given to poverty,
discrimination, deprivation and so on. In response, I explained that in process
thought, because of its connection with metaphysics (which is understood as a
generalised interpretation of every experience), this means an affirmative answer.
[26] Whitehead, *Religion in the Making,* p. 15.

promotes the transformation of society through its moral energy.[27] On the other hand, unlike Kant, Whitehead also maintains that while religion is valuable for ordering one's life, conduct is merely an inevitable by-product. It is not the mainstay of religion. In fact, the overemphasis on rules of conduct can be detrimental to religion. What should emerge from religion is individual worth of character. But Whitehead warns us that worth is positive or negative, good or bad. Thus, in a rather startling observation, but perhaps a more realistic one, he points out that religion is by no means necessarily good and therefore that it may be evil.[28] Along similar lines Hartshorne, who describes human beings as fragments of reality, maintains that our reaction to that fragmentariness is what characterises our religion. Our religion is good if we accept our relative insignificance in the best possible way, poor or non-existent if we close our eyes to this situation. We could persuade ourselves into thinking that our limitation in space and time is only of slight importance; or we could consider ourselves the centre of the universe, with everything else revolving around us.[29]

Whitehead's conception of religion also clearly establishes its link with human thought not only because of his constant recourse to the word "rational" but also because of his distinction between religion and mere sociability. Religion, he says, emerges from ritual, emotion, belief, and rationalisation. But it is only when belief and rationalisation are well established that solitariness itself is discernible as of essential religious importance.[30] Without these, religion is in decay and returns to mere sociability.[31] Thus, religion as a human reaction is a conscious reaction. Furthermore, it is a conscious reaction to the world we find ourselves in. While religion appeals to the direct intuition of special occasions and emanates from what is special, it encompasses everything through conceptualisation.[32] This is accomplished with the help of human reason. Progress in religious truth, Whitehead tells us, is "mainly a progress in the framing of concepts, in discarding artificial abstractions or partial

---

[27] *Ibid.*

[28] *Ibid.,* 17.

[29] Charles Hartshorne, "The Modern World and the Modern View of God," *Crane Review* 4.2 (Winter 1962), 73. See also his "Man's Fragmentariness," *Wesleyan Studies in Religion* 41.6 (1963-64), 17-28.

[30] Whitehead, *Religion in the Making*, 18-19.

[31] *Ibid.* 23. Also, his *Adventures of Ideas* (Cambridge University Press, 1942), 207.

[32] *Ibid.* 32.

metaphors, and in evolving notions which strike more deeply into the root of reality.'[33]

Religion and Metaphysics

For this reason, Whitehead shares the tendency, rooted in Western philosophical tradition but criticised in some quarters, to connect religion with metaphysics. It must be noted, however, that metaphysics for Whitehead is understood and developed differently from the dominant metaphysical schools of thought in the West. He describes metaphysics as "the science which seeks to discover the general ideas which are indispensably relevant to the analysis of everything that happens".[34] Whitehead argues that rational religion—and as we have already noted, rationality for Whitehead is an integral part of religion—must have recourse to metaphysics.

Metaphysics enables religion to scrutinise itself. Whitehead regards the dispassionate criticism by metaphysics of religious beliefs to be of utmost necessity. "Religion will not regain its old power," he points out, "until it can face change in the same spirit as does science. Its principles may be eternal, but the expression of these principles requires continual development."[35] He strongly insists that the foundations of dogma must be laid in a rational metaphysics which criticises meanings, and endeavours to express the most general concepts adequate for the all-inclusive universe.[36] Moreover, for Whitehead the dogmas of religion are "clarifying modes of external expression", signaling the return of individuals from solitariness to society. Since there is no absolute solitariness, everything taking place in an environment, religious dogmas as modes of expression are thus important. The interaction between religion and metaphysics is regarded by Whitehead as one great factor in promoting the development in religion

---

[33] *Ibid.* 131.
[34] *Ibid.* 84. See also, 88-89.
[35] Whitehead, *Science in the Modern World,* 189. Prof Richard Dawkins in his documentary "The Root of All Evil?" aired on Channel 4 (Britain) on January 9, 2006 maintains that religion and science are poles apart. Whitehead shows that this need not necessarily be the case nor must religion be equated with irrationality as Dawkins alleges. See also, "Religion, Science and Hartshorne's Metaphysics," in my *Religion, Reason and God: Essays in the Philosophies of Charles Hartshorne and A.N. Whitehead* (Peter Lang Publishers, 2004), 101-123.
[36] Whitehead, *Religion in the Making*, p. 83.

of an increasing accuracy of expression, disengaged from adventitious imagery.[37]

At the same time, however, metaphysics can benefit from its connection with religion by taking into account the evidence furnished by religion. While religion must reckon with metaphysics in formulating and developing its teachings, it makes its own contribution of immediate experience to that pool of knowledge.[38]   In this way, metaphysical knowledge becomes truly all-inclusive. Thus, metaphysics and religion are not only related but also, and more importantly, mutually beneficial.

Whitehead offers yet another definition of religion, which incorporates what has been presented so far, particularly with reference to metaphysics, and adds another dimension:

> Religion is the vision of something which stands beyond, behind, and within, the passing flux of immediate things; something which is real, and yet waiting to be realised, something which is a remote possibility, and yet the greatest of present facts; something that gives meaning to all that passes, and yet eludes apprehension; something whose possession is the final good, and yet is beyond all reach; something which is the ultimate ideal, and the hopeless quest.[39]

John Cobb explains that religion for Whitehead is not a means to any end beyond itself, not even to the good of society. Instead religion is a vision of that whose possession, although unattainable, is the final good. Cobb adds that the reason for worshipping—we have already heard that the reaction to this vision is worship—is not to achieve some good, but because that which one dimly apprehends evokes worship.[40]   In other words, religion is the attempt to see beyond the ephemeral; and what one sees, although not too clearly, inspires a worshipful attitude.

This vision that Whitehead mentions has an effect on one's life.[41] John Cobb makes the observation that Whitehead's own general mood in life was of quiet confidence in the worthwhileness of living. But this confidence was not derived from any assurance about history or about nature.[42]   Indeed, Whitehead maintains that the worship of God, which is the

---

[37] Whitehead, *Science in the Modern World*, p. 266. Whitehead adds that the interaction between religion and science also promotes religion's development.
[38] Whitehead, *Religion in the Making,* 79.
[39] Whitehead, *Science in the Modern World*, pp. 267-268.
[40] Cobb, *A Christian Natural Theology,* pp. 217-217.
[41] M. Sivaramkrishna illustrates this point in the context of Hinduism in *Hindu View of Life: a Contemporary Perspective* (Dharmaram Publications, 2001).
[42] Cobb, *Christian Natural Theology*, 218.

outcome of this vision, is "not a rule of safety—it is an adventure of the
spirit, a flight after the unattainable. The death of religion comes with the
repression of the high hope of adventure."[43] He accepted that there is
perpetual perishing, loss as well as gain, sorrow as well as joy. In rather
poetic terms, he refers to human life "as a flash of occasional enjoyments
lighting up a mass of pain and misery, a bagatelle of transient
experience."[44] And yet, whatever may be its temporal outcome, what
guarantees the worthwhileness of life for Whitehead, remarks Cobb, is the
vision of God. When we respond positively to that vision, contributing our
share to the world, then it is a vision that indeed can give meaning to life.
"The vision of God was for Whitehead," as Cobb sums it up, "the basis for
all reality of meaning and all depth of feeling."[45]

Religion and Human Experience

No doubt, Whitehead's conception of religion, culled from his basic
insights, raises some important questions as we enquire into how it can
serve as a philosophical basis for inter-religious dialogue: To what extent
is this helpful in determining what could be classified a religion? Does it
nullify the claim that special experiences are themselves religious? Is
religion merely a human phenomenon? Does this mean that while
solitariness is universal, religion itself is not so insofar as one may not
reach, for whatever reason, that state of doing something about one's solitariness? How does this conception of religion relate to the major
religions of the world? These are fundamental concerns which need to be
addressed carefully.

Although Whitehead accepts that there are special occasions which can
lead to religious consciousness, religion as far as he is concerned emerges
from ordinary human experience.[46] We have noted that he refers to "the
human search" or "the longing of the spirit" for something which
transcends everything, but the search or the longing for it is deeply rooted
in mundane matters, in everyday experience. This search or longing results
in solitariness. Solitariness, however, is more than just the common
experience of loneliness. Solitariness, as has been pointed out, is the sense

---

[43] Whitehead, *Science in the Modern World*, 276.
[44] *Ibid.*, 275.
[45] Cobb, *Christian Natural Theology*, 223.
[46] According to Whitehead, "experience" is one of the most deceitful words in
philosophy. He provides a brief analysis of it in his *Symbolism: Its Meaning and
Effect* (Cambridge University Press, 1928), 19f. For a more extensive and technical
discussion, see his *PR*, particularly Part III.

of separateness, the initial experience having been that of belongingness. It enables one to become aware of one's individuality, which is a further stage from one's previous pre-conscious experience of sociality and relatedness. Since religion is a response to solitariness, it means that solitariness itself is actually pre-religious, despite being a further stage in one's search for the transcendent. Strictly speaking then, religion is not to be equated with individuality. And unlike the sense of solitariness, religion itself is more than a stage. There has been an evolution in one's experience and not just a prolongation. In addition, there has been a development since there is an active element: religion after all is what one *does* with one's own solitariness. It is the response to one's search or longing. There is a purposeful consciousness in religion that is merely latent in solitariness but is developing as one becomes aware of one's individuality.

It is interesting that Whitehead should regard the human experience of longing and searching, which leads to solitariness, as the fundamental context in which religion can emerge. Some of the modern critics of religion had attacked it for preying, as it were, on such experiences. Freud, tracing religion back to the need for emotional comfort, especially relief from disasters, accidents, sickness, and other natural evils that surround us, accused religion of perpetuating human immaturity through its teachings and practices. He regarded religion as an infantile neurosis that ought to be cured before we can grow into mature, healthy adults. Once cured of such a sickness, human beings, he alleged, can achieve maturity as a race. It will then no longer be necessary to invent fanciful beings personalised by religion for us to be able to face this impersonal and at times brutal world of ours. Marx criticised religion for enslaving people through its preaching of acceptance of one's miserable lot in life and its championing the virtues of patience, humility and self-denial. Religion, he claimed, misleads us in not recognising the real causes of our alienation and suppresses our desire to improve the economic and political conditions of life. Both of these influential thinkers would hardly agree with Whitehead that true religion stems from the human experience of longing and searching. If anything, such an experience in their view is being misinterpreted and misled by religion.

But these experiences of life, as our pre-reflexive starting point, are part and parcel of human life itself. While agreeing with Freud that religion is based on emotional needs, Jung rightly criticised him for not taking into account that they are basic to human nature and that we cannot deny them without inducing neurosis. What is called for therefore is not the abandonment of religion as demanded by Freud. Rather, it is our response to those needs that is really in question. It will determine the kind of religion that we have in mind, as Whitehead clearly states. Our response to human longing or yearning for something more does not have to be, and should not be, in the form severely criticised by Freud and Marx.

Unless religion embarks on its journey with our everyday experiences, including emotional ones, as the place of departure, it can easily become so abstract as to be rendered irrelevant. Worse, it makes nonsense of many religious practices and customs, which have arisen in response to specific life-situations. Religion—and one can notice in the various religions— cannot ignore deep-felt hunger or yearning for "something more" even if it is not always clear what that "something more" is or even if the expression of this desire is simplistic or unreflective. Whitehead correctly underscores this point whereas Plato neglects it. In the Western world Plato led the way in freeing religion from the particularistic, anthropomorphic expressions of it as exemplified by the Greek divinities. He insisted that true religion is concerned with fundamental and comprehensive questions rather than with emotional concerns. His own theory of religion was grounded in his desire to understand the universal attributes of reality, far removed from the transient, ever-changing environment which surrounded him. But by sharply establishing a line of demarcation between the established interpretation of religion in his day—understandably so, given its crudities—and his own one, Plato unfortunately cut off an important link with concrete life. He wanted to construct a theory of religion that had left behind the world of sense experience. While there were good reasons for dissociating genuine religion from the so-called religious practices and be- liefs of his time, Plato's hard-line attitude resulted in a rather intellectual- ised, and even elitist, version of religion. Whitehead's conception of relig- ion, on the other hand, rightly shows that it is in the midst of everyday life, experienced in various fashions and expressed in concrete ways, that we begin to ask questions which take us beyond the particular situation that we find ourselves in and lead us to what he refers to as "solitariness". And our reaction, also part of human living, to that solitariness shapes religious thought.[47]

Religion and Rational Thinking

Our further attempts to make sense of our experiences of and in life lead to something more general and more complex as we yield to the urge for something more. There is in human life what Whitehead calls "a noble

---

[47] In *From Suffering to God* (Basingstoke: Macmillan/N.Y. St. Martin's Press, 1994), we tried to illustrate how the experience of suffering leads to the question regarding what we can say about God.

discontent", which is "the gradual emergence into prominence of a sense of criticism, founded upon appreciations of beauty, and of intellectual distinction, and of duty."[48] Such a discontent distances us from particular experiences and inevitably prods us to seek conceptual expressions and rational support.[49] It is therefore inevitable that religion (or more accurately, what Whitehead calls rational religions) would be concerned with the intellectual dimension resulting in the formulation and adoption of beliefs, creeds and doctrines.[50]

Whitehead reminds us that "religion is concerned with our reactions of purpose and emotion due to our personal measure of intuition into the ultimate mystery of the universe," and that here we must "not postulate simplicity."[51] Rational thinking has a major contribution to religion. Situations in life have a way of pressing challenging questions on us, and

---

[48] Whitehead, *Adventures of Ideas*, 12.

[49] Whitehead outlines the process in this particularly helpful passage: "Our consciousness does not initiate our modes of functionings. We awake to find ourselves engaged in process, immersed in satisfactions and dissatisfactions, and actively modifying, either by intensification, or by attenuation, or by the introduction of novel purposes. This primary procedure which is presupposed in consciousness I will term Instinct. It is the mode of experience directly arising out of the urge of inheritance, individual and emotional. Also, after instinct and intellectual ferment have their work, there is a decision which determines the mode of coalescence of instinct with intelligence. I will term this factor Wisdom. It is the function of wisdom to act as a modifying agency on the intellectual ferment so as to produce a self-determined issue from the given conditions." *Ibid.*, 58. Whitehead sets this out for the purpose of understanding social institutions, but I have used it in this context because it also shows how he understands the process from experience to conceptualisation. He does add that this division must not be made too sharply.

[50] It had been pointed out to me during discussion that a certain understanding of the Koran would not accept this point. I acknowledge this. It seems to me, however, that Asghar Ali Engineer, an Islamic scholar, would actually agree with me. He argues that it is necessary to separate what is divine from what is the opinion of the medieval "ulana", claiming that even the most eminent Islamic thinker cannot escape various human factors which influence one's understanding of the divine. He makes the distinction between laws and values, for example, asserting that laws are merely temporal expressions of the values in the Qu'ran. Cf. *A Modern Approach to Islam* (Dharmaram Publications, 2003), 7. See also, Yoginder Sikand, "Asghar 'Ali Engineer's Quest for a Contextual Islamic Theology," *Studies in Interreligious Dialogue*, 15: 2 (2005), 211-231.

[51] *Ibid.*, 207. Whitehead maintains that history and common sense have testified that systematic formulations are potent engines of emphasis, of purification, and of stability. Without resorting to reason, Christianity would have sunk into superstition.

for the sake of intellectual credibility in religion, these questions cannot remain ignored. While religion is not, and should not be, a purely rational enterprise, it does involve careful, deliberate and logical thinking. Whitehead frequently uses the phrase "rational religion". On this point his reference to the obvious link between religion and metaphysics is especially notable. It is obvious not in the sense that the link is generally accepted since there are those who do not wish to associate religion with metaphysics or with any other kind of philosophical trappings and even argue that such an association is detrimental and dangerous. Rather, there is a clearly recognisable tradition which closely connects the two even if the kind of the connections is variously interpreted. As we have already seen, Whitehead, following in that tradition, accepts and defends that linkage. For him both religion and metaphysics are based on human experience and represent a common search for ultimacy. They help shape human thought and influence human life. Whitehead's understanding of the relationship between the two indicates that for him the formation of religious thought is inevitably connected to a metaphysical view of reality.[52]

One area where metaphysics features in religion—and of particular relevance to the conference theme—is in the development of religious doctrines.[53] We have seen that Whitehead maintains that progress in religious truth comes about "in the framing of concepts, in discarding artificial abstractions or partial metaphors, and in evolving notions which

---

[52] It is also grounded in his theory of knowledge. Whitehead rejects "mere knowledge". He claims that knowledge is always accompanied with accessories of emotion and purpose and that there are grades in the generality of ideas (Cf. his *Adventures of Ideas*, 5). All knowledge, according to him, is derived from, and verified by, intuitive observation. All knowledge is conscious discrimination of objects experienced (Cf. *Ibid.*, 227-228). He regards ideas as explanatory of modes of behaviour and of inrushes of emotion dominating our lives. Although ideas do modify practice, practice mainly precedes thought; and thought is mainly concerned with the justification or the modification of a pre-existing situation (Cf. *Ibid.*, 140; also, 127).

[53] There has been talk of course of the demise of metaphysics, particularly during the era of logical positivism. However, it is probably more accurate to speak of the decline of certain metaphysical ways of philosophising rather than of metaphysical thinking itself. It should be noted that Whitehead's notion of metaphysics and his metaphysical view of reality are quite distinctive. Cf. *Process and Reality*. Because of its emphasis on becoming (as well as relatedness and events), his metaphysical system has been referred to, among other descriptions, as process metaphysics although he himself referred to it as the philosophy of organism.

strike more deeply into the root of reality,"[54] all of which are achieved with the aid of metaphysics. But it is also useful to recall that for Whitehead religious truths are generalised truths, which originated in particular instances, expanded into a coherent system and *then applied to the interpretation of life.* The criterion for acceptance or rejection of these truths is their success in the interpretation of life.[55] Whitehead's well-known metaphor to describe speculative philosophy as the flight of the aeroplane is equally applicable to the discovery and formulation of religious truths: after taking off from life's experiences and being borne aloft by rational thinking, religion must touch down in life's fields again.

Religious doctrines, in Whitehead's view, represent a further stage in the process of making more explicit what one has held implicitly or has experienced. Ideally, they should express faithfully these pre-reflexive experiences. If they do, then one's appreciation of religion becomes richer and possibly more profound. But sometimes the process of conceptualisation does not do justice to the earlier stage; hence the need to rethink and re-interpret doctrines.[56] As Vincent Brümmer observes, "Changes in the circumstances and demands of life bring about changes in cultural and hence also in the conceptualisation forms that people find adequate, including the concomitant beliefs that they hold to be true. Because of changes in the demands of life, our conceptual forms cannot remain eternally adequate."[57] This is why the task of formulating religious doctrines is an on-going one. This is just as true for a particular religion as it is in inter-religious dialogue.[58] It is not surprising then that an urgent

---

[54] Whitehead, *Religion in the Making*, 131. Cf. my "Process Thought as Conceptual Framework," *Process Studies* 19, 4 (Winter 1990), 248-255. For a very useful discussion, based on Whitehead's thought, on the relationship between doctrinal beliefs and experience, see John B. Cobb Jr. & David Ray Griffin, *Process Theology: An Introductory Exposition* (Belfast: Christian Journals Ltd., 1977), 30-40.

[55] Whitehead, *Religion in the Making,* 124.

[56] See Kuncherian Pathil, *Trends in Indian Theology* (Bangalore: ATC Publications, 2005.).

[57] Brümmer, *Speaking of a Personal God*, 20.

[58] In reply to a question by Matthew Lopresti at the conference on this point, I explained that an important consideration in inter-religious dialogue is really an epistemological issue: how one understands and accepts the status of religious belief. In process philosophy, a distinction is made between absolute truths and our relative knowledge of such truths. Unlike relativism, process thought accepts that there are indeed absolute truths; but unlike absolutism, it rejects the absoluteness of our knowledge of such truths. Furthermore, the certainty with which one holds one's beliefs does not justify the absoluteness of those truths. In response, a

challenge today is to formulate religious doctrines which are not only based on concrete life but also, in an intellectual and systematised manner, express adequately the realities of life. What is called for therefore is the integration of religion with both human thought and life.[59] The following quotation from Whitehead is particularly appropriate here:

> Religion is an ultimate craving to infuse into the insistent particularity of emotion that non-temporal generality which primarily belongs to conceptual thought alone. In the higher organisms the difference of tempo between the mere emotions and the conceptual experiences produce a life-tedium, unless this supreme fusion has been effected. The two sides of the organism require a *reconciliation* in which emotional experiences illustrate a conceptual justification, and conceptual experiences find an emotional justification.[60]

Concluding Remarks

Despite some questions which will remain, Whitehead's conception of religion does, in my view, result in a clearer understanding of religion by showing how religion arises in the first place and how it also serves as the criterion for religious truths. At the same time it underlies the need to transcend our experiential starting point through rational thinking and to integrate the doctrinal expression with concrete human life. To what extent these considerations can form a basis and facilitate inter-religious dialogue remains to be seen.

---

further question was posed regarding a situation when one does not accept such a theory of knowledge. It seems to me that Martin Buber's insights into the life of dialogue can be particularly helpful in creating what I would call "the cultural context" that should precede philosophical and religious conversations. I would, therefore, agree with Mariola Paruzel's comment at the conference that psychology has a positive role to play in inter-religious dialogue.

[59] G.C. Nayak attempts to understand religion from diverse perspectives in *Understanding Religious Phenomenon* (Dharmaram Publications, 1997). He shows how sincere faith commitments do not prevent adherents from embracing expansion and growth in their beliefs.

[60] Whitehead, *Process and Reality*, p. 16. Italics added.

Santiago Sia is Professor and Dean of the Faculty of Philosophy of Milltown Institute (a recognized college of the National University of Ireland). He was previously Professor of Philosophy at Loyola Marymount University, Los Angeles, USA. Author/editor of several books and journal articles in the philosophy of religion, in ethics, and in process thought, he has lectured at universities in various countries throughout the world and presented papers at a number of international conferences. His most recent book is (with Ferdinand Santos): *Personal Identity, the Self and Ethics* (Palgrave Macmillan, 2007). He is completing a book manuscript titled "Ethical Thinking: Contexts and Issues".

BETWEEN ECSTASY AND ESCHATOLOGY: IMMANENCE, TRANSCENDENCE, AND THE METAPHYSICS OF PROCESS

JONATHAN WEIDENBAUM

I. Introduction: The Problem of Religious Diversity

In *A Common Faith*, John Dewey argues that there is no such animal called "the religious experience." There is in fact a wide variety of experiences which have been labeled as religious. Between the "trances and semi-hysteria" brought on by fasting, the "mystical ecstasy" of Neo-Platonism, the visions of William Blake and the "mysticism of sudden unreasoning fear"- there is neither a common denominator nor an underlying unity.[1] One must speak instead of religious *experiences*, the existence of which Dewey in no way denies. "On the contrary," he states, "there is every reason to suppose that, in some degree of intensity, they occur so frequently that they may be regarded as normal manifestations that take place at certain rhythmic points in the movement of experience."[2] It is likewise for the object of these experiences. Dewey points out that a diversity of absolutes exists even within one religion: "The contemporary emphasis of some Protestant theologians upon the sense of inner personal communion with God, found in religious experience, is almost as far away from medieval Christianity as it is from Neoplatonism or Yoga."[3]

Few scholars of comparative religion or philosophically-minded theologians have a quarrel with Dewey's grasp of the world's many spiritual traditions. It is the consequences drawn out by him which presents a problem for the adherents of any particular denomination. Indeed, one of the major themes of this small but powerful critique of religion is the tendency of human beings to project the content of their

---

[1] John Dewey, *A Common Faith* (New Haven: Yale University Press, 1934), pg. 35-6.
[2] Ibid, pg. 37.
[3] Ibid, pg. 36.

religious experiences out upon the cosmos, reifying them into objectively real forces or entities. Given the sheer diversity of gods, spirits, and principles held as sacred at different times and places, who is to claim that their particular object of ultimate concern -to borrow a phrase from Paul Tillich- is the ultimate reality? The biologist Richard Dawkins, perhaps the most scathing and unrelenting of the "new atheists", is fond of labeling all of us as non-believers. After all, Jews, Christians, and Muslims alike reject Zeus, Apollo, and Thor- among other popular deities of the past. That those who rejected the official gods of the Roman Empire were once branded as atheists adds more than a little historical weight to Dawkins' gleeful accusation.

Dewey's analysis if fine as far as it goes: There are many kinds of religious experience, and as many absolutes to correspond with each of these themes. But he overlooks the fact that not all have had the same impact upon the spiritual sensibilities of humankind, that a few have exceeded the others in enjoying a sustained influence upon centuries or even millennia of thought, belief, and expression. For it can be argued that there are invariants within the diversity; essential structures or modes of the spiritual life which have either persisted or continually resurfaced while others have vanished.   Perhaps there is a reason why the mortification of the body or the invoking of hallucinations have either died away or remained only among those cultures largely marginalized from the world's major civilizations.

However, the problem of religious diversity does not go away if those few remaining invariants of the spiritual life remain at odds with one another. In fact, the problem increases. To affirm a wide plurality of religious worldviews is to leave room for the standards and methods of preference- an art more than congenial to an era of multiculturalism. But when two or more worldviews have endured the scrutiny of near-endless criticism and reflection, and yet are found to contrast with one another, then we are left with a formidable impasse. Standing before a number of perspectives, both possessing an equal measure of inner coherence and outer appeal, is akin to finding oneself at a fork in the road without a map.

Two such contrasting invariants of the religious life include the contemplative worldview- the goal of which is to nullify the ego and merge into or commune with an impersonal absolute (often called *mysticism*); and the more existential worldview- the goal of which is to further individuate the self and foster a living relationship to a transcendent and personal deity (often called *faith*). In our time, process theologies inspired by the groundbreaking work of Alfred North Whitehead have presented a schema through which these perspectives are to be integrated into a single vision. In particular, it is the doctrine of the "two absolutes" elaborated by David Ray Griffin and John Cobb Jr. which is said to have harmonized these two forms of the religious life. The point of this essay is to evaluate just this claim.

My strategy is as follows: In section II, I discuss a fundamental divide between the contemplative and faith-centered versions of the religious experience, and employ the theologies of Advaita Vedanta and Johannes Climacus (a pseudonym of Søren Kierkegaard) as examples of each. I choose these philosophies for one reason: They are strong yet definitive representatives of the two perspectives. Thus, the possibility (or impossibility) of their inclusion is an ample test of the claim made by process theologians. In section III, I present an interpretation of the metaphysics of Whitehead along with his innovative notion of a dipolar God. In section IV I examine the doctrine of the two absolutes, and assess the extent to which it can incorporate *either* Advaita Vedanta or the theology of Johannes Climacus. Finally, I conclude by reviewing the implications all of this presents for a process philosophy of religion. If the pages which follow offer something to the woefully belated and much needed dialogue between religions, it would have fulfilled any larger purpose.

II. The Sages and the Pseudonym

Two Invariants

Sifting through the myriad theological positions entertained throughout history, particularly those which seek as their end the salvation or liberation of humankind, one comes across two predominant types. Of course, they do not exhaust the full story of religion. But that they are major strands running through the fabric of human spirituality is evident to anyone who cares to examine the world's great texts and traditions.

The first of these positions claims that we victims to a number of illusions- chief of which is our attachment to an individualized ego-identity. Overcome this separation, this perspective states, and one is reconciled with a supra-mundane reality, a primordial unity or a ground of being.

The second position claims that we are victims not to the illusion of a self but to self-satisfaction; or more accurately, a false sense of security. We are to redirect ourselves, according to this perspective, away from our pride and complacency, and towards an external and supernatural agent- one highly particularized and paradoxical to the understanding.

The reader may be tempted to label the first of these as Eastern and the second Western. This is correct only in the grossest and most general sense. In truth, the two are found within both Asian and Occidental traditions. The varieties of Hindu theism (*Vaishnavism, Shaivism…etc.*) and the many Bodhisaatva cults within Mahayana Buddhism are examples of the second tendency. Likewise, the predominant line of Occidental mysticism from Plotinus through Meister Eckhart, not to mention the Sufi traditions of Islam, falls under the first type. Every religion, and every *stage* of every religion, may very well bear out the two perspectives. For instance, the reader may benefit from perusing one of the most classic essays in Judaic studies, Joseph Weiss's "Mystical Hasidism and the Hasidism of Faith; A Typological Analysis."[4] This piece outlines the two perspectives as they are found within Hasidic Judaism, the pietistic revival movement which originated among Eastern European Jewry in the eighteenth century.

Throughout the rest of this section, I provide a definitive example of both forms of the religious life.

The Upanishads and Advaita Vedanta

The *Vedas*, the main holy texts of the Hindu tradition, are comprised of hymns to the various deities, details for the fire sacrifices, and instructions for the Brahman priests. The *Upanishads* are a series of books added to the end of the *Vedas*. They are a product of the Axial Age, that extraordinary period in the history of culture (labeled by the German thinker, Karl Jaspers) which saw the rise of Buddhism, Greek philosophy, Jewish prophecy, and the ideas of Taoism and Confucianism in China. Meaning "sitting devotedly near," the *Upanishads* were gathered together by the disciples of gurus and sages scattered throughout the forests and retreats of ancient India. If the *Vedas* are formal and ceremonial in character, the *Upanishads* are more concerned with intuitive insight into the nature of reality. They are, in fact, direct expressions of such an insight, and employ narrative, parable and allegory in order to convey experience beyond the limits of ordinary language and communication. One such parable selected from the *Chandogya* Upanishad captures the major themes of these seminal texts quite effectively.

A student is asked to place a pinch of salt in a glass of water and observe it the next day:

---

[4] The essay is included in Shaul Magid's *God's Voice from the Void; Old and New Studies in Bratslav Hasidism,* (Albany: State University of New York Press, 2002), pg. 277-285.

"Sip the water and tell me how it tastes."

"It is salty, sir."

"In the same way," continued Uddalaka [The Guru], "though you do not see Brahman in this body, he is indeed here. That which is the subtle essence- in that have all things their existence. That is the truth. That is the Self. And that, Svetaketu [The student], THAT ART THOU."[5]

Brahman is the Absolute of the *Upanishads*. Inseparable from the cosmos, it pervades the universe like a pinch of salt spreading through a glass of water. But more: The cosmos itself is a manifestation of Brahman- to borrow another analogy found in this principal *Upanishad*- like nuggets fashioned out of gold ("and the truth being that all are gold").[6]

At the very end of the parable, the guru recites what is perhaps famous line of the *Upanishads*: "That art thou."[7] And this is the second major theme of these holy books: That the true self is not the individualized personality or psyche, but the immortal and impersonal soul. Called the Atman, the Self is really Brahman by another name. If Brahman pervades, contains, and *is* the cosmos- it is most readily found within the human being. In what Aldous Huxley would later reformulate as the "the perennial philosophy" (a term borrowed from Leibniz), what is deepest in us is part and parcel of what is deepest in reality.

Advaita Vedanta is the school of thought based upon the *Upanishads*. Vedanta means "end of the Vedas," and Advaita translates as "non-dual." The latter points to the unity subsisting between our true selves (Atman) and the transcendental origin of all being (Brahman). Hence, the Absolute and the soul are not two, but one. The creator (or in some interpretations, the consolidator) of Advaita Vedanta is the legendary Indian philosopher Sankara, and it is to this eighth century sage we may very well owe some of the most imaginative thinking in the history of religion.

Surveying the world of appearance, we are confronted with a wide variety of things: Stars and suns, cups and cars, teeth and toenails- and, above all, individual human beings. All of this, claims Sankara, is *Maya*- what is commonly translated as "illusion." Scholars of Advaita Vedanta never tire of explaining that this is a poor and even misleading translation, and that *Maya* is nothing less than the creative power of Brahman in taking on the appearance of the many. Thus *Maya*, according to one

---

[5] From *The Upanishads; Breath of the Eternal*, (Swami Prahbavananda and Frederick Manchester, trans.) (New York: Mentor Books, 1957), pg. 70.

[6] Ibid, pg. 68.

[7] In Sanskrit, the phrase is: *Tat Tvam Asi*. See John M. Koller's illuminating chapter on the *Upanishads* in his *The Indian Way,* (New York: Macmillan Publishing Co., Inc., 1982).

scholar, "is a kind of screen or magic illusion but, at the same time, it is the reverse side of Brahman itself."[8] A word commonly used alongside of *Maya* is the term *Lila-* meaning "play" or "sport." Brahman, the sole reality, is involved in a game, and this is why we perceive a universe composed of different objects. It is notable that even within the midst of *Maya* we encounter Brahman: The computer upon which I type this essay, and the fingers with which I press the keys, are in fact the One Reality in disguise. A question however arises: How have we duped ourselves into taking keyboards, computer, and fingers as fundamentally separate and non-spiritual things?

The answer to this question, as well as to the subsequent one of how we may once again perceive Brahman, reveals Sankara to be a philosopher as well as a mystic. In short, we are victims of our own ignorance (*avidya* in Sanskrit), and are in the bad habit of projecting conceptions and labels derived from our memory and previous lives onto the external world. Sankara calls this activity *adhyasa* or "superimposition," and famously compares it to encountering a rope and immediately mistaking it for a snake.[9] *Moksha*, or liberation, is simply a matter of reversing this process. The main tool and organ through which this is accomplished is called "sublation," the art of overturning false conceptions of reality for increasingly stable and less illusory ones. Poking the rope with a stick for instance, we discover that the snake was a hallucination. In similar manner, by sublating layer after layer of false understanding, we retrieve a vision of the One through the multiplicity of forms. Seen against this light, Brahman can further be defined as that which can never be sublated.[10] Here, the student of comparative religions may recognize a parallel with the West: The practice of negative theology. By endlessly listing what God is *not* ("not this"…"not that") the mind is brought before a vision of the divine. In Hinduism this is known as *Jnana Yoga*, the practice of disclosing the eternal and the unchanging through the persistent practice of discrimination.[11]

Advocates of Advaita Vedanta stress *ad nauseam* that the mundane world of everyday experience is not completely unreal, and that the charge of an otherworldly *acosmism* -the doctrine that the physical universe does

---

[8] Natalia Isayeva, *Shankara and Indian Philosophy*, (Albany: State University of New York Press, 1993), pg. 3.

[9] Sankara, *A Thousand Teachings; The Upadesasahasri of Sankara.* (Segaku Mayeda, trans.), (Albany: State University of New York Press, 1992), pg. 211.

[10] See Ramakrishna Puligandla's *Fundamentals of Indian Philosophy,* (New Delhi: D.K. Printworld (P) Ltd., 2005), pgs. 231-5.

[11] Ibid, pg. 253.

not exist- is simply false. There are levels of reality according to the thought of Sankara, and as far as practical concerns go the empirical realm is not to be ignored. It is true that our *higher* knowledge perceives reality from the Absolute's point of view, and grasps the existence of Brahman behind the illusion of multiplicity. But the illusion is still real as an illusion, and requires our attention for the more pressing affairs of day-to-day living. Both the incoming train and my car are ultimately Brahman in disguise- but I must drive off the tracks unless I want them to collide. Hence, the empirical world is understood to be *derivative* rather than non-existent. One suspects that the frequency in which scholars of Indian thought emphasize this point belies a fundamental insecurity.

If the world of appearances is of secondary status in Advaita Vedanta, so is temporality. The ecstasy of *moksha* need not wait for death, and still less for some far-off messianic era. "History and the empirical world," explains Puligandla, "both being time-bound, cannot serve as means for liberation and freedom from bondage and ignorance."[12] Penetrating through the folds of outer appearance and inner consciousness are achievable in the here and now. At the end of the journey we realize that the One reality, the final destination for all religions, all spiritual paths, has been waiting silently for our return since the very beginning. Brahman has reunited with Brahman, and even the voyage home is relevant only from our delusional and embodied perspective. From God's point of view – which is to say our true Self- very little has occurred.

The Incarnation

There are styles of spirituality found in the West which parallel and even resemble the vision of Sankara. The religious experience espoused by Plotinus, the figure standing at the very foundation of much Occidental mysticism, is that of the soul stripping away all vestige of particularity and disappearing into the Absolute- a being undifferentiated, impersonal, and beyond (or underlying) time and space. The spiritual life is not that of a self standing before a transcendent deity, but the flight of the "solitary to solitary;" a part of God's very being, purified of the body and the senses, returning to its source.[13]

But the scholastic and mystical traditions of the West had to wrestle with the Biblical and Quranic concept of God. The deity of mainstream Judaism, Christianity, and Islam is the God of history, a personal and

---

[12] Ibid, pg. 285.
[13] Plotinus, *The Enneads.* (Stephen MacKenna, trans.), (New York: Penguin Books, 1991), pg. 549.

volitional being who constructed the cosmos out of nothing (or more accurately, a primordial chaos according to Genesis), revealed his Word through a line of prophets, and guides the universe to its end and culmination. In Christianity, the personal character of God is raised a notch: The divine became man; and not Man in general, but a *particular* man. The Absolute incarnated Himself into a Jewish peasant in first century Palestine. His life, teachings, and most importantly, the blood shed by him on the cross, provides humankind with its much longed-for redemption.

Now other traditions have incarnations (or *avatar* in the context of Hinduism). Thinkers in Vedanta for instance draw a distinction between *Nirguna* Brahman, the Absolute without qualities, and *Saguna* Brahman, the Absolute with qualities. The great bulk of spiritually-needy human beings require a personal face on their object of devotion, and for this reason Brahman has expressed Himself through the innumerable deities of the Hindu pantheon, the Buddha (to the chagrin of most followers of Buddhism, a non-theistic faith), Christ, and the founders of every religion.[14]

Even here, there are severe qualifications. First, Brahman-with-qualities, at least for Sankara's Advaita Vedanta, is derivative- since the true god-head is ultimately devoid form, distinction, and personality. Secondly, the individual incarnations taken by Brahman, being so various and inclusive, become less important when taken in isolation. After all, what need do I have for Christ if I decide upon Krishna, Zoroaster, or the Bahaullah for my vehicle to God? What relevance is Mohammed, the last and greatest of the prophets according to Islam, if I can employ elephant-headed Ganesha as my path to the Absolute? There is something almost frivolous in accepting the Gods and prophets of every culture. Arguably, the affirmation of every tradition means true devotion to none. Nothing can be more opposed to the Abrahamic tendency to spiritualize, in such a highly specific and exclusive manner, specific figures and historical events.

For some religions, it is the sheer *particularity* of the divine expression which provides the conditions for salvation. This is especially the case for the role of the Incarnation in Christianity. For many thinking and feelings Christians, those influenced by the Greek and Scholastic traditions in particular, this concept has been scandalous enough. Mystics and philosophers of the West have sought to see it as allegorical in nature, as symbolic for processes taking place within the depths of the human soul.

---

[14] See Pravrajika Vrajaprana's *Vedanta; A Simple Introduction*, (Hollwood: Vedanta press, 1999), pg. 50-1.

There is a type of religious sensibility however, from Tertullian and Luther and onward to the neo-orthodox and postmodern theologians of recent times, which have converted the scandalous centerpiece of Christian piety into the very means of personal and spiritual transformation. One of the most seminal figures in this tradition is the Danish philosopher and theologian, Soren Kierkegaard.

Johannes Climacus

If Advaita Vedanta seeks to liquidate the ego into some transcendental ground, Kierkegaard centered his polemic against the similar pantheistic tendencies of both liberal theology and Hegelian idealism. It is precisely this loss of the self into an impersonal whole –whether this understood as the systems of the philosophers or the conformity of the masses- which the Danish philosopher diagnosed as spiritlessness, the fundamental malaise of late modern Europe.

The true life of the spirit for Kierkegaard is precisely the further individuation of the self- with the latter understood as project rather than a thing. The human being, an uneasy synthesis of finite and infinite, temporality and eternity, is always in the making. The ego cannot attain a state of completion through its own efforts, let alone achieve a god's eye perspective on reality. None of Kierkegaard's numerous pseudonymous voices has emphasized this last point more than Johannes Climacus, the author of the *Philosophical Fragments* and the voluminous *Concluding Unscientific Postscript*.

It is arguably through Climacus wherein Kierkegaard's talent for satire reached its highest expression, for the Postscript is replete with one analogy after another crafted to mock the efforts of the speculative thinker. It is not the erecting of philosophical systems alone which Kierkegaard/Climacus objected to, but the presumptuousness of including the human subject within a static and final picture of reality. The metaphysician and pantheist alike –Climacus perceived them as one and the same- are likened to an author attempting to write himself into a paragraph within his own book, a lunatic seeking to lift himself up by his own bootstraps, and a Munchhausen striving to break the laws of gravity and fly through space. In the eyes of Climacus, becoming an abstraction is just not an option for a concretely existing human being. If Advaita Vedanta, as well as the thought of Hegel, aims to go beyond the subject/object divide, Climacus seeks to heighten the distinction. "The systematic idea is subject-object, is the unity of thinking and being; existence, on the other hand, is precisely the separation."[15]

It is in fact the *separation* between the human and the divine which makes the spiritual life is possible. Immersing oneself within the godhead, whether in mysticism or Advaita Vendata, removes the need for faith. Though the infamous "leap of faith" is nowhere found in his writing, it is not entirely inappropriate for labeling the form of religion championed by Kierkegaard's pseudonymous authors. Faith is, after all, belief stretching beyond the limits of both reason and experience. Climacus explains:

> Without risk, no faith. Faith is the contradiction between the infinite passion of inwardness and the objective uncertainty. If I am able to apprehend God objectively, I do not have faith; but because I cannot do this, I must have faith. If I want to keep myself in faith, I must continually see to it that I hold fast the objective uncertainty, see to it that in the objective uncertainty I am "out on 70,000 fathoms of water" and still have faith.[16]

It is in the *Philosophical Fragments* where Climacus presents another key statement on the nature of faith. The *Fragments* is in large part a thinly disguised presentation of traditional Lutheran and Protestant themes, particularly those of sin, grace, and the paradoxical nature of the Incarnation. Here, Climacus essentially contrasts the Christian vision of human existence with that of the Platonic Socrates- which is itself a disguise for Hegelian Idealism. While the Hegelian and the idealist (or the Advaita Vedantist!) places truth within the depths of the self, the Christian sees otherwise. For the Christian, truth comes is brought to us from the outside- and in the form of a savior. Caught within the pincers of sin, we are in need of the very *condition* for receiving the truth. In other words, it is only by an act of grace that we are able to receive Christ, a decision through which we are transformed into new individuals. The occasion in which all of this occurs is instantly transformed into "the fullness of time," and experience is flooded with a sense of eternity.[17]

---

[15] Soren Kierkegaard, *Concluding Unscientific Postscript to Philosophical Fragments,* (Howard V. Hong and Edna H. Hong, editors and translators), (New Jersey: Princeton University Press, 1992), pg. 123.

[16] Ibid, pg. 204.

[17] Soren Kierkegaard, *Philosophical Fragments* (Howard V. Hong and Edna H. Hong, editors and translators), (New Jersey: Princeton University Press, 1985), pg. 18.

Later in the *Fragments*, Climacus would further unpack what is entailed in the act of salvation. Just as eternity enters time in the person of Christ, so a similar process occurs in our personal response to this historical fact. The Incarnation is labeled by Climacus the Absolute Paradox, and is a truth which is, and *must* be, beyond our range of understanding. Throughout Kierkegaard's pseudonymous writings it is not only the self which defies the great systems of the metaphysicians, but the very object of Christian belief.

The Eternal Self

Both Advaita Vedanta and the thought of Climacus possess the salvation of the individual as their overriding goal and purpose. Both seek to engender a radical transformation of the human being; a reorientation of the self away from the distracted and worldly form of life and towards a communion with eternity. In other words, both promote the death of the ego and the birth of an entirely new self-understanding- what William James has called the "twice-born."[18] It is the manner in which Advaita Vedanta and Johannes Climacus direct us toward eternity which speaks the most of their differences.

For Advaita Vedanta, the eternal lie at the very base of the soul as well as in reality in general. It is by peeling layer after layer of illusion -that of the individuated ego-personality as well as an apparent world of multiple things and persons- which discloses the one reality lying at the core of both. For Climacus, the eternal first makes its appearance to us incognito and from outside the self. We must first be granted the grace to believe the ultimate paradox: The occasion of God becoming man in first century Palestine. Our defense mechanisms and our intellectual vanity must shipwreck themselves before this paradoxical truth, after which peace and eternity come crashing into our experience.

It should be noted that for Advaita Vedanta, the true Self was *always* eternal, while for Climacus the human being is first stuck in sin and untruth, and then receives an eternal self through devotion to an external and supernatural being. It can be argued that on closer inspection of Kierkegaard's writings, Christ has always been forgiving us our sins- it is only our active resistance to it which keeps us from salvation. That is, beneath the active and volitional self is the already-redeemed self, and the faith-act merely yields its discovery.

---

[18] This is found in a number of places in his classic *Varieties of Religious Experience*, (New York: Penguin Books, 1958).

But even then, the knowledge of our redemption, the eternal self, must come by way of faith in a particular figure: The god in time. And drawing upon another of Kierkegaard's pseudonymous authors, Johannes de Silentio, the faith-act must be perpetually re-achieved. The Christian must continually relate himself or herself to the Absolute Paradox, and receive eternity in a brief and ephemeral sense only. A final reconciliation of the self with eternity is not available to a living human being- at least not in the present. "An existing person," states Climacus, "can relate himself forward to the eternal only as the future."[19] This is nothing less than the *eschatological* sensibility; the tendency of the Abrahamic religions to invoke a more forward and anticipatory style of existence.[20]

To summarize: The perspective of Advaita Vedanta is one of radical *immanence*: Eternity is found both within the self and in the present. The religions of immanence are labeled by Climacus in the *Postscript* as "religiousness A." For Climacus, eternity is also located in the present, what he calls the "fullness of time." But it is not found there from the outset. According to Climacus's own position, "religiousness B," the eternal can only be gained by directing ourselves away from our own experience and immediacy, and towards both the incarnation and an eschatological future. We may call this position that of *transcendence*.

Here is an even finer distillation of the two positions: In bridging the gap between the human and the divine, Advaita ("non-dual") Vedanta has us overcome our finitude. Our truest self already resides within the source and foundation of the cosmos. By contrast, Climacus's theology is essentially an anti-totalizing perspective, and has us brush up against our intellectual and experiential limits. "This, then, is the ultimate paradox of thought: to want to discover something that thought itself cannot think."[21] In regards to our cognitive capacity, we are finite through and through. As I have shown earlier, this is the very pre-requisite of faith.

III. The Ontology of Process

Metaphysics Beyond Totalization.

The process ontology of Whitehead is as detailed as it is broad, and possesses a synoptic and comprehensive character reminiscent of Aristotle

---

[19] *Concluding Unscientific Postscript*, pg. 424.
[20] Eschatology, or "knowledge of last things," is the branch of theology which deals with the end of history. Topics include the day of judgment, the messianic era, and the final stages of the universe.
[21] *Philosophical Fragments*, pg. 37.

and Aquinas, Spinoza and Hegel. There are differences however between Whitehead and these earlier philosophical giants. Process metaphysics, also called "the philosophy of organism," is nothing less than a gigantic hypothesis, a series of generalizations from experience rather than a system of concepts deduced from self-evident axioms. There is a reason for this: The cosmology of Whitehead is one fashioned under the influence of William James- a philosopher whose polemic against the totalizing tendency of traditional metaphysics matches the force and intensity of Kierkegaard. In the words of an eloquent introduction to existentialism, James "plumbed for a world which contained contingency, discontinuity, and in which the centers of experience were irreducibly plural and personal, as against a 'block' universe that could be enclosed in a single rational system."[22]

It is in and though the legacy of James, among others, that the British-born Whitehead would join the venerable tradition of American philosophy, inheriting some of its cardinal themes and redefining them for generations to come. First, from Peirce through James, Dewey, Whitehead and beyond, is found the notion of an open cosmos, a universe perpetually adding to itself and whose laws are always in the making.[23] For Kierkegaard, the self cannot be subsumed within a closed picture of any kind. For Whitehead (and James), the whole of reality possesses this character. A second theme is the preoccupation with what European thought would come to call *phenomenology*- the art of describing the texture of experience free of all metaphysical bias. Together, these themes assist process ontology in avoiding both the overly abstract character of traditional metaphysics as well as the charge of totalization so often leveled by existentialist and postmodern thinkers against the more systematic kinds of philosophy. This will play a crucial role in section IV.

Whitehead's version of speculative philosophy is outlined in *Process and Reality* as "the endeavor to frame a coherent, logical, necessary system of general ideas in terms of which every element of our experience can be interpreted."[24] That Whitehead, a consummate scientist and mathematician, would employ the use of logic and coherence as standards for his system is to be expected. But the stress here on experience is no mere gesture offered to appease the "softer" disciplines of theology or

---

[22] William Barrett, *Irrational Man*, (New York: Anchor Books, 1962), pg. 19.
[23] While Whitehead spoke of unchanging eternal objects, pure potentials, the overall behavior of the cosmos reflects the nature of the cosmic epoch we are living in. These epochs change.
[24] Alfred North Whitehead, *Process and Reality; Corrected Edition.* (David Ray Griffin and Donald W. Sherburne, ed.), (New York: The Free Press, 1978), pg. 3.

comparative literature. For creating his system, Whitehead seeks to include a broad array of human experiences, including:

> ...experience drunk and experience sober, experience sleeping and experience waking, experience drowsy and experience wide-awake, experience self-conscious and experience self-forgetful, experience intellectual and experience physical, experience religious and experience sceptical, experience anxious and experience care-free, experience anticipatory and experience retrospective, experience happy and experience grieving, experience dominated by emotion and experience under self-restraint, experience in the light and experience in the dark, experience normal and experience abnormal.[25]

That process ontology is a scheme based upon the full range of experience is what makes its categories relevant to the philosophy of religion. In the pages which follow, particularly in section IV, we will examine the extent to which these categories can integrate the experiential core found in both Sankara and Climacus. The point of the rest of this section is to outline the major themes of the philosophy of organism.

Monism and Pluralism

The cosmology of Whitehead largely consists of droplets of experience; each of which are complex, interdependent, and possessing of both subjectivity and a measure of self-determination. These droplets of experience, called *actual occasions*, are the fundamental units of reality. In different combinations, they constitute suns and stars, cars and trees, persons and plants. Each actual occasion is alive insofar as it is in the midst of forming; the minute this formation is complete it loses its inner life, and serves to influence the successive wave of fresh actual occasions.

Each occasion is constituted, in no small part, by its relationship to other occasions- and the very character of this relationship might be one of Whitehead's most important contributions to the history of Western metaphysics. The influence of James is apparent even here, whose doctrine of radical empiricism breaks with classical rationalism and empiricism by placing causal relationships within the very tissue of experience. Whitehead has greatly expanded the concept, unpacking it in fine detail and setting out its relevance in regards to the whole of reality.

---

[25] Alfred North Whitehead, *Adventures of Ideas,* (New York: The Free Press, 1933), pg. 226.

The result is, in the words of Charles Hartshorne, genuine "metaphysical discovery."[26]

Labeled by Whitehead as a *prehension*, the relationship between actual occasions is a kind of pre-theoretical grasping, a form of perception occurring beneath the level of explicit cognition. Prehension is thus a form of primitive experience, and serves as the causality subsisting between actual occasions as well as ingredients in the constitution of each. This concept contains revolutionary implications. First, causality is here defined as internal as opposed to external in nature, and more akin to the capturing of an object within the film of a camera rather than the banging of one billiard ball into another. Second, the more explicit forms of thinking and awareness enjoyed by human consciousness are only a more complex and high-grade version of a tendency shared by the rest of the cosmos. Sometimes labeled as *pansychism* –David Ray Griffin has insisted on the term "panexperientialism"- experience is a quality pervading the structure of reality.[27] Matter for process ontology is not the hollow or neutral stuff of traditional philosophy. From Aristotle to Descartes and Newton, the physical world has typically been portrayed as bereft of everything except what the sublime Huxley describes as "only such attributes as render it amenable to mathematics."[28] Whitehead calls this position the fallacy of "vacuous actuality."

The concept of prehension also possesses significance for what James has called "the most central of all philosophical problems."[29] Is the cosmos a One or a Many? Is the universe a unity, or an assortment of disparate and independently existing things? The former position is held by religions with a transcendental bent, and stresses the completion already found beneath appearances. The latter, more pluralistic model entails a universe where individualism counts, where the future matters and human effort makes a difference in the course of history. For moral reasons, James chose pluralism and fought off a generation of neo-Hegelian idealists as well as his own father's pantheistic mysticism.

---

[26] Charles Hartshorne, *Creative Synthesis & Philosophical Method,* (La Salle: The Open Court Publishing Co., 1970), pg. 91.

[27] See David Ray Griffin, *Reenchantment without Supernaturalism; A Process Philosophy of Religion,* (Ithaca: Cornell University Press, 2001).

[28] Aldous Huxley, "The 'Inanimate' is Alive." from *Huxley and God: Essays.* (Jacqueline Hazard Bridgeman, ed.), (San Francisco: HarperSanFrancisco, 1992), pg. 235.

[29] William James, *Pragmatism and The Meaning of Truth,* (Cambridge: Massachusetts, 1975), pg. 64.

Whitehead's doctrine of prehension goes beyond both while retaining the philosophical core of each.

Each actual occasion is constituted, at least in part, by its prehensions of earlier actual occasions, and these are partly composed of still earlier occasions- and so on. What results is a picture in which a single unit of becoming reflects the entire cosmos from its own standpoint. Yet the end product is far from the simple all-in-all or undifferentiated unity found in some mystical traditions. An actual occasion has some freedom in shaping itself out of prior occasions; an indeterminacy negligible in some occasions (those which constitute rocks) but of decisive significance in others (human states of consciousness). Thus, a single actual occasion, though shaped initially by prior ones, possesses its own integrity and initiative. For describing the relationships between actual occasions, it is hard to surpass Whitehead's famous and succinct formulation: "The many become one and are increased by one."[30]

It is instructive to pause and appreciate the vision afforded us by *Process and Reality*. It is one of reality as fluid, simultaneously multiple and yet forming of unities, endlessly rolling forward in novel forms and patterns throughout eternity. The endless journey of the cosmos is called the *creative advance*, and the dynamism pervading everything, the process by which each stage of the universe gives rise to new ones, is called *creativity*. Together with "the many" and "the one," creativity constitutes what Whitehead names the Category of the Ultimate.[31]

The God of Process Thought

We have seen that the metaphysics of Whitehead is, in no small part, an attempt to reconcile the full range of human experience within one scheme. This includes the great contraries of life expressed through nature and human culture. Whitehead lists these as flux and permanence, order and novelty- and labels the general relationship and clash of these tendencies (or "ideal opposites") as the Cosmological Problem. Clearly related to the tension created by these factors of existence is the core evil of the process cosmos- that with each new stage of becoming, *something* is lost. Whitehead labels this sorrowful truth "perpetual perishing," and the issue it presents us as The Religious Problem. Yet there is no reason, Whitehead states, "why this should be the whole story."[32]

---

[30] *Process and Reality*, pg. 21.
[31] Ibid, pg. 21.
[32] Ibid, pg. 340.

The resolution of these problems not only provides the scaffolding for which all of the details of process metaphysics are granted their place and significance, but reverberates through all contemporary theologies and philosophies of religion. This is Whitehead's highly original concept of deity.

For Whitehead, each actual occasion possesses a physical and mental pole: The former receives the influence (or prehends) all prior actual occasions, the latter decides upon a possibility though which to form its final shape. God, being an actual occasion, is different in detail and not in principle from the other actual occasions. The deity of Whitehead is not the infamous "god of the gaps" employed by philosophers to cover the weak spots of their systems, but as far as the major categories of process thought goes- their "chief exemplification."[33]   Thus, the deity of Whitehead is dipolar, and possesses both a *primordial* and *consequent* component. The process God is an actual occasion to house all the others, and serves as both the underlying condition of their structure as well as the means though which they attain their final unity.

The primordial aspect of the deity serves as the ground of the world's design, both envisioning and ordering the abstract possibilities (or "eternal objects") employed to form each actual occasion. The consequent nature of God is the integration of all existing actual occasions along with the abstract possibilities found in his primordial nature. God thus *prehends* the cosmos in its entirety, witnessing and in fact feeling what each occasion feels. Since actual occasions possess their own freedom of becoming –adding their contributions to an increasingly growing and expanding universe- the consequent nature of God, though never perishing, is as plastic as the cosmos. Both conscious and receptive to the experiences of each occasion, the deity of process thought is described by Whitehead as "the fellow sufferer who understands."[34]   Here, we have come as far as possible from the passive, immutable and static deity of Greek and Scholastic theology.

The God of process metaphysics neither creates the universe wholesale ("he is not *before* all creation, but *with* all creation"), nor exerts total control over its destiny.[35] Process theism thus avoids the most intractable

---

[33] Ibid, pg. 343. The term "god of the gaps" has a history, but was most pointedly formulated by the theologian and concentration camp victim Dietrich Bonhoeffer.
[34] Ibid, pg. 351.
[35] Ibid, pg. 343. Though Whitehead employed the term "He" for God, he did not attribute masculinity to the deity. Process metaphysics has in fact opened new avenues for feminist theology. See John B. Cobb and David Ray Griffin, *Process*

sticking point of Western theology, the problem of evil. Out of all the previous conceptions of deity, the God of process is neither the stern moralizer of the prophets nor the heavenly dictator of Calvinism, but the "Galilean" understanding of a being who "dwells upon the tender elements in the world, which slowly and quietness operate by love."[36]   The primordial aspect of God does not thunder commands at actual occasions, but sends "initial aims" into the world of fact, mere suggestions for their optimal development. Meanwhile, the consequent part saves the story of each occasion within its ever-growing (and never-dying) reality.

It is this last fact which yet again distinguishes the metaphysics of Whitehead from earlier systems, and speaks not to origins but to ends, not to the underlying condition of the cosmos but its culmination. For the consequent nature of God not only preserves the legacy of each stage of the world process, but threads the final story in such a way that every little bit of good is made to echo for eternity, and every evil relegated to a minor discord in a greater and ultimately triumphant picture. And yet, the great story of Whitehead's cosmology does not end here: Just as every actual occasion, after forming, lends its finished product to future occasions, so the consequent nature of the deity sends its completed and victorious nature back into the realm of becoming.   Hence, the final benefit bequeathed by God to the universe is found not just at the end of the drama, but within every step on the way. As Whitehead poetically if cryptically states: "For the kingdom of heaven is with us today."[37]

This last component of deity, God's completed nature spilling into the present, is labeled his "superjective nature."[38]   Together with the consequent part, it provides harmony to the whole system, solving both the "cosmological" and "religious" problems and balancing the experience of anxious anticipation with that of immediate spiritual fulfillment.

IV. The Two Absolutes: A Reconciliation?

God and Creativity

In the previous section, we have seen that process thought rejects the traditional doctrine of creation *ex nihilo*, and advocates a God co-eternal with the universe. Moreover, process theism rejects an omnipotent picture

---

Theology; An Introductory Exposition, (Louisville: Westminster John Knox Press, 1976).

[36] Ibid, pg. 343.
[37] Ibid, pg. 351.
[38] Ibid, pg. 87.

of a deity with absolute control over the cosmos, and replaces it with the more loving image of a God sending out "initial aims" to each existing entity, gently prodding each to realize its potential. Since actual occasions possess a measure of autonomy, they are free to accept or reject the call from God and choose their own path of becoming. This indeterminacy is *creativity*; the never-ending succession of actual entities joining into new ones, exercising their own volition and expanding the cosmos without end. God, in prehending the cosmos (and being prehended by it) is no exception. Thus, both God and the world "are in the grip of the ultimate metaphysical ground, the creative advance into novelty."[39]

Subsequent process theologians have made much use of the co-existence between God and creativity in Whitehead's system, and have articulated the promise it holds for a dialogue between religious worldviews. This is particularly the case for the contrast set out in the introduction and beginning of section II: The contemplative perspective through which the devotee is to overcome his or her ego-self and merge within an impersonal and divine reality, and the faith-centered perspective through which the individual is to revere and obey the will of a personal and mostly transcendent deity. Both John B. Cobb and David Ray Griffin perceive creativity as the object of the contemplative approach, and the have skillfully incorporated the complex God of process theism (influenced as much by metaphysician Charles Hartshorne as Alfred North Whitehead) into the Triune deity of Christian piety.[40] Noting Whitehead's preference for Jesus's understanding of deity, they interpret the primordial nature of God to the Father, his incarnation into the world through "initial aims" to be the Son (the Logos of John), and his subsuming of all actual occasions into his consequent nature as the Holy Spirit.[41]

Cobb and Griffin have called this position the doctrine of the Two Absolutes. In "Emptiness and God," Cobb calls creativity the "metaphysical ultimate," and God –with his initial aims and gradation of value- as the "principle of right."[42] Griffin, in *Reenchantment without Supernaturalism*, labels God the "personal ultimate" and creativity as the

---

[39] Ibid, pg. 349.

[40] Of course, they have been more than respectful and encouraging to the other theistic traditions. For instance, see *Jewish Theology and Process Thought,* Sandra Lubarsky and David Ray Griffin, ed., (Albany: State University of New York Press, 1996).

[41] *Process Theology; an Introductory Exposition*, chapter six.

[42] My copy of Cobb's essay is found in Gary Kessler's *Philosophy of Religion; Toward a Global Perspective.* (Gary E. Kessler, ed.), (New York: Wadsworth Publishing Company, 1999). The quotes are from page 78.

"impersonal ultimate."[43]   In both cases, Whitehead's distinction between God and creativity is set out for a rapprochement between religious worldviews unprecedented in the history of theology.

It remains to be asked however, can either representation of the contemplative and faith-centered perspectives I have outlined in section II be subsumed within the categories of process ontology? That is, can either one be incorporated within process metaphysics when taken *individually*-let alone reconciled or harmonized with the other, contrasting perspective?

Sankara and Creativity

David Ray Griffin has employed Nirguna Brahman of Advaita Vedanta thought as a prime example of the creativity side of the Two Absolutes, and at first this makes perfect sense. Taken as an ultimage, creativity very much satisfies the sense of *immanence* found in the contemplative version of the religious experience. The notion of an abiding and essential ego-self persisting through the changes of experience is a metaphysical illusion. Every part of the cosmos is to a great extent intertwined with every other, and there is true ecstasy available to those willing to discipline themselves into grasping their connectedness with the rest of existence.

But this is where the similarity ends, for on closer inspection, creativity has little in common with Nirguna Brahman. Here it is instructive to move from Griffin's *Reenchantment without Supernaturalism* to Cobb's earlier "God and Emptiness," for Cobb is adamant in pointing out that Advaita Vedanta, like the monisms of Western mysticism and theology, remains a *substance* ontology, and holds static being over becoming. Creativity, with its endless passing of multiplicities into unities, resembles the *sunyata* or void of Mahayana Buddhism far more accurately than the Brahman of Vedanta. The former is an ever-changing relation between entities, each lacking an absolutely independent existence, and not the One of Sankara.

Next to the ceaseless activity of creativity in Whitehead's later thought, there is something too sterile in the Brahman of Advaita Vedanta, something against which the Jamesian presence in process metaphysics rises in protest. Creativity yields a cosmos always in the making, and the interconnectedness of actual occasions does not liquidate the integrity of each. One is reminded of a lone reed in the foreground of a Chinese

---

[43] Chapter seven, pg. 269.

landscape painting. Slightly bent, it takes on even more significance when placed against the background of empty white space.

The scholar of Indian thought may remind us over and over again that sunsets and cigarette butts lying in puddles are not *completely* unreal, just derivative to the supreme unity of Brahman. Next to creativity however, such an absolute resembles what James describes as "too buttoned-up and white-chokered and clean-shaven a thing to speak for the vast slow-breathing unconscious Kosmos with its dread abysses and its unknown tides."[44] Whitehead's creativity yields what James called a "thick" universe: One richly textured, personal, and beset with possibilities- and not the "thin" and anemic metaphysics predominant among the idealists and transcendentalists of his own time.[45] It should be remembered that Vedanta-inspired interpretations of the Bhagavad Gita were a strong influence upon the kind of philosophies James fought against.

Climacus and the Process God

We have seen how congenial is the deity of process metaphysics to the incarnated and Triune deity of Christian theism. Moreover, there is much in process thought to support the experiences depicted by Kierkegaard's pseudonym, Johannes Climacus. Within process ontology, the human self, a succession of high-grade actual occasions, is always in the making. The philosophy of organism is thus congenial to existentialist anthropology. Rather than stressing its composition out of other actual entities (as in Buddhism), the self may choose to intensify its sense of purpose and destiny and increase its receptivity to the "initial aim" sent it by God. Overcome by grace, it may recognize Jesus of Nazareth as embodying the will and character of the deity, as do Christian process theists- from Whitehead's inspiration from the "Galilean" vision to the more explicitly theological works of Cobb and Griffin. "Whereas Christ is incarnate in everyone," states Cobb/Griffin, "Jesus *is* Christ because the incarnation is constitutive of his very selfhood."[46]

It should be noted that in any single act of prehension, not everything about one occasion is prehended by the other. Like the moon showing its face to the earth while concealing its far side, actual occasions may possess a component beyond the reach of other occasions. It can be

---

[44] William James, "Absolutism and Empiricism." From *Essays in Radical Empiricism*, (Lincoln: University of Nebraska Press, 1996), pg. 277-8.
[45] See William James, *A Pluralistic Universe,* (Lincoln: University of Nebraska Press, 1996), pg. 135-6.
[46] *Process Theology; An Introductory Exposition*, pg. 105.

argued that Whitehead therefore does justice to the position of thinkers like Levinas, for whom the face of another human being, "the Other", must elude each and all of my attempts to subsume it completely within my perception and understanding. This is certainly the case for the prehension of the deity by all finite actual occasions. I may feel God's initial aim as well as his presence to my joy and suffering. But I cannot grasp the entirety of God's being, including his sometimes opaque and unfathomable will. The fact is that the larger part of God's primordial and consequent natures stretch beyond my field of awareness. Thus, the relationship between God to the self remains mostly one of *transcendence*.

Furthermore, in dedicating ourselves to God's aims, we heed the deity's plans for the cosmos at large. We have seen how the consequent nature of God ensures the triumph of good over evil, and how the "superjective" component of God floods the present with his completed nature ("For the kingdom of heaven is with us today.") Thus, in relating to eternity as embodied in Jesus and the eschatological future, we are granted an experience of it in the midst of our life- what Climacus has called "the fullness of time." Here, we are rescued from our self-centered and sinful nature, and created anew as compassionate and selfless beings in conformity to the will of an equally compassionate deity.

There are differences however between the absolute of Climacus and that of process Christology. Although actual occasions transcend as well as include each other, the Christ of Johannes Climacus is the Absolute Paradox; a truth permanently outside the boundaries of human understanding. Process theism however is a form of *natural* theology. Whitehead's unique doctrine of prehension is, after all, a theory of how entities incarnate themselves within one another. Employed by Griffin, Cobb and others, it is used to make perfect sense out of the significance of Jesus in traditional Christianity. "It is difficult to believe that God actually was decisively revealed through Jesus," explains Cobb/Griffin, "unless we have some motion as to how this was possible."[47] There is no real paradox in this picture; no stumbling block to other religions and no offense to reason. Even the current author, a non-Christian, can appreciate the profound logic at work in process Christology. It seems that process thought can speak to the conversion experience, the upheaval of the self gained through the *kerygma* or "proclamation" issued by the Gospel message- without the starkness of Tertullian's absurdity, Luther's theology of the cross, or Kierkegaard's leap of faith. In other words: While there might be aspects of the divine which elude the understanding of a process theist, the Incarnation is not one of them.

---

[47] Ibid, pg. 106.

V. Conclusion: A Proposal

In the "Pragmatism and Religion" chapter of *Pragmatism*, James questions whether transcendentalist and monistic philosophies are compatible with the more pluralistic ones in which possibilities are real and salvation not guaranteed.

> Can it be that the disjunction is a final one? That only one side can be true? Are a pluralism and monism genuinely incompatibles?
> ...If this were so, we should have to choose one philosophy or the other. We could not say 'yes, yes' to both alternatives. There would have to be a 'no' in our relations with the possible.[48]

I have argued above that the mysticism of Sankara and the theology of Climacus share a focus on the liberation and transformation of the human being. Yet the metaphysics of both, what James calls their "over-beliefs," are clearly opposed to one another. I have also argued that the doctrine of the Two Absolutes, a position designed to harmonize both personalistic theism and the impersonal ground of Asian and Western mystical traditions, fails to fully incorporate the absolute of *either* Sankara or Climacus- both of which are, admittingly, strong representations of each.

To the monism of Advaita Vedanta and the Absolute Paradox of Kierkegaard, process metaphysics offers, in the words of James, a double "no." To the former, the philosophy of organism is too attentive to the richness of concrete human experience; to the latter, process thought has married its concern for lived experience with a tendency toward bold and unfettered speculation. In short, the ontology of process is too existential for Sankara, and too metaphysical for Kierkegaard. In lieu of the inability of process metaphysics to include the worldview of either Sankara or Climacus, here is a proposal. Rather than advertise itself as a grand synthesis of the absolutes held dear by the traditions of the world, process theology should instead promote itself for what it is: A genuine and unique alternative.

However, I have also argued that the *experiences* found in both perspectives are accounted for in the cosmology of Whitehead and his descendents. To both the ecstasy of Sankara and the eschatological vision of Climacus, process thought offers a resounding "yes, yes."

---

[48] *Pragmatism*, pg. 141.

Jonathan Weidenbaum is a professor of Liberal Arts at Berkeley College, in New York City. He teaches ethics, world religions, and philosophy, and specializes in the philosophy of religion. He has publications in the *Journal of Media and Religion*, *Journal of Liberal Religion* (online), and *Transcendent Philosophy*. Though his work was once informed by the Continental tradition, Dr. Weidenbaum now sees the relevance of John Dewey, William James and Alfred North Whitehead for his ideas.

RELIGIOUS EXPERIENCE IN WILLIAM JAMES AND WHITEHEAD AND THE QUESTION OF TRUTH

HELMUT MAAßEN

Whitehead relies to a large extent on William James' concept of experience, which was a rejection of a purely mechanistic understanding of reality. In doing so James particularly stresses the importance of religious experience. Though not explicit, the cosmic ocean, in which the experiencing "I" finds itself embedded, is one of his major metaphysical presuppositions. For Whitehead and for James, the question remains of how to evaluate experience and, especially in our context, religious experiences. In my view, it is not sufficient to measure religious experience in a Jamesian way purely based on pragmatic results. Whitehead seems to go beyond this. But are his criteria for truth claims adequate? My aim in this paper is to point out some difficulties as well as possible solutions in his metaphysics of experience.

William James was confronted with a mechanistic view of the universe in the second half of the 19th Century, which he later called a 'block-universe'[1]. Realizing this led him into deep depression.

---

[1] William James, *A pluralistic universe. Hibbert Lectures at Manchester College on the present situation in philosophy*, (New York; London: Longmans, Green & Co. 1909). 'Can a plurality of reals be possible?' asks Mr. Bradley, and answers, 'No, impossible.' For it would mean a number of beings not dependent on each other, and this independence their plurality would contradict. For to be 'many' is to be related, the word having no meaning unlessthe units are somehow taken together, and it is impossible to takethem in a sort of unreal void, so they must belong to a largerreality, and so carry the essence of the units beyond their properselves, into a whole which possesses unity and is a larger system....Either absolute independence or absolute mutual dependence--this,then, is the only alternative allowed by these thinkers. Of course'independence,' if absolute, would be preposterous, so the onlyconclusion allowable is that, in Ritchie's words, 'every single eventis ultimately related to every other, and determined by the wholeto

Whilst in this state of philosophic pessimism and general depression of spirits about my prospects, I went one evening into a dressing-room in the twilight to procure some article that was there; when suddenly there fell upon me without any warning, just as if it came out of the darkness, a horrible fear of my own existence. Simultaneously there arose in my mind the image of an epileptic patient whom I had seen in the asylum, a black-haired youth with greenish skin, entirely idiotic, who used to sit all day on one of the benches, or rather shelves against the wall, with his knees drawn up against his chin, and the coarse gray

Undershirt, which was his only garment, drawn over them inclosing his entire figure. He sat there like a sort of sculptured Egyptian cat or Peruvian mummy, moving nothing but his black eyes and looking absolutely non-human. This image and my fear entered into a species of combination with each other THAT SHAPE AM I, I felt, potentially. Nothing that I possess can defend me against that fate, if the hour for it should strike for me as it struck for him. There was such a horror of him, and such a perception of my own merely momentary discrepancy from him, that it was as if something hitherto solid within my breast gave way entirely, and I became a mass of quivering fear. After this the universe was changed for me altogether. I awoke morning after morning with a horrible dread at the pit of my stomach, and with a sense of the insecurity of life that I never knew before, and that I have never felt since. ..It was like a revelation; and although the immediate feelings passed away, the experience has made me sympathetic with the morbid feelings of others ever since. It gradually faded, but for months I was unable to go out into the dark alone... In general I dreaded to be left alone. I remember wondering how other people could live, how I myself had ever lived, so unconscious of that pit of insecurity beneath the surface of life. My mother in particular, a very cheerful person, seemed to me a perfect paradox in her unconsciousness of danger, which you may well believe I was very careful not to disturb by revelations of my own state of mind (I have always thought that this experience of melancholia of mine had a religious bearing).

On asking this correspondent to explain more fully what he meant by these last words, the answer he wrote was this:

> I mean that the fear was so invasive and powerful that if I had not clung to scripture-texts like 'The eternal God is my refuge,' etc., 'Come unto me, all ye that labor and are heavy-laden,' etc., 'I am the resurrection and the life,' etc., I think I should have grown really insane.[2]

---

which it belongs.' The whole complete block-universethrough-and-through, therefore, or no universe at all!", 664.

[2] This he first wrote in his letters in 1870. *Letters of William James*, 2 vols. (1920)Vol I, 146ff and later, without reference, he put this text into his Gifford

It took James quite some time to deal with this depression, in theory as well as in practice.

He realized that freedom of the will cannot be proved. Somewhat similarly to Kant, who stated that Freedom is (one of three) postulates of pure practical reason. Or, to put it ethically, 'ought implies can'.[3] But, unlike Kant, James claims, 'My first act of free will shall be to believe in a free will'. On April 30, 1870 he notes in his diary:

> I think that yesterday was a crisis in my life. I finished the first part of Renouvier's second *"Essais"* and see no reason why his definition of Free Will – 'the sustaining of a thought because I choose to when I might have other thoughts' – need be the definition of an illusion. At any rate, I will assume for the present – until next year – that it is no illusion. My first act of free will shall be to believe in free will.
>
> I will see to the sequel. Not in maxims, not in *Anschauungen*, but in accumulated acts of thought lies salvation. *Passer outre*. Hitherto, when I have felt like taking a free initiative, like daring to act originally, without carefully waiting for contemplation of the external world to determine all for me, suicide seemed the most manly form to put my daring into; now, I will go a step further with my will, not only act with it, but believe as well; believe in my individual reality and creative power. My belief, to be sure, can't be optimistic but I will posit life (the real, the good) in the self-governing resistance of the ego to the world. Life shall [be built in]   doing and suffering and creating.[4]

This makes his concept of the free will an act of the will. It can only be experienced as enaction, not in theoretical terms. Of course, this enaction again has to be an act of free will and cannot be forced onto somebody; otherwise it would be a contradiction in terms.

Lectures, The Varieties of Religious Experience: *The varieties of religious experience*, (New York ; London: Longmans, Green & Co. 1902), 160ff.

[3] Immanuel Kant (1900-) *Kant's gesammelte Schriften (Kant's Collected Works)* , ed. Royal Prussian (subsequently German, then Berlin-Brandenburg) Academy of Sciences, Berlin: Georg Reimer, subsequently Walter de Gruyter, 29 vols, in 34 parts , Theory and Practice 8: 287.A major part of the present discussion concerning Free Will, seems to neglect Kant's and James' earlier thoughts. Cf section II of the article on Kant in: GUYER, PAUL (1998, 2004). Kant, Immanuel. In E. Craig (Ed.), *Routledge Encyclopedia of Philosophy*, (London: Routledge. Retrieved August 11, 2008), from http://www.rep.routledge.com/article/DB047SECT11.

[4] John Locke*, An Essay Concerning Human Understanding,* (Oxford 1975 I), 148.

The free-willist believes the appearance to be a reality: the determinist believes that it is an illusion. I myself hold with the free-willists,—not because I cannot conceive the fatalist theory clearly, or because I fail to understand its plausibility, but simply because, if free *will were* true, it would be absurd to have the belief in it fatally forced on our acceptance. Considering the inner fitness of things, one would rather think that the very first act of a will endowed with freedom should be to sustain the belief in the freedom itself. I accordingly believe freely in my freedom; I do so with the best of scientific consciences, knowing that the predetermination of the amount of my effort of attention can never receive objective proof, and hoping that, whether you follow my example in this respect or not, it will at least make you see that such psychological and psychophysical theories as I hold do not necessarily force a man to become a fatalist or a materialist.[5]

All knowledge and theoretical considerations have an ethical character, basically. It explains the otherwise puzzling title of one of his famous books: The Will to Believe. Consequently this ethical assumption bears in it the pragmatic criterion, as a method of judging human action; actions are judged by their consequences. The utilitarian principle is the basic thought in his book 'Pragmatism' (1907), which he dedicated with good reason to the memory of John Stewart Mill.

After having overcome his pessimism and depression, the question arose: what are the sources of knowledge, how do I get beyond the ethical self (I)? James assumes experience, or more precisely, as he calls it, pure experience, as the key to all knowledge. He follows the line of British empiricist tradition, which was initiated by John Locke in the famous paragraph of his Enquiry:

> 2. ... Let us then suppose the mind to be, as we say, white paper, void of all characters, without any ideas:- How comes it to be furnished? Whence comes it by that vast store which the busy and boundless fancy of man has painted on it with an almost endless variety? Whence has it all the materials of reason and knowledge? To this I answer, in one word, from **EXPERIENCE.** In that all our knowledge is founded; and from that it ultimately derives itself. Our observation employed either, about external sensible objects, or about the internal operations of our minds perceived and reflected on by ourselves, is that which supplies our understandings with all the materials of thinking. These two are the fountains of

---

[5] Wiliam James, *Talkes to teachers on psychology: and to students on some life's ideals*, (New York; London: Holt and Longmans, Green & Co. 1899), 93.

knowledge, from whence all the ideas we have, or can naturally have, do spring.[6]

The process of experiencing is not one which applies not only to humans and to living organisms but to reality as a whole. "There is no thought-stuff different from thing-stuff, I said; but the same identical piece of 'pure experience' (which was the name I gave to the 'materia prima' of everything) can stand alternately for a 'fact of consciousness' or for a physical reality, according as it is taken in one context or in another." [7] Reality is a process of experiencing which manifests itself primarily as a phenomenon. The world of experience is one in the experience of each self.[8]

> The individualized self, which I believe to be the only thing properly called self, is a part of the content of the world experienced. The world experienced (otherwise called the 'field of consciousness') comes at all times with our body at its centre, centre of vision, centre of action, centre of interest. Where the body is is 'here': when the body acts is 'now'; what the body touches is 'this'; all other things are 'there' and 'then' and 'that.'[9]

James' ontology, therefore, is a metaphysics of relations, which successfully tries to overcome the Subject-Object dualism.

We become conscious of ourselves as experiencing entities. These entities are not isolated but part of an oceanic multitude.

> Out of my experience, such as it is (and it is limited enough) one fixed conclusion dogmatically emerges, and that is this, that we with our lives are like islands in the sea, or like trees in the forest. The maple and the pine may whisper to each other with their leaves, and Connecticut and Newport hear each other's fog-horns. But the trees also comingle their roots in the darkness underground, and the islands also hang together

---

[6] John Locke, An essay Bk II, Cht1, 2.

[7] William James, *Essays on radical empiricism*, (New York; London: Longmans, Green & Co. 1912), 137/138: 1, [Reprinted from The Journal of Philosophy, Psychology and Scientific Methods, vol II,, No. 11, May 25, 1905.].

[8] Eilert Herms notes with good reason though, that experience in James has a duadic structure: 'Thought with something in it', but , at least since Charles Sanders Peirce, it is being thought of thought to have a triadic structure: the relation of the self to itself.' In: Eilert Herms, William James, *Die Vielfalt religiöser Erfahrung, Eine Studie über die menschliche Natur, Übersetzt, herausgegeben und mit einem Nachwort versehen von Eilert Herms*, Walter-Verlag, Olten/Freiburg 1979. Nachwort, II. James' Religionspsychologie im Zusammenhang seines Lebenswerks, 501.

[9] William James, *Essays on radical empiricism*.

through the ocean's bottom. Just so there is a continuum of cosmic consciousness, against which our individuality builds but accidental fences, and into which our several minds plunge as into a mother-sea or reservoir.[10]

The Will to be free and the notion of experience as the starting point to philosophise and to live beg the question of how to differentiate experiences and how one can judge them. James was of course aware that mental illness should be regarded as a state of mind which needs to be healed. But which state of mind needs to be healed and which should be accepted, even if it is exceptional, as is very often the case with religious experiences?

If this connectedness with everything gets disturbed, the reason for it is a false judgment of ours or in our experience. True ideas lead to useful concepts and lead away from isolation:

> True ideas lead us into useful verbal and conceptual quarters as well as directly up to useful sensible termini. They lead to consistency, stability and flowing human intercourse. They lead away from excentricity and isolation, from foiled and barren thinking. The untrammeled flowing of the leading- process, its general freedom from clash and contradiction, passes for its indirect verification; but all roads lead to Rome and in the end and eventually, all true processes must lead to the face of directly verifying sensible experiences SOMEWHERE, which somebody's ideas have copied.[11]

Different opinions are to be accepted, since they spring out of experience, even though they can be true or false.

> A new opinion counts as 'true' just in proportion as it gratifies the individual's desire to assimilate the novel in his experience to his beliefs in stock. It must both lean on old truth and grasp new fact; and its success (as I said a moment ago) in doing this, is a matter for the individual's appreciation. When old truth grows, then, by new truth's addition, it is for subjective reasons. We are in the process and obey the reasons. That new idea is truest which performs most felicitously its function of satisfying our double urgency. It makes itself true, gets itself classed as true, by the way it works; grafting itself then upon the ancient body of truth, which

---

[10] End of chapter VIII, William James, *Memories and Studies (1911)*.
[11] William James, *Pragmatism: a new name for some old ways of thinking*, (London ; New York: Longmans, Green & Co. 1907), 103.

thus grows much as a tree grows by the activity of a new layer of
cambium.[12]

In the process of experience, parts of it get lost, abolished, do not
continue (unlike in Whitehead). Its predecessors set the framework for
later experiences, but they do not necessarily continue.

> Some experiences simply abolish their predecessors without continuing
> them in any way. Others are felt to increase or to enlarge their meaning, to
> carry out their purpose, or to bring us nearer to their goal. They 'represent'
> them, and may fulfill their function better than they fulfilled it themselves.
> But to 'fulfill a function' in a world of pure experience can be conceived
> and defined in only one possible way. In such a world transitions and
> arrivals (or terminations) are the only events that happen, though they
> happen by so many sorts of path. The only function that one experience
> can perform is to lead into another experience; and the only fulfillment we
> can speak of is the reaching of a certain experienced end. When one
> experience leads to (or can lead to) the same end as another, they agree in
> function.[13]

It is experience all the way down. James' relational metaphysics,
therefore, is a new type of metaphysics, because of its relational character
based in experience.

What about religious experience in particular? James finds it hard to
believe in principles 'which make no difference in Facts'.[14]

Religious experience creates a difference concerning natural facts.
Though most people would regard personal immortality as the major
difference in fact, James thinks it to be a secondary point.[15] In the interest
of intellectual clearness he says: 'I feel bound to say that religious
experience, as we have studied it, cannot be cited as unequivocally
supporting the infinitist belief. The only thing that it unequivocally

---

[12] Ibid., 36.
[13] William James, *Essays on radical empiricism.* 'According to my view,
experience as a whole is a process in time, whereby innumerable particular terms
lapse and are superseded by others that follow upon them by transitions which,
whether disjunctive or conjunctive in content, are themselves experiences, and
must in general be accounted at least as real as the terms which they relate. What
the nature of the event called 'superseding' signifies, depends altogether on the kind
of transition that obtains. Some experiences simply abolish their predecessors
without continuing them in any way. Others are felt to increase or to enlarge their
meaning, to carry out their purpose, or to bring us nearer to their goal.', 62.
[14] William James, *The varieties of religious experience*, (New York ; London:
Longmans, Green & Co. 1902), 361 (Postscript).
[15] Ibid. 363.

testifies to is that we can experience union with SOMETHING larger than ourselves and in that union find our greatest peace. '[16] And he goes on to specify the particular practical needs, religious experience requires:

> ...the practical needs and experiences of religion seem to me sufficiently met by the belief that beyond each man and in a fashion continuous with him there exists a larger power which is friendly to him and to his ideals. All that the facts require is that the power should be both other and larger than our conscious selves. Anything larger will do, if only it be large enough to trust for the next step. It need not be infinite, it need not be solitary. It might conceivably even be only a larger and more godlike self, of which the present self would then be but the mutilated expression, and the universe might conceivably be a collection of such selves, of different degrees of inclusiveness, with no absolute unity realized in it at all.[17]

If that is so, the conclusion for the different contents of such experiences would very likely support a kind of polytheism or, more philosophically, a pluralistic universe.

> I think, in fact, that a final philosophy of religion will have to consider the pluralistic hypothesis more seriously than it has hitherto been willing to consider it. For practical life at any rate, the CHANCE of salvation is enough. No fact in human nature is more characteristic than its willingness to live on a chance. The existence of the chance makes the difference, as Edmund Gurney says, between a life of which the keynote is resignation and a life of which the keynote is hope.[18]

Consequently, James calls himself a supernaturalist of the piecemeal type.

It has to be noted that in his Principles of Psychology religious experience is missing totally and one wonders how that relates to the Gifford Lectures which were published as The Varieties of Religious Experience. I think that for James, religious experience is not one experience among others, but plays a major role in the dynamics of the psyche. This becomes evident e.g. in the following passage from the Varieties of Religious Experience:

> There was not a mere consciousness of something there, but fused in the central happiness of it, a startling awareness of some ineffable good. Not vague either, not like the emotional effect of some poem, or scene, or blossom, or music, but the sure knowledge of the close presence of a sort

---

[16] Ibid.
[17] Ibid. 364.
[18] Ibid. 365.

of mighty person, and after it went, the memory persisted as the one perception of reality. Everything else might be a dream, but not that.[19]

James' criteria for falsehood are rather tentative, since no objective truth is possible. Every experiencing subject is part of the community of experiencing subjects, none being outside this community. Therefore, even classical forms of truth, according to James, were human.

> They also mediated between still earlier truths and what in those days were novel observations. Purely objective truth, truth in whose establishment the function of giving human satisfaction in marrying previous parts of experience with newer parts played no role whatever, is nowhere to be found. The reason why we call things true is the reason why they ARE true, for 'to be true' MEANS only to   perform this marriage-function.[20]

Experience and criteria for truth in Alfred North Whitehead

The similarities between James' and Whitehead's concept of experience are striking. In the following sections of my paper I shall concentrate on the differences. Let me begin with a brief consideration of Whitehead's concept of religion.

In Whitehead's "theory of religion," the development of religion leads to a *rationalization* of religious experience. [21] Although, at first, religious concerns were preoccupied with rituals, partial myths, and emotional stabilization, later religious consciousness evolved increasingly towards the recognition of universal connectivity, leaving behind provincial rituals and social bounds.[22] For Whitehead, this process of the "rationalization" of religion occurs within reciprocal movements towards *solitariness* and *solidarity*. These opposite features reveal the meaning of "religious intuition," namely, to be the *universal mediation of uniquely experienced events*.

In Whitehead's words: The contrast of *singularity* and *universality*, *solitariness* and *solidarity*, illuminates "the origin of rational religion"[23]. "Religion is what the individual does with his own solitariness"[24] *and*

---

[19] Ibid.
[20] William James, *Pragmatism: a new name for some old ways of thinking*, 35.
[21] Alfred North Whitehead, *Religion in the Making* (1926). 1974, New American Library, 20-63.
[22] Ibid. 23.
[23] Ibid. 58.
[24] Ibid. 16.

"religion is world-loyalty"[25]. Thus the religious experience of uniqueness is both the experience of "solitariness" *and* that of the "loyalty" to the world[26]. Whitehead's theory of "religious intuition" has a dual structure:

> Rational religion appeals to the direct intuition of special occasions and to the elucidatory power of its concepts for all occasions. It arises from that which is special, but it extends to what is general. The doctrines of rational religion aim at being that metaphysics which can be derived from the super-normal experience of mankind in its moments of finest insight.[27]

"Religious intuition," therefore has two aspects: (1) *Singularity:* religious intuition is a "*direct* intuition" which cannot be resolved by general terms (such as rationality, metaphysics), but may only be *experienced.* Hence, religious intuition cannot be conceptualized completely, but is bound to the *uniqueness* of the experiencing subject over against all conceptual generalities.[28] This uniqueness of religious intuition constitutes "the ultimate religious evidence, beyond which there is no appeal"[29]; (2) *Rationality:* although "intuitions" occur as events under *unique* conditions, they must, due to their accessibility for others, be subject to a process of communicability by theoretical transformation, i.e., the process of their *"rationalization"*[30]. "Intuitions," as it were, introduce the uniquely new into the world. However, at the same time, they must be generalized to be accessible for others experience.[31] Or, as Whitehead says, the relevance of its concepts can only be distinctly discerned in moments of insight, and then, for many of us, only after suggestion from without.[32]

It is important to realize that, in Whitehead's thought, "religious intuition" has *irreplaceable* meaning for any general "theory of the world." On the one hand, it allows for a unique base of experience, or "one select

---

[25] Ibid. 59.
[26] Ibid. 86.
[27] Ibid. 31.
[28] Whitehead compares this experience of the unpronounceable, that is nevertheless known, with the knowledge of the mother, who "can ponder many things in their hearts which their lips cannot express." See Ibid. 65.
[29] Ibid.
[30] Ibid. 63: "But reason is the safeguard of the objectivity of religion: it secures for it the general coherence denied to hysteria."
[31] This applies in particular to the religious experience in which "novelty" cannot be expressed by any "formula." Nevertheless, religious experience becomes (and remains) accessible by its rational generalization: Ibid. 129 ff.

field of interest"[33] On the other hand, it maintains that concepts of religion, "though derived primarily from special experiences, are yet of universal validity"[34]. For a general theory of the world, the *irreplaceable* contribution of *religious* experience consists in the fact that it proceeds from the "super-normal experience of mankind in its moment of finest insight"[35].

In Whitehead's description of experience, his arguments of proof are different to James'. The pragmatic test of truth is accepted as one component of truth. But there is a final link of experience to reality as a whole. While agreeing with James on coherence and the value character of every experience, he goes further:

> The truth itself is nothing else than how the composite natures of the organic actualities of the world obtain adequate representation in the divine nature."[36]
> Similarly, applying truth criteria to religious experience, he writes:
> "Religious truth must be developed from knowledge acquired when our ordinary senses and intellectual operations are at their highest pitch of discipline. To move one step from this position towards the dark recesses of abnormal psychology is to surrender finally any hope of a solid foundation for religious doctrine.
> Religion starts from the generalization of final truths first perceived as exemplified in particular instances. These truths are amplified into a coherent system and applied to the interpretation of life. They stand or fall, like other truths, by their success in this interpretation. The peculiar character of religious truth is that it explicitly deals with values.[37]

What follows is an stimulating evaluation of dogmata[38]: their truth and their limitations: how much they can stimulate and express experience as well as in what way and in which circumstances they can cause the opposite effect: 'a one-sized formulation may be true, but may have the

---

[33] Alfred North Whitehead, *Religion in the Making*, 31: "a small selection from the common experience," or "one among other specialized interests of mankind whose truths are of limited validity."

[34] Ibid. 31.

[35] Ibid.

[36] Allfred North Whitehead, *Process and Reality*, 12.

[37] Alfred North Whitehead, *Religion in the Making,* 120.

[38] 'But the dogmas, however true, are only bits of the truth, expressed in terms which in some ways are over-assertive and in other ways lose the essence of truth. When exactly understood in relation to an exact system of philosophic thought, they may - or may not - be exactly true.' Ibid. 139.

effect of a lie by its distortion of emphasis'[39]. Coming back to the pragmatic evaluation of religious experience, Whitehead relates it to the evaluation of scientific development. "Progress in truth - truth of science and truth of religion - is mainly a progress in the framing of concepts, in discarding artificial abstractions or partial metaphors, and in evolving notions which strike more deeply into the root of reality."[40]

If religion for Whitehead is primarily individual,[41] it inevitably entails the problem of expression. This would involve 'individual expression' and rituals, which are communal forms of expression.[42] But that would have to be the subject of another paper. In my view, the surprising statement concerning religion in Whitehead is his insistence on 'every day experience' as a basis, although there can be extraordinary ones as well.

> The final principle of religion is that there is wisdom in the nature of things, from which flow our direction of practice, and our possibility of the theoretical analysis of fact. It grounds this principle upon two sources of evidence, first upon our success in various special theoretical sciences, physical and otherwise; and secondly, upon our knowledge of a discernment of ordered relationships, especially in aesthetic valuations, which stretches far beyond anything which has been expressed systematically in words.[43]

Truth claims play an important role in religious discussion. At the same time one should keep in mind, Whitehead's famous statement concerning any scheme of philosophy in mind:

> If we consider any scheme of philosophic categories as one complex asser-
> tion, and apply to it the logician's alternative, true or false, the answer

---

[39] Alfred North Whitehead, *Religion in the Making*, 123.

[40] Ibid., 127.

[41] 'Thus religion is primarily individual, and the dogmas of religion are clarifying modes of external expression. The intolerant use of religious dogmas has practically destroyed their unity for a great, if not the greater part, of the civilized world.' Ibid. 132.

[42] 'The later phases of the antecedent communal type of religion are dominated by the conscious reaction of human nature to the social organization in which it finds itself. Such reaction is partly emotion clothing itself in belief and ritual, and partly reason justifying practice by the test of social preservation. Rational religion is the wider conscious reaction of men to the universe in which they find themselves.' Ibid. 41.

[43] Ibid., 137/138.

must be that the scheme is false. The same answer must be given to a like question respecting the existing formulated principles of any science.[44]

'It would be cosy to get a neat theory without error. "James' service to metaphysics [lies] in bringing out error and patting it on the back. Always on the side of the underdog – one side of it."[45] In a similar fashion Whitehead writes: 'Philosophers can never hope to formulate these metaphysical first principles...[46] There is not even the language in which to frame them.'[47] These are distinct statements regarding relationalism as the suitable forms of philosophizing, to avoid the Scylla of absolutism and the Charybdis of relativism.[48]

Thus, the major problem for philosophy and theology is dealing with symbols concerning experience.

> So much of human experience is bound up with symbolic reference, that it is hardly an exaggeration to say that the very meaning of truth is pragmatic. But though this statement is hardly an exaggeration, still it is an exaggeration, for the pragmatic test can never work, unless on some occasion in the future, or in the present there is a definite determination of what is true on that occasion. Otherwise the poor pragmatist remains an intellectual Hamlet, perpetually adjourning decision of judgment to some later date.[49]

For a further discussion of symbolic reference and a fully developed system of signs, one should turn to Charles Sanders Peirce's philosophy.[50]

---

[44] Allfred North Whitehead, *Process and Reality*, 8.

[45] Jennifer Hamlin von der Luft,. „The Harvard Lectures for 1924-25." In: *The Emergence of Whitehead's Metaphysics*, von Lewis S. Ford, 262-302, (Albany: State University of New York Press, 1984), 288.

[46] Allfred North Whitehead, *Process and Reality*, 4.

[47] Ibid. 13.

[48] See also Maria-Sibylla Lotter, *DIE METAPHYSISCHE KRITIK DES SUBJEKTS, Eine Untersuchung von Whiteheads universalisierter Sozialontologie,* (Hildesheim, Zürich, New York: Georg Olms, 1996), 20-48.

[49] Allfred North Whitehead, *Process and Reality*, 181.

[50] There is so far only a German edition of Peirces Writings of Philosophy of Religion avaiable: Charles Sanders Peirce, *Religionsphilosophische Schriften* , Übersetzt unter Mitarbeit von Helmut Maaßen, eingeleitet, kommentiert und herausgegeben von Hermann Deuser.PhB 478. , Verlag Felix Meiner, Hamburg, 1995.

Helmut Maassen (European Society for Process Thought, Geldern, Germany) is an independent scholar. He has taught Philosophy and Religion at several Colleges and Universities (USA, Germany, India). His areas of research are Indian Philosophy (Gandhi, Ambedkar), Metaphysics, especially Leibniz, Spinoza, Peirce and Whitehead, Philosophy of Religion and Comparative Religion. He has published several books on Whitehead and Peirce. He is the Editor of the European Studies in Process Thought and is recently preparing a German edition of Herbert Wildon Carr's *Cogitans Cogitata*. He is a founding member of the German Whitehead Society.

INTER-RELIGIOUS DIALOGUE: BY WHOM, FOR WHAT PURPOSE OR: HOW TO OVERCOME THE CLASH OF RELIGIONS

LOUWRENS W. HESSEL

Summary

There is no philosophical basis for inter-religious dialogue, but philosophy is indispensable for minimising derailments and for preventing stagnation.

The parties involved

The usual way of organising inter-religious dialogues is to arrange for theologians and other religious professionals to meet together and discuss their various doctrines, in order to find similarities and to overcome vicious disagreements. As theologians are the most knowledgeable about religious doctrine they are considered to be best qualified to enter into dialogue. But because they must be loyal to their spiritual home and because they are strongly attached to the outlook of their own group it is desirable to have philosophers as moderators. These can bring in the broader view which is necessary to come to acceptable conclusions.

In real life at least two more parties are involved. There are the founders and prophets of each religion and, although they are no longer with us, we know enough about their personalities and cultural environment to imagine what their partaking in the dialogue would be like. A participating philosopher now becomes much more involved because he must point out discrepancies between the visions of founding prophets and what theologians under the influence of the culture of their day have made of them.[1]) *Inter*-religious dialogue becomes entangled with *intra*-religious argument[2].

The fourth, and most important group are the common people for whom religion is not a calling or a profession but part of their identity. As long as they live in peace with believers of other religions, doctrinal issues are not very important to them. They are busy living, which for the majority of mankind means trying to survive. For people in distress any call to religious dialogue is out of season. Their fate depends on the quality of their leaders[3].

Good leaders help people to recognise the similarity between their own struggles and those reported in their religious traditions[4]. They will stress the saving power of the Eternal One, which then becomes a source of comfort and inspiration, even in the face of defeat. Resistance, not dialogue must characterise the position of the oppressed but they will bring in invaluable experiences once their time has come. They then can show the way to true progress.

There are also leaders that have not outgrown their evolutionary heritage in terms of dominance and hierarchy. When they are religious, they will emphasise coercive power as the major divine characteristic. They may incite to great deeds of bravery (sometimes offering eternal reward), but once in power there is no further incentive except territorial expansion and internal control. Dialogue is considered as disloyalty and stagnation sets in.

Thus to make wars into religious wars seems to be a specialty of monotheistic religions.[5] Tribal societies had their gods who served them in winning their battles; monotheistic chiefs claimed that it was they who served God (or his prophet) by winning battles for Him. Until recently not

---

[1] Of course a philosopher is himself a child of his time but he will not have recourse to unassailable revelations, and he is not necessarily bound by loyalty to some school of philosophy..

[2] Theologians claim to explain and develop the visions of the founders. But derailments are frequent, from the saddening quarrels of the Church Fathers to Muslims debating the uncreatedness of their holy book, branches of Judaism reducing the Torah to a code of Law, perversions of the karma doctrine in Buddhism etc.

[3] For a long time in human history tribalism with dominant leaders provided the best survival strategy, just as in the animal kingdom.

[4] Cf. Jesus citing from the Psalms when dying on the cross.

[5] Cf. Whitehead's dictum: "When the Western world accepted Christianity, Caesar conquered" in: A.N.Whitehead, *Process and Reality* (The free press, 1978) 342. Western belligerence may have its roots in the traditional belief that the power of the Eternal One is coercive, rather than persuasive.

much help in the way of peace has come from these quarters. Conferences of more moderate leaders are not always useful either. At the "Millennium World Peace Summit of Religious and Spiritual Leaders" the Dalai Lama, Nobel prize winner for the peace, was not invited.[6]

Truth and certainty

As long as philosophy is considered as a failure when it does not yield certainty and truth, it does not contribute much to this situation. It is easy to expose the sophistry in saying that truth is what is revealed by God or to point out how often this has become an instrument of evil. It is not easy to pass judgment on its value for (group)survival. Revelationists would dismiss such judgments as beside the point, defeatist and faithless.

It seems that in Western philosophy and theology certainty and truth have been felt as a kind of substantial entities, independent, objective, absolute and unchanging.[7] This may be understandable in view of the vagaries of western history, but a philosopher must admit that absolute truth can arise only by confrontation with the totality of experience and is never in the possession of any human institution. He would not deny the value of certainty and truth, but he must admit that they remain ideals, forever beckoning, forever beyond our grasp. What we do have is relative certainty and partial truth, which is not nothing. They are attainable and can be judged by their trustworthiness, i.e. their reliability for humans to act upon. Truthfulness in one's deeds rather than truth tables for one's words.

"As being is to becoming, so is truth to belief"[8]. Plato used it as evidence for the superiority of being over becoming and of truth over belief. We know what it lead to in his later years. Living human beings will turn it around: because we live in a world which always becomes and never really *is*. We have only belief to act upon. There is no escape from risk taking, and that is why we must live by faith.

Truth and life

This contrast reflects a wider re-orientation in western philosophy: from believing in (putative) timeless substances to recognising time-bound

---

[6] "Snubbing the Dalai Lama at the U-N. A sample of American editorial comments in *www.fas.org/news/2000/000811*.
[7] Linguisticists went to the other extreme by considering truth as nothing more than a property of propositions.
[8] Plato, Timaeus 29C.

experiences as the ultimate elements of reality. This is in line with postmodernism, but in a constructive way. It transforms many time-honoured religious concepts. Transcendence and revelation are now recognised as aspects of every event; the idea of unqualified divine omnipotence is shown to be irrational; being is felt as always entangled with becoming; persuasion, not coercion, as worthy to be obeyed. Truth and certainty are acknowledged as excellent but not supreme. Whitehead would say that behind their pursuit there must be an even more important purpose i.e. the promotion of the art of life, expressed as: "how to live, how to live well, how to live better", and that it is philosophy's mission to promote these.[9] Not just for a human elite, but for common people and for the world at large. Understanding eastern religions becomes now more easy, understanding the dominant form of Abrahamic religions[10] is made more difficult.

Role of philosophy

Philosophy's critical task is to be formulated as to try and clear up "doctrines, ignorantly entertained"[11]. For the monotheistic religions it involves questioning the way traditional metaphysics has conceptualised divine saving events which lead to assertions like "if there is one God, then He/She must be omnipotent" or "if God is not omnipotent then He/She is not powerful enough always to save".

Taking philosophy as basic is trying to escape from the particularity of important events. And because ignorances can only be recognised from the outside, dialogue plays a crucial role, painful and unsettling as it may be. Philosophy does have the task to generalise, but there is no "view from nowhere". Religions are inexorably particular, both in their origins as in their call to individuals to listen and get transformed.

In a critical sense philosophers must make bold to formulate criteria for judging religious doctrines, not for providing foundations or dismissals of foundations. In the present world there is falsity, or at least inadequacy, in any religion which recommends isolation from the world as a superior virtue, or which refuses to give the highest priority to the sufferings of the

---

[9] Cf. A.N. Whitehead, *The function of reason* (Boston: Beacon Presse, 1929), pg. 8.

[10] At the conference Dr. Krajewski objected to implicitly undervaluing the unique position of Judaism by subsuming it under "Abrahamic religions". I repent. To give priority to deeds over dogma has always been one of the excellencies of Judaism.

[11] A.N.Whitehead, *Modes of thought* (Free Press, 1968) 171.

world.[12] Most importantly, unselfishness (not loss of self but allowing the momentary self to be surpassed) must be recognised as a supreme virtue. In the words of John Hick, religions must be judged by their power to transform the lives of their adherents from self-centeredness to "Reality-centeredness". But again, this is a limit, not a foundation.[13] These are modest and largely negative contributions, comparable to the *via negativa* of medieval theologians.

Risk taking

Globalisation appears to work in two opposite directions. There is generalisation: the inescapable evolution from tribal security to world consciousness, and there is individualisation: an increase in feelings of personal identity and responsibility. Morality evolves from collective ritualism to personal conscience. What philosophy has to offer is no substitute for the comfort found in trusted religious authority. Rather it must stress that religion is "what the individual does with his own solitariness".[14] This is a conscientization, carrying a moral incentive: first to fully interiorise the tradition of one's own upbringing (which is a condition for authenticity in any dialogue) and then the willingness to allow one's foundations to be shaken[15]. This carries a high price. There is no longer the security to be found in existing power structures and no comfort in meetings in churches, mosques or temples. There may be accusations of unbelief, apostasy. But the voice of the old faith must never

---

[12] Dr Sia, in note 25 to his paper for this conference, points out that giving attention to the miseries and injustices in life is given as part of "a generalised interpretation of every experience", that is of philosophy at large. This is true, but for liberation theologians it is not enough. For them analysis and redress are the primary tasks to which any valid philosophy would assist. Cf. the critical review essay *Process philosophy, social thought, and liberation theology* in Zygon 19(1) 65-81 (1984) an a more balanced discussion in: M.F.Sia and S.Sia, *From suffering to God* (St. Martin's Press 1994).

[13] Cf. J.V. Apczynski, "John Hick's theocentrism: revolutionary or implicitly exclusivist", *Modern theology* 8, 1 (Jan. 1992), pg. 39-51.

[14] A.N.Whitehead, *Religion in the making* (New American Library, 1926), pg. 16. The saying has been criticised as overly individualistic. But it was the individual conscience of prophets, and pre-eminently Jewish prophets, to which "the word of the Lord" came. Prophets open new vistas to the ultimately real One and His/Her call to righteousness and beauty. Communities are not individuals and have no conscience.

[15] The shaking may involve all three monotheistic religions as process theologians question unilateral creation, omnipotence and divine impassibility.

be silenced, even when it speaks unfairly[16]. It is an ongoing affair with the character of oscillation between different convictions, which may find rest only "at the end of times", and which results in mutual transformation[17] without loss of continuity.

The outcome will be uncertain and this is where faith comes in, which is the courage to act according to one's conscience. Conscience, however, cannot be static; it is shaped and sharpened by one's religion and it is permanently being transformed by life itself. Dialogue is an essential part of it. It is difficult to see how any religion could do without. This is not relativism; relationality precludes relativism.

New religious communities may spring up, old ones may rejuvenate themselves but they will offer no escape from individual responsibility. Dialogue must lead to world solidarity, but it is not for free.

Louwrens W. Hessel, Ph.D., worked for many years as chemistry lecturer and as college chaplain in Pakistan, Tanzania and the Philippines. Later he was deputy director of the Gaubius Institute TNO Leiden, for cardiovascular diseases. He holds university degrees in chemistry and philosophy from Leiden University, the Netherlands.

---

[16] Silencing the voice of the old faith is what happened when the early Christian church severed its bond with Judaism. The results have been disastrous. A new attitude is evident from the attention given by Christian leaders to books like T. Frymer-Kensky et al, eds., *Christianity in Jewish terms* (Westview Press, 2000).

[17] Sharply to be distinguished from syncretism as described by: David Novak, *Jewish-Christian dialogue* (Oxford University Press, 1989), pg. 20.

INTER-RELIGIOUS DIALOGUE AND RELIGIOUS PLURALISM: A PHILOSOPHICAL CRITIQUE OF POPE BENEDICT XVI AND THE FALL OF RELIGIOUS ABSOLUTISM

MATTHEW LOPRESTI

Introduction

This paper does not concern itself with a dialogue between those who share, or think they share, a common vision of reality. Rather, the focus is on those who generally *do not* share a common vision of reality. By focusing on this second, more interesting, group we are presented with a challenging philosophical and practical problem in our examination of inter-religious dialogue, specifically, we are faced with the question: *is it possible to hold an absolutist view of the truthfulness of one's own traditions and still engage in an open inter-religious dialogue with other religions?* The importance of this question cannot be overemphasized: and this paper is aimed at answering this question in as affirmative a way as possible, but with the ironic twist that absolutists who wish to engage in inter-religious dialogue must adopt a pluralistic outlook if they are to remain faithful to the unconditional[1] truth-claims of their own tradition. This paper is dedicated to framing the question in a way that highlights the need for an agreed upon philosophical basis for this dialogue, and in so doing demonstrates the intimate connectivity of inter-religious dialogue with religious pluralism.

---

[1] A religious absolutist holds that one's religious tradition—especially its conception of a religious ultimate—is based on unconditional truth-claims. Because one's tradition is thought to have uniquely true insights of ultimate reality, that tradition's dogma, soteriological path, and spiritual praxes are understandably thought to teach and prescribe the only, if not perhaps the most, correct and efficacious religious beliefs and practices.

This paper is divided into three main sections. This first defines what is meant by "inter-religious dialogue." The second demonstrates the necessary relationship between religious pluralism and inter-religious dialogue: inter-religious dialogue is a practice that needs to be informed by the theory of religious pluralism, and religious pluralism is a theory that is strengthened and furthered by the practice of inter-religious dialogue. The third somewhat counter intuitively argues that if a tradition is committed to religious absolutism (and its practitioners are to remain faithful), then it (and they) must also be committed to genuine inter-religious dialogue and therefore, surprisingly, must also commit itself (and themselves) to a religious pluralism.

Joseph Ratzinger's[2] writings on these issues lead to a more thorough understanding of the challenges and possibilities afforded to religious traditions in their struggle to strike a balance between commitments to authentic (rather than polemical) inter-religious dialogue and commitments to absolutist religious dogma. Attention to the interplay between views of religious pluralism and interfaith dialogue in his scholarship uncovers assumptions that may either preclude or foster the possibility for open and genuine inter-religious dialogue and pluralism itself.

On Inter-religious Dialogue

A.   Theological Bases for Inter-religious Dialogue?

Prescribing a shared vision of reality is hardly a popular thing to do when setting a groundwork for possible dialogue with traditions (religious or otherwise) quite different from one's own. It is nevertheless necessary for any inter-religious dialogue to take place. If the prescribed vision of reality comes from or blatantly resembles some one religious tradition or another, adherents of different traditions will rightly feel excluded or violated and this may even turn potential participants in the dialogue off, or implicitly render the "dialogue" moot, because of an inability to begin the dialogue from a shared perspective (i.e., a perspective of non-superficial similarities and differences). If, on the other hand, this shared

---

[2] Throughout this paper I will often use the name "Ratzinger" rather than "Pope Benedict XVI" because I do not want to be perceived as trying to undermine the Pope, per se, or Catholic dogma, but rather am analyzing and critiquing the philosophical ideas and implications of the man. At certain times, when it is appropriate to draw attention to his role as the head of the Roman Catholic Church, I may use his pontific name or title.

perspective is prescribed by a sensible, a-religious philosophical understanding of reality, then I argue that there is a better chance for inter-religious dialogue to get off the ground. But, such a dialogue is apt to seem vacuous and of little if any interest to those who are unwaveringly committed to truth and see a particular worldview as true, and even worse for those committed to an absolutist view of their particular metaphysical understanding of that worldview. These are the two possibilities of religious absolutism and I make this distinction here between a commitment to the objects or aims of greatest religious concern identified in one's tradition as universal truths (e.g., the religious ultimates or salvific paths and aims) and a commitment to a way of seeing the world because later I will argue that if one is committed to the former, then, being committed to truth, one must also be committed to inter-religious dialogue.[3] If one is committed to the later, however, then one ends up, in Abrahamic terms, worshipping his worldview instead of God.[4] In essence this means that aligning oneself with dogma rather than the reality that this dogma is supposed to accurately portray.

Dutch philosopher Louwrens W. Hessel[5] argued at the conference that discussing the possibility for a shared vision of reality is a handicap for theologians who—if they are "good theologians"—are committed to a particular, and largely non-negotiable, vision of reality. This wrongly

---

[3] In certain traditions, for example, there is an obligation for adherents to actively seek out wisdom and understanding equal to their intellectual ability (e.g., Islam) and specific teachings geared towards people with different levels of insight and wisdom (e.g., Buddhism's pragmatic notion of *upāya*, or skill-in-means). Such understanding is not attained by abject surrender of the intellect to dogma but demands an active engagement in not only intra-religious dialogue but inter-religious dialogue as well so that one can more fully realize the deepest wisdom of the dharma, for Buddhists, or more fully and more faithfully surrender one's soul unto Allah, in Islam. Taking a cue from T.S. Eliot, I argue that to be faithful to the claims of one's tradition one must actively engage in an understanding of these claims, and just as one only knows oneself through engagement with the Other, one does not begin to understand one's own religious tradition until one comes back to it (from an engagement with another tradition) for the first time.

[4] In non-theistic Buddhist terms, we could say that one ends up being attached to the teachings rather than embodying them. In secular Whiteheadian terms we might accurately say that one ends up fallaciously concretizing a conceptual scheme as foundational rather than adventuring with these fluid and largely pragmatic abstractions.

[5] In *Interreligious Dialogue—by whom, for what purpose. How to Overcome the Clash of Religions*. Presented at the conference on The Philosophical Basis for Inter-Religious Dialogue in Katowice, Poland (May 2008) and also appearing in this volume.

implies that theologians are equally committed to explicit metaphysical systems, but I contend that the metaphysics theologians often find themselves committed to are not so much necessary to their respective religions as they are inherited explanations of the dogma of those religions, expressed in terms of one rather than another metaphysical system (e.g., Roman Catholicism and Thomistic philosophy). I favor a thesis contra Hessel, namely that it is not possible for theologians to fully engage in inter-religious dialogue unless they are able and willing to temporarily bracket their theological and supposed metaphysical commitments and engage other traditions *qua* philosophers.[6] In this sense, inter-religious dialogue is a philosophical, not a theological, activity and can also constitute a furthering of one's religious practice.

B.   A Philosophical Basis for Inter-religious Dialogue

Understanding inter-religious dialogue as a philosophical rather than theological activity means that there is no need to attempt to provide inter-religious *theological* bases for dialogues between traditions (especially given the total lack of *theo*logy in some major religious traditions). Getting parties to agree on a theological basis from which their dialogue can grow would require a specifically tailored basis for each dialogue that differs with each new tradition that engages in or disengages from the dialogue. As a philosophical activity, however, inter-religious dialogue avoids this un-navigable minefield completely.

Locating a philosophical basis for inter-religious dialogue means, in this paper, articulating a vision of reality that offers the most fertile ground for effective inter-religious dialogue. I see that ground to be a deep religious pluralism and informed by the philosophy of Whitehead and Hartshorne, whose search for a general vision or understanding of the cosmos is grounded in a process perspective.[7] It is this general process

---

[6] To be fair, Hessel argues that philosophers are required as mediators in inter-religious dialogue, but dismisses the possibility that theologians can themselves fully participate on their own. It seems that he and I agree insofar as we both see inter-religious dialogue as a philosophical rather than theological practice.

[7] The most recent and concise articulation of this pluralism can be found in David Ray Griffin, *Deep Religious Pluralism* (Louisville: Westminster John Know Press, 2005). John B. Cobb, Jr. originated the theory and it has been most thoroughly explicated and promulgated by David Ray Griffin. The basis of this religious pluralism is the ontological plurality of Alfred North Whitehead's process metaphysics. Whitehead's metaphysical schema involves three ontological ultimates as generic, irreducible aspects of the world. They are creativity, God, and actual occasions. Cobb takes these ontological ultimates as schemata for

perspective that I believe offers the most fertile ground for a cross-cultural, trans-traditional shared vision of reality. Nevertheless, this paper limits its argument to showing only that a pluralistic perspective will have to be adopted by any who wish to engage in inter-religious dialogue. This pluralistic perspective need not, however, push us into the arms of a Whitehead-specific pluralism. In the end, however, I clearly see this as the most likely candidate for a stable philosophical basis for not only inter-religious dialogue but a deep religious pluralism as well. But if one sees absolutism and relativism as the only available options for attempting an explanation of religious diversity—and this is the mistake I argue that Joseph Ratzinger makes in the second section of this paper—then where is the basis for commitment to unconditional religious truths, let alone inter-religious dialogue? This brings us back to the idea that the purpose of inter-religious dialogue depends upon whether one adopts a relativist, pluralist, or absolutist outlook towards religious diversity.

C.   The Relative Purpose of Inter-religious Dialogue

No tradition-respecting religious practitioner chooses relativism. Even if one did, what could be the point of dialogue from a relativistic perspective? To pass the time? It will be shown that Ratzinger feels compelled to choose absolutism, because he rejects relativism and sees no other alternative, having conflated pluralism with relativism. In Ratzinger's hands, religious absolutism leads to confusing imperatives regarding inter-religious dialogue and along with his writings on the topic, makes his endorsement of inter-religious dialogue suspect. Having demonstrated how Ratzinger's negative view of religious pluralism negatively effects[8] his view of inter-religious dialogue, which he sees as a tool for conversion, we will then turn to a deeper examination of absolutism as a viable response to the diversity of religious traditions and their truth claims. Where does absolutism leave people committed to inter-religious dialogue and is there a role for genuine inter-religious dialogue in a religious absolutism beyond what Ratzinger envisions?

---

interpreting different multiple religious traditions—specifically their general conceptions of religious ultimates—as compossibly true. By arguing that there a plurality of religious ultimates can simultaneously obtain, Cobb establishes a "deep" religious pluralism wherein a plurality of religious traditions can be true at the same time.

[8] "Effect" because I am arguing that there is an implicit counterfactual relation between religious pluralism and inter-religious dialogue and vice versa.

Pluralism calls for engagement in genuine inter-religious dialogue to further the depth of understanding of one's own tradition and of the traditions of others on their own terms. Above all, it requires David Ray Griffin's positive and negative criteria for a generic religious pluralism.

> The negative affirmation is the rejection of religious absolutism, which means rejecting the a priori assumption that [one's] own religion is the only one that provides saving truths and values to its adherents, that it alone is divinely inspired, that it has been divinely established as the only legitimate religion, intended to replace all others. The positive affirmation, which goes beyond the negative one, is the acceptance of the idea that there are indeed religions other than one's own that provide saving truths and values to their adherents.[9]

But absolutists are in no way inclined to accept these two pluralistic demands, because it may seem as if the "negative" demand requires one to reject one's faith and the "positive" demand is a descent into relativism, if not blasphemy. Do these pluralistic criteria then exclude absolutism by mere fiat? Why ought an absolutist accept these criteria? As we shall see, Vatican II's *Nostra aetate* might be interpreted as an attempt by Catholicism to grant both of these pluralistic assumptions. But without getting into intra-religious theological debate, suffice it to say that some, like Joseph Ratzinger and Marcello Pera, see *Nostra aetate* as espousing relativism. Instead can we locate a direct link between religious absolutism and Griffin's pluralistic criteria? After demonstrating the necessary link between one's view of inter-religious dialogue and one's view of the viability of a religious pluralism in the second section, I argue in the third and final section of this paper that we can, because religious absolutism is argued to require genuine inter-religious dialogue, and since this dialogue requires a pluralistic basis for it to get off the ground, a viable religious absolutism would be paradoxically reliant upon these pluralist assumptions.

Joseph Ratzinger, Inter-religious Dialogue, and Religious Pluralism

In May 1996, Pope Benedict XVI, then Cardinal Joseph Ratzinger, identified the "theology of religious pluralism as the gravest threat facing

---

[9] Griffin, Deep Religious Pluralism, 3.

the church today."[10] His reasoning behind this statement was two-fold: first he criticized religious pluralism for being what he calls a "religious indifferentism" (i.e., relativism)[11], and second, he is gravely concerned with what he sees as religious pluralism's challenge to the unique saving role of Christ.[12] The concern for truth over indifferentism toward truth and the preservation of the basic tenets of one's tradition are theological concerns that many of the world's religious traditions and their practitioners share. These are issues that Ratzinger ought to be concerned about. I argue that as a philosopher, however, Joseph Ratzinger makes scholarly errors in his characterization of pluralistic theologies as relativisms. These errors have a dramatic and deleterious effect on his two concerns above and also on his stated positions re inter-religious dialogue.

There is a unique paradox in Ratzinger's commitment to inter-religious dialogue in his actions as Pope and in his ostensible disdain for genuine dialogue in his worlds as a scholar. In his recent actions as pontiff, Ratzinger has clearly made gestures towards open dialogue with other traditions (Islam and Orthodox Christianity in particular), however, in his writings as Prefect for the Congregation for the Doctrine of Faith, I argue, he views inter-religious dialogue as a tool for evangelism, and thus sees no real role for open dialogue at all.

This section of the paper is directed at an examination of the philosophical reasoning that informs Pope Benedict XVI's views on religious pluralism and how this directly impacts his views on inter-religious dialogue. Ratzinger's views discussed herein fit with most recent and well-known articulations of the Church's hardened position on dialogue and pluralism. This should be expected, seeing as he was the Prefect of the Congregation of the Doctrine of Faith for a quarter of a

---

[10] Reported by John L. Allen, Jr. in "Perils of Pluralism - History of Vatican opposition to relativism among world religions," *National Catholic Reporter*, September 15, 2000.

[11] "Religious indifferentism" carries an epistemic meaning for Ratzinger. Anyone who adheres to religious indifferentism regards the truth of one religion to be equal with the truth of others, and so, for Ratzinger, his use of this term clearly denotes relativism. This phrase was also used by Ratzinger (when he was still the Prefect of the Congregation of the Doctrine of Faith) to criticize the work of Indian Jesuit Fr. Anthony de Mello, whom he accused of uncritically blending ideas from Eastern and Western traditions.

[12] This is *the* essential roadblock to Christian consideration of pluralism, and no faithful Christian can ignore it. Due to limited space, I am unable to address this issue here, though it is addressed in Chapter 5 of my dissertation, from which this paper is derived.

century prior to becoming Pope.[13] The Prefect's job is to determine what is and what is not appropriate Catholic theology.[14] One might defend Ratzinger by saying that it is not entirely fair to criticize a Pope, of all people, for "protecting the faith" or preserving the philosophical lineage of his tradition. Indeed, given his past role as Prefect and his new role as a Shepard, such unwavering and unapologetic protectionism ought to be expected in his theology. But my critique is neither theological nor personal, nor is it a critique of the Roman Catholic Church itself; rather it is a purely philosophical critique of the writings of the man who also happens to currently head it. Responses that point to Ratzinger's role as prefect or pontiff rather than his reasoning are more defenses of the man rather than the positions he is taking. Similarly, responses that point to the larger context of Catholic doctrine rather than the arguments presented in his writings are more defenses of Catholicism than the positions this one man is taking. Either type of response will miss the point of my critique. Besides, if there is a Western religious tradition that has thrived from critical inquiry, it is the Roman Catholic Church and this sort of philosophical analysis of Ratzigner's views is certainly warranted and worth undertaking.

What follows is the first English language philosophical critique of Pope Benedict XVI's writings. It begins by arguing that he reduces all religious pluralisms to relativism. As a result, it is more than understandable that he deeply distrusts pluralism. I argue, however, that his wholesale reduction of pluralism to relativism is related to his narrow conception of the possible utility of inter-religious dialogue. Ratzinger's writings are critiqued to demonstrate that, for him, inter-religious dialogue is desirable only to the extent that it offers an opportunity to convert others to Catholicism. I argue, to the contrary, that *genuine* inter-religious dialogue must be concomitant with an authentic and demonstrably deep

---

[13] Ratzinger was Prefect of the Congregation for the Doctrine of Faith from 1981 until the time he was elected Pope in 2005 and he was Cardinal and Archbishop of Munich and Freising for five years prior to that (1977- 1982).

[14] Rather than focus on how Roman Catholics have historically addressed pluralism and how exactly the current pontiff fits in here, it is sufficient in this article to note the kind of attention that has been paid to Roman Catholic clergy and academics who have addressed the challenge of pluralism since Vatican II. The fallout of Ratzinger's attention in this area has lead to a number of censured works (some posthumously), a list of theologians deemed to be either unfit to teach Catholic Theology, and, in some instances, has resulted in excommunication for what seems to have been the crime of taking Vatican II a little too seriously, a little too soon. Even Pope John-Paul II found himself and his ecumenical outreach the object of CDF corrections.

religious pluralism, and is thereby exclusive of any intentional attempts at conversion.

A.   Misunderstanding Pluralism: A Note on Taxonomy

Religious pluralism calls for a normative philosophical response to the fact of religious diversity. Paying attention to the *ism* we ought to be sure to distinguish it from the basic descriptive fact of religious diversity as well as from more generic plural*istic* theologies. Pluralism, as a philosophical response to religious diversity, must also be distinguished from the cosmopolitan and democratic ideals of tolerance and acceptance of this multiplicity of religious traditions. Tolerance of plurality is not plural*ism*; neither is diversity itself plural*ism*. A religious pluralism is a hypothesis that claims the truthfulness of multiple *seemingly contradictory* religious traditions (or aspects of various traditions) can simultaneously obtain without contradiction. Relativism, which is plural*istic* in its intent, is the far more radical claim that "*all* traditions are equally true" (and therefore equally false). So whereas pluralism is not necessarily committed to embracing all religious traditions, relativism declares all religious traditions to be right, just not in a meaningful way. Harder, absolutist responses include: exclusivism, inclusivism, and identism.[15] Ratzinger

---

[15] Exclusivism claims that one's own tradition is the only veridical one, to the exclusion of others. Inclusivism allows for the truthfulness of other traditions (or aspects of some traditions) to be explained by means of determining the extent to which they approximately express the truths of one's own tradition. Identism, which Griffin identifies as John Hick's position, is a bit more complicated. While it is more pluralistic than inclusivism it is not quite a plural*ism*. This is because identism is more closely aligned with inclusivism than pluralism insofar as it purports to ascertain the truthfulness of other traditions (or aspects of some traditions) by means of determining the extent to which they participate in a generic view of reality that just happens to resemble one type of tradition to the exclusion of others. Identism, therefore, attempts to cast a wider inclusivist net by trying to explain wildly divergent religious traditions in generic terms that are utterly foreign to some and intimately familiar to others. The most profound error of identism is the claim that there is just one transcendent religious ultimate. Regardless of how much Hick, and identists in his vein, claim that no single quality can rightfully be said to characterize this religious ultimate to the exclusion of others (e.g., personal or impersonal), one thing is for certain in Hick's Kantian characterization of the religious ultimate, it is explicitly noumenal, transcendent. A transcendent ultimate reality is a concept that is utterly foreign to several major world religions (e.g., the religious ultimates of Daoism and Buddhism, among others, are radically immanent) and therefore, an identism, which has pluralistic intent, ironically denies these traditions an explanation of themselves in their own

does not address these three harder responses to religious diversity and so we will part from further explication of them here.

In order to demonstrate that pluralism does not pose a relativistic threat to Christianity, as Ratzinger seems to think it does,[16] it is worthwhile at this point to also recap the basic distinctions between pluralism and relativism prior to arguing against Ratzinger's conflation of the two. In its most generic form religious pluralism is distinguished, according to Griffin, by an adherence to two basic assumptions – one negative, the other positive (quoted previously). From these two assumptions alone, a number of different responses to religious diversity can occur – even relativism. Indeed, these two assumptions are what give a family resemblance to plural*istic* theologies in general, but it is what they do with these assumptions that determines whether or not their pluralistic response forms an identism, a pluralism, or a relativism.

The distinction for us here is that whereas religious relativism lacks any epistemic standard for the determination of a tradition's truth claims, and is thus rightly rejected by Ratzinger as religious indifferentism, religious pluralism allows for standards for endorsing or denying various traditions, or aspects of those traditions, as veridical. The minimum standard that separates pluralism from relativism is pluralism's basic adherence to the law of non-contradiction. Any pluralism should, therefore, be logically distinct from the kind of "debilitating relativism" identified by Alan Race, which takes all religions as equally true, and therefore as equally false.[17]

B.   Absolutist or Relativist Soteriologies: A False Dichotomy

Prior to becoming Pope Benedict XVI, Joseph Ratzinger co-authored a book with Marcello Pera (President of the Italian

---

terms in an absolutist manner that resembles an inclusivism more than it does a pluralism.

[16] To be fair, Ratzinger does admit to there being different varieties of pluralism, but not once has he explicated anything other than a relativist or an identist position in his scholarship, at times even conflating the two.

[17] For Race's statement of the challenge of avoiding a debilitating relativism for any pluralistic theologies see Alan Race, *Christians and Religious Pluralism* (Maryknoll, New York: Orbis Books, 1982), 78.

Senate), *Without Roots: The West, Relativism, Christianity, Islam.*[18] In it Pera observes:

> At Vatican II, in the declaration *Nostra aetate* (1965), the thesis was approved according to which the different religions 'often reflect a ray of Truth which enlightens all men' (article 2). While it recalls the principle that Christ is 'the way, the truth, and the life,' ...[Pera protests that this declaration *did not* specify] that He is the *only* way. The orientation... seemed to allude to parallel roads to salvation...thus running the risk of relativism.[19]

Twenty-five years later, the Church issued the encyclical *Redemptoris missio* (1990), in which the first chapter is entitled "Jesus Christ is the *only* Savior" and warns against "widespread indifferentism...characterized by a religious relativism which leads to the belief that 'one religion is as good as another'" (article 36). A full decade later, Cardinal Joseph Ratzinger, Prefect of the Congregation for the Doctrine of Faith, took this "correction" even further in *Dominus Iesus* (2000)[20], which declared "that the other [Christian] churches and other religions...were in a 'gravely deficient situation.'"[21] Ratzinger's commitment to religious absolutism is made clear here in no uncertain terms.

To be sure, I regret—as should other pluralists—the fact that persons, of whatever faith, hold any sort of simplistic indifferentism as alluded to by Ratzinger. Moreover, let me be absolutely clear in my agreement with Ratzinger that it is philosophically untenable for anyone to adhere to relativistic beliefs or a view that would simply equate one religion or salvation to be as good as another. This is, after all, an elementary and widely agreed upon truth dictated by the basic tenets of logic: the competing truth claims of the myriad religious traditions *cannot* all be true, and thus, pragmatically speaking, cannot sensibly be said to be of equal worth, so long as it is assumed that at least one is more factually true

---

[18] Joseph Ratzinger and Marcello Pera, *Without Roots: The West, Relativism, Christianity, Islam*, Trans. George Weigel (New York: Basic Books, 2006). Published in 2006, prior to his Papacy, Ratzinger and Pera support and endorse one another's views on a number of issues involving modern societies' response to the Church and the Church's response to modern challenges. In it they both deride inter-religious dialogue and religious pluralism.

[19] Pera in *Without Roots*, 144 n. 31.

[20] Paul Elie, called the wording of *Dominus Iesus* a "graceless" approach that used "wounding words." "The Year of Two Popes: How Joseph Ratzinger stepped into the shoes of John Paul II – and what it means for the Catholic Church," *The Atlantic Monthly*, January/February 2006. Vol. 297, No. 1., 64-92, page 76.

[21] *Ibid.*

or efficacious than the others. Sadly, Ratzinger's philosophical analysis and complete rejection of the varieties of religious pluralism, which we will come to momentarily, effectively throw the baby out with the bathwater[22] since he mistakenly views all pluralistic theologies as various forms of logically untenable relativistic positions.

While relativism is clearly an undesirable position, it is vital to point out at this point that I am not making any value judgment or assumption about absolutism being somehow inherently bad. While no prejudice should be held against absolutism, in the end, I will argue that it is not a tenable position. Indeed, the major world religious traditions generally conceive of themselves as being absolutely true, so I am also not singling out Catholicism (or Christianity for that matter) as absolutist. My point in critiquing absolutism via one particular thinker (Ratzinger) from one particular tradition (Catholicism) is simply to demonstrate that absolutist practitioners will find themselves in a paradox when they insist that their tradition presents absolute truths and simultaneously assume that inter-religious dialogue is desirable or are required by the tenets of their faith to participate in such dialogue.

C.   "Pluralistic Indifferentism": Conflating Religious Pluralism with Relativism

Despite the clear differences between relativism and pluralism Ratzinger is quite fond of reducing pluralism to what *he* sees as a modern Hickian relativism,[23] which reduces Christianity, as Ernst Troeltsch suggested, to a revelatory tradition that simply shows the side of God's face that just happens to be facing the Europeans. Ratzinger also sees this "pluralism" as nothing particularly new – locating other times in history when Christianity had to face down the specter of religious relativism. He writes, for example, of the oration of the late fourth century Roman senator Symmachus (d. 402) who spoke before Emperor Valentinian II, "in defense of paganism and advocating the restoration of the statue of the goddess 'Victoria' in the Roman senate."[24] It is Symmachus whom

---

[22] The bathwater, of course, being pluralistic religious sentiments (some of which admittedly tend towards relativistic theologies) and which Ratzinger identifies as heretical, and the baby being authentic religious pluralism, which I identify as a perspective that is capable of being faithful to his and to other religious traditions.
[23] See Joseph Ratzinger, *Truth and Tolerance: Christian Belief and World Religions*, Trans. Henry Taylor (San Francisco: Ignatius Press, 2004), 117-122 for his most specific identification of Hick's theory as a relativism.
[24] *Ibid.* 176.

Ratzinger considers to offer the classical formulation of "religious pluralism:"

> It is the same thing that we all worship; we all think the same; we look up to the same stars; there is one sky above us, one world around us; what difference does it make with what kind of method the individual seeks the truth? We cannot all follow the same path to reach so great a mystery.[25]

Given our taxonomy, however, we see this more clearly as a religious relativism rather than a pluralism, because it conflates religious ultimates and thought while disregarding method entirely. I call this strain of poor philosophical reasoning that hastily blends various pluralistic theologies into relativism, "pluralistic indifferentism"—contra Ratzinger's "religious indifferentism."

Indeed, according to Ratzinger, the contemporary trend towards relativising religious truths, is merely a return to the theory of religion of late antiquity, specifically, as reflected in the dialogue *Octavius*, by Minicius Felix (circa 200 C.E.) and Varro's theory of religion.[26] Even so, Ratzinger is fond of lamenting what he sees as the particularly *modern* relativist indignation, which regards any statements that Catholicism is true and correct as imperialistic.[27] Furthermore, he complains that "to claim to know the truth" these days is to be attacked as an arrogant threat to tolerance and freedom.[28] Ratzinger and I can agree, however, that "The cost of countering absolutism by relativising truth and goodness is too high," as Maria Baghramian writes in her book, *Relativism*,[29] however, the perceived arrogance Ratzinger objects to is not due to any proclamation that Christianity represents *a* correct view, but rather, because he arrogates

---

[25] *Ibid.* Ratzinger quoted this from Gnilka, *Chresis*. In his footnote, Benedict notes further "[o]n pp. 19-26, Gnilka offers a detailed analysis of the text."

[26] See *Ibid.* 74 and 176.

[27] Interestingly, Ratzinger also protests that pluralism "denies the unity of mankind" (*Ibid.* 81). However, it really reinforces the commonality of humanity as spiritual beings, but what it specifically does deny—at least Cobb's pluralism does this—is the *unity of religion*. It does this by upholding difference in doctrines and paths which are understood to be cultivated as particular responses to particular challenges facing the human condition, and which direct us towards certain goals in light of these (often different or differently characterized) challenges.

[28] *Ibid.* 114.

[29] Maria Baghramian, *Relativism* (New York: Routledge, 2004), 304. Hence the importance of developing a coherent pluralism (or pluralisms) in response to religious, metaphysical, ontological, moral, and aesthetic absolutisms and relativisms. Thus, the pluralism endorsed herein can be seen as a part of a much larger pluralistic project across the philosophical spectrum.

truth in its entirety for the Catholic faith—proclaiming it to be a *complete* truth, and therefore also the *only* truth.[30]

Just as Ratzinger is rightfully indignant of relativism as a reactionary position to absolutism, his reassertion of an unwavering absolutism (in response to what is largely layperson's relativist tendencies) in an increasingly pluralistic world understandably draws ire. I contend that the indignation that has met the new Pope's old scholarship is not a response by religious practitioners of other traditions who feel the same way about their own traditions as absolutely true. Instead, it is reflective of a growing pluralistic sentiment (as described in its generic form by Griffin's two pluralistic assumptions above) that seeks to allow for a multiplicity of truths that may originate from a multiplicity of religious traditions. What is desperately needed for spiritual people of the world to move beyond sentimentality, however, is a positive, non-sentimental, non-relativistic theory like the deep religious pluralism argued for by Cobb; what is needed in addition to that is a negative, non-sentimental, formal argument against absolutism to justify one in making the move from one view (absolutist) to the other (pluralist).

Prior to presenting this negative argument, we turn to an explication of Ratzinger's view of inter-religious dialogue in order to demonstrate the negative effect that his view of "pluralism" has on what he sees as the possibility for open and genuine dialogue from an absolutist perspective.

D.   Ratzinger's Evangelical View of Inter-religious Dialogue

In Ratzigner's most recently translated book, *Without Roots*, Marcello Pera voices his and Ratzinger's concern regarding inter-religious dialogue by posing two important questions: "what is the *purpose* of this dialogue; and what is its *subject*?"[31] Regarding its purpose, he argues that it cannot be to discover truth, because revelation plays that role for Christianity. And though he admits that dialogue can lead to truth in areas other than the Christian religion, he sees no point in Christians engaging in dialogue

---

[30] In fairness to the Catholic Church, Vatican II reintroduced the Augustinian notion (from *The City of God*) of a "pilgrim church" (*ecclesia peregrima*). In effect this can be understood as meaning that there are still truths to be discovered beyond Catholic dogma. It does not seem a stretch to suggest that some of these truths may be found in other religions. And since other truths are presumed, the faithful are obliged to seek them out, and therefore, I argue, obliged to engage in genuine inter-religious dialogue.

[31] Pera in *Without Roots*, 28.

to learn any of these truths from other religious traditions. Pera, at least, is thus willfully blind to even the possibility that, although these other traditions may have very different worldviews and salvific goals, this does not imply that they wholly lack salvific knowledge or are mutually exclusive. Pera and Ratzinger thus seem to wholeheartedly endorse David Hume's famous declaration that whatever is different in religion is contrary. Indeed, Pera does not even consider it worth examining the fact that many of the truths of other religions are acquired via revelation as well, and that perhaps a dialogue about these revelations might be fruitful for Christians and non-Christians alike.

Ratzinger does not seem to recognize the complementary possibilities of different religious traditions and thus his view of the potential purpose of inter-religious dialogue is corrupted by this misinformed view. As an absolutist, it is not easy to see any other purpose to dialogue other than convincing another of the truth of one's own tradition. Naturally, then, he is fearful that a lay Christian's *open* engagement (i.e., an engagement wherein participants honestly open themselves and their traditions to critical inquiry from other traditions) in inter-religious dialogue could jeopardize her commitment to the attainment of salvation through Jesus Christ. Because of this dual aversion to genuine inter-religious dialogue it is no surprise that Ratzinger promulgates the use of dialogue as an evangelical tool.

E.   Evangelical Tool or Relativist Credo?

Pera's sentiments (just above) and his view that inter-religious dialogue can have only two purposes: "to foster mutual understanding; and to preach"[32] are echoed by Ratzinger later in the text when writing on multiculturalism. Ratzinger notes that multiculturalism would be unable to survive without an acknowledgement of some "common foundations."[33] This is a basic hermeneutic fact, so what is of interest here is what Ratzinger takes these *common foundations* to be. In a presentation of his views on this topic,[34] he was very clear about this commonality being the "unity of the human condition"[35] and this is presumably his meaning here as well. In talking of dialogue between people of different cultures and faiths, he says of this unity of the human condition, that it is:

---

[32] *Ibid.*
[33] Ratzinger in *Without Roots*, 79.
[34] In Salzburg, Austria during the Salzburg Higher Education week 1992.
[35] Ratzinger, Truth and Tolerance, 79.

not estranged from the sacred.... [for multiculturalism] teaches us to approach the sacred things of others with respect.... We can and we must learn from that which is sacred to others. [Because w]ith regard to others, it is our duty to... show the face of the revealed God ... the God who is so human that He Himself became man.[36]

Saying that it is the Christian's duty in inter-religious dialogue to "show the face of the revealed God" (i.e., Christ) seems appropriate and harmless on its own. But the reason for engaging in inter-religious dialogue at all, he says above, is to learn what others count as sacred, because it is "our duty" to correct them by showing them "the face of the revealed God." Thus, we can see that what Ratzinger is saying, within the context of this plausible interpretation is that *we ought to learn about others so as to better evangelize them.* This meaning is validly inferred from what he writes.

The encyclical *Redemptoris missio* states that "[i]nter-religious dialogue is part of the Church's evangelizing mission" (article 55), and where the normative statement is written in this mission that "dialogue does not dispense from evangelization", it seems quite clear that this intends the opposite to be true, namely, that *evangelization ought to dispense from dialogue.* Besides, Ratzinger makes it very clear that he understands that

the concept of dialogue... has become the very epitome of the relativist credo.... [D]ialogue in the relativist sense means setting one's own position or belief on the same level with what the other person believes, ascribing to it, on principle, no more of the truth than to the position of the other person. Only if my fundamental presupposition is that the other person may be just as much in the right as I am, or even more so, can any dialogue take place at all.... [As a result] the relativist elimination of Christology, and most certainly of ecclesiology, now becomes a central commandment of religion.[37]

It is no surprise from conclusions about the purpose of inter-religious dialogue such as this that Ratzinger has no qualms about utilizing inter-religious dialogue as an evangelizing tool in today's world.

The sad implication of is that both Ratzinger and Pera seem to see only two purposes of inter-religious dialogue—at least insofar as the Christian ought to be concerned: first, to work towards mutual understanding, and second, to use that gained understanding

---

[36] Ratzinger in *Without Roots*, 79.
[37] Ratzinger, *Truth and Tolerance*, 120-121.

to effectively exploit the vulnerability of the other's honest and open engagement so as to undermine her faith in her own tradition. Unfortunately, for people seduced by this view, nothing that could truthfully be counted as *understanding of the Other* could ever be attained in this so-called "dialogue" of conversion. The mere intent of employing inter-religious dialogue as a subversion tactic would prohibit any genuine understanding from the outset. In short, subterfuge would necessarily exclude the possibility of inter-religious dialogue.[38]

F.   Pluralistic Evangelism?

To be sure, genuine inter-religious dialogue is not, and should not be, polemical. Neither does it merely serve those who seek greater understanding of the Other, because it ultimately brings greater clarity of one's own position. It is no less than an open-ended discussion that ought to be transformative in this way for all its participants. I am in agreement with Cobb and Griffin, who understand genuine inter-religious dialogue as *necessarily* leading to mutual transformation.[39] I agree with this and argue further that such an understanding does more than just foster greater understanding of the valuable common ground between religious traditions, it brings their unique differences into greater focus as well.

A deeper appreciation of many traditions promotes an understanding of the possibility that different traditions can make separate but veridical claims about ostensibly contrary notions of reality and salvation such that epistemic dissonance does not arise. Ratzinger's ostensible assumption that religious truth-claims are, by definition, mutually exclusive can thus be undermined by a more thorough understanding of the myriad traditions themselves, each from its own vantage point. This kind of understanding is an essential foundation component of any religious pluralism, and it is also informs Cobb and Griffin's Whiteheadian religious pluralism.

If the fruit of genuine inter-religious dialogue is to be "mutually transformative", any transformation, from the Pope's perspective, may

---

[38] This is not to say that any communication involving deceit is somehow meaningless or not worthwhile, otherwise, areas like diplomacy, for example, would amount to nothing more than futile murmurings. Rather, it simple means that genuine dialogue, no matter what the topic of discussion, requires a mutual openness and receptivity for all participating parties.
[39] For example, see John B. Cobb, Jr., *Beyond Dialogue: Toward a Mutual Transformation of Christianity and Buddhism* (Philadelphia: Fortress, 1982). Griffin endorses Cobb's views in, among other places, *Deep Religious Pluralism*.

very well be seen as threatening. Such transformations could be seen as furthering the project of pluralism and thereby the very nature of genuine inter-religious dialogue appears to be an evangelical ruse for promoting pluralism! Indeed, Ratzinger suggests that this is the case when he declares that dialogue means "the relativist elimination of Christology."[40] This would understandably deepen Ratzinger's mistrust of such dialogue and further his disdain for "religious pluralism" – giving yet another perspective for understanding his view that inter-religious dialogue should not be used for anything other than conversion. Ratzinger's opportunistic view of inter-religious dialogue is thus, I argue, an understandably defensive result of his view of its purpose and its effect. Even so, it is still excessive and reactionary. After all, what could such a man feel he has to gain from dialogue with, in his own words, the deluded adherents of "second-hand religion"[41] who are in a "gravely deficient situation" (*Dominus Iesus*, 2000) when it comes to spirituality and religion and who, he fears, may be using inter-religious dialogue themselves (intentionally or not) to weaken a Christian's chances at salvation through Christ?

To see genuine inter-religious dialogue as an evangelical practice that works to convert people to pluralism is to assume both that a transformation of one's understanding of one's own tradition is somehow anathema to one's own tradition, and that an appreciation of the claims of other traditions somehow relativizes one's own. But this is not at all the case in a genuine inter-religious dialogue. Instead, the focus is on the positive influx of new perspectives, while, according to Cobb, affirming one's own "as universally valid! What we cannot do, without lapsing back into unjustified arrogance, is to deny that the insights of other traditions are also universally valid."[42] The point is to recognize truth in other traditions, not to abandon the truth in one's own.

G.   Genuine Inter-religious Dialogue

My understanding of mutual transformation is perhaps more broadly construed than Cobb or Griffin's. It does not necessarily require that one's beliefs be altered or that one disassociate oneself from one's inherited

---

[40] Ratzinger, *Truth or Tolerance*, 120-121.

[41] One of the most depressing remarks made publicly by Ratzinger was his regard for non-theistic religions as being, at best, "second-hand religion." The implication of his view therefore seems to be that a Catholic ought not go *slumming* by engaging in inter-religious dialogue with degenerate religions.

[42] John B. Cobb, Jr., *Transforming Christianity and the World: A Way beyond Absolutism and Relativism* (Maryknoll, NY: Orbis Books, 1999), 137.

dogma. These may in fact occur, but at minimum transformation means enriched by contact. Transformation thus occurs as a result of any hermeneutic activity, but this does not mean abandoning one's own position, but seeing some of its gaps and places for it to grow. We are unavoidably (and sometimes uninterestingly) changed by the activity of dialogue; amending our loyalties to particular ideas or themes is not a necessary aim. Rather, the aim is to transform one's views of one's own tradition and that of others simply by engaging in inter-religious dialogue with traditions other than one's own. At minimum, an understanding of one's own tradition is effectively altered insofar as it is now understood in the greater context of alternative views. This transformation is mutual for all involved in the dialogue and is why I do not say that this dialogue must be *potentially* transformative, but rather that it *is* transformative. This is neither a platitudinous nor a vacuous aim. At one level, this transformation is an unavoidable result of dialogue; to say, then, that the aim of dialogue is transformation is admittedly to say, in effect, that the purpose of dialogue is dialogue. This is true. But the secondary benefit of getting people talking across traditions in an open and receptive way is that the more this occurs, the more focus and attention will be directed to *the need for commensurable common ground* between people across traditions in order for this dialogue to even take place or have meaning. If, a dialogue between divergent traditions is ever going to get off the ground, the common ground they must meet on needs to be philosophical rather than theological. Furthermore, if there is to be any edifying purpose to this dialogue for its participants, the impetus of dialogue must be an assumed pluralistic, rather than absolutist or relativist, perspective.

What Ratzinger fails to realize in his reduction of pluralism to relativism and his reduction of dialogue to a "relativist credo" is that the assumed equality of the other's tradition and one's own is merely the *necessary starting point* for a conversation involving the extremely sensitive subject matter of religious belief. When it comes to inter-religious dialogue, such assumed possible equality is absolutely necessary for any conversation aiming at mutual understanding from each other's perspective to even get off the ground. What counts as genuine inter-religious dialogue requires mutual openness and some degree of understanding from the outset, but it certainly does not involve conversion or even actual equality as a goal or even as a necessary by-product. The pluralist's presupposition of one tradition being as truthful as another for the purposes of inter-religious dialogue is nothing more than a launch pad for dialogue to take place. But it is just that, a *starting point*; it is *not* an underlying philosophical assumption that must be unquestioningly held.

Therefore, genuine inter-religious dialogue does not insist on a relativism that surrenders the meaningfulness of the central components of one's tradition. This helps to help expose Ratzinger's leap from before from "[o]nly if my fundamental presupposition is that the other person may be just as much in the right as I am, or even more so, can any dialogue take place at all," to the notion that this necessitates "the relativist elimination of Christology."[43]

There is absolutely no need to permanently "relativize our beliefs" in order to engage in dialogue.[44] Explaining Cobb's position further, Griffin writes, "he must provisionally bracket his tradition's claims to what he, as a Christian, sees as most important is truly the most important thing."[45] Even so, Cobb does *not* claim that what is bracketed is:

> the content of what I find supremely important... nor the conviction that this is important for all, but only the opinion that it is *more* important for all than what others regard as supremely important. *Perhaps* becoming empty is just as important![46]

The fact of the matter is that there are significant spiritual truths that are attainable through a variety of religious traditions, but if one does not recognize that this is even possible, then it seems that there will be nothing of value that a dogmatist or absolutist will immediately see in dialogue aside from conversion.

H.   Generic Pluralistic Assumptions as the Hermeneutical Basis for Genuine Inter-religious Dialogue

Griffin's two generically pluralistic assumptions are absolutely necessary for genuine inter-religious dialogue to take place, because one must first negatively assume that you or your tradition does not have the only legitimate view, and second, you must positively assume that the Other may have a familiarity with a saving truth that you lack. In the first case, people who are committed to even absolutist views are obviously not incapable of thinking philosophically and therefore they are not incapable of engaging in inter-religious dialogue; even though their positions are informed by their native theologies, they can have the humility to break

---

[43] Ratzinger, *Truth and Tolerance*, 120-121.
[44] Cobb, *Transforming Christianity and the World*, 137.
[45] Griffin, *Deep Religious Pluralism*, 63.
[46] John B. Cobb, Jr. in Leonard Swidler, et al., *Death or Dialogue? From the Age of Monologue to the Age of Dialogue* (London: SCM Press, 1990), 11.

beyond these dogmatic limitations and imagine the negative pluralistic possibility necessary for engaging in inter-religious dialogue. Moreover, in the second, positive pluralistic possibility they can also have the fortitude to either expose themselves to critical inquiry or make themselves receptive to the spiritual insights of others.

For the discerning participant in this dialogue, the hermeneutical basis provided by these two pluralistic assumptions may be too soft, too vague for any meaningful transformation to occur. It seems that with these assumptions alone, we are left wanting a more robust ground on which divergent traditions can to meet, but it is clear that these assumptions are a necessary doorway to that ground.

I. Whitehead's Metaphysical Pluralism as a Philosophical Basis for Genuine Inter-religious Dialogue

While Griffin's positive and negative assumptions are dialogical necessities, they are insufficient as a robust philosophical basis for this dialogue. How then might they lead us to a more robust philosophical basis for genuine inter-religious dialogue? For starters, they leave open a wide range of philosophical possibilities wherein these two assumptions might make sense. In my dissertation research I argue that our choices are limited to only generically pluralistic theologies as the meta-philosophical perspectives that can make broader sense of these two assumptions: identism, pluralism, and relativism. Neither relativist nor identist positions, however, offer viable explanations of religious diversity. This leaves us with only one remaining option to provide the philosophical basis for meaningful inter-religious dialogue, namely authentic religious pluralism.

A process philosophical system adequately informs an authentic religious pluralism because it allows for an explanation of multiple religious ultimates.[47] While other philosophical systems might be able to adequately inform an authentic pluralism, the Whiteheadian-based process philosophy employed by Cobb and Griffin is (currently) the only fully articulated process system that adequately satisfies the explanatory scope that an authentic religious pluralism aspires to. That is to say, it answers the philosophical challenges presented by religious diversity with the deepest, broadest, sensible explanation with the greatest simplicity; other schemata may very well invite authentic pluralisms, but they have yet to

---

[47] The multiple religious ultimates of creativity, God, and actual occasions serve as the basis of Cobb's Deep Religious Pluralism. See footnote 7.

be fleshed out as a basis for a genuine religious pluralism to the same extent as the schemata of Cobb's Deep Religious Pluralism.

A Whiteheadian process view of reality, therefore, functions as the metaphysical and philosophical basis (that informs the hermeneutical basis) for this inter-religious dialogue, because it offers a philosophical narrative for making sense of the pluralistic assumptions required for inter-religious dialogue to take place. Without a shared view of reality that makes sense of these positive and negative pluralistic assumptions, any attempt at inter-religious dialogue would falter into relativism or be co-opted by one tradition's religious interpretation of reality over another.

Religious Pluralism is the Necessary Ground for Religious Absolutisms in Dialogue

Much ink has been spilt over and against relativism. Similarly, whether pluralism can possibly provide a viable basis for a theology of religions has been subjected to much debate. But what about religious absolutism? Is it a viable position? In this final section I argue that strict religious absolutism is untenable.[48] In critiquing the epistemic implications of committing oneself to absolute truth claims, I argue that inter-religious dialogue becomes necessary for faithful adherents of the world's absolutist religions. This is largely because fidelity to the idea of absolute truth forces one towards a more pluralistic openness to the potentially transformative wisdom of the interpretive claims of other religious traditions.

The problem with absolutism is largely an epistemic one. If there are absolute truths, then knowledge of these truths cannot be absolute.[49] Santiago Sia more clearly articulated this position at the conference. In his paper from the conference he writes:

> In reply to a question by Matthew Lopresti... I explained that an important consideration in inter-religious dialogue is really an epistemological issue: how one understands and accepts the status of religious belief. In process philosophy, a distinction is made between absolute truths and our relative knowledge of such truths. Unlike relativism, process thought accepts that

---

[48] I am extremely grateful to Amy Donahue for her assistance in the development of this argument, as well as for both her and Ben Lukey's insightful comments and suggestions during my writing of this paper.

[49] I thank Santiago Sia for more precisely articulating this aspect of my argument against absolutism during question and answer after his presentation and in his gracious comments after mine.

there are indeed absolute truths; but unlike absolutism, it rejects the absoluteness of our knowledge of such truths. Furthermore, the certainty with which one holds one's beliefs does not justify the absoluteness of those truths.[50]

Rather, the certainty with which one holds one's beliefs undermines the absoluteness of the realities that these beliefs purport to be about. This is clearly an idea that we share, and it is the essential idea that informs the argument I made against religious absolutism during my conference paper.

The profound power and simplicity of the pluralistic turn lies in the change of the article *the* to *a*, as in, "my tradition is *the* true religion" to "my tradition is *a* true religion." The first and necessary step in achieving this article shift is the recognition and admission that any tradition, being the historical progression of beliefs and ideas that it is, cannot possibly be faithfully thought to have fully grasped and infallibly interpreted *all the answers* for *all people* for *all times*. It may in fact have. But agents of the tradition cannot be sure of this unless they substitute their present collection of beliefs and ideas for the ultimate that these beliefs and ideas purport to be about.

We will begin the argument from the perspective of a religious absolutism. Let us say that "P", the path of Roman Catholicism, for example, claims to have articulated the full truth of ultimate reality or P. Naturally, "P" is true if and only if P. Absolutists insist on the unconditional truth of "P", and we see the justification for this provided by the alleged literal truth of its dogma. The problem for absolutists who are averse to inter-religious dialogue is that the only standard of truth for "P" is God (i.e., P), not the Catholic Church's opinion of its own articulations of God (i.e., not "P"). Now, either (A) the Vatican thinks that it knows it has a complete knowledge of P, or (B) it is not the case that the Vatican thinks that it knows it has a complete knowledge of P. The first disjunct, A leads to either an epistemic relativism or an infinite regress of epistemic justification. The second disjunct, B leads to the humble admission of fallibilism. (Let me explain the reasoning of what A and B lead to immediately following this summary of the larger argument.) Because A is not feasible, religious absolutists are obliged to be fallibilists. As fallibilists who are nevertheless committed to P, they must arguably engage in open and receptive inter-religious dialogue with others who

---

[50] Santiago Sia, *Whitehead on Religion: A Philosophical Basis for Inter-religious Dialogue?* Presented at the conference on The Philosophical Basis for Inter-Religious Dialogue in Katowice, Poland (May 2008) and also appearing in this volume.

claim to have access to P, if they are to remain faithful to their objects of veneration. As already argued, engaging in genuine inter-religious dialogue requires that one assumes two basic pluralistic assumptions, which, in the end can only be made sense of in the context of a deep religious pluralism. Religious absolutism is therefore committed to religious pluralism.

In returning to the disjunct above, we see that disjunct A, where the Vatican thinks that it knows it has a complete knowledge of P, has two possibilities. To arrive at these possibilities we must ask, how do they know that they know P? In the first case if they say that their knowledge of P is based on "P", but if there is no external justification of their dogma ("P"), then this leads to an epistemic relativism. The supposedly unconditional truth of "P", rather than being derived strictly from P, would be contingent on the Vatican's conception or articulation of it. In the second case, they might say that they know that "P" is true because God has certified their knowledge that "P" is true. Indeed, they might say, God alone can certify that one has complete knowledge of P. But how do they know that God has certified that "P" is true? This conception or conviction that "P" is certified by God has two possibilities, either their knowledge that "P" is certified by God is based on "their knowledge God has certified that ' "P" is certified by God' "—but then how do they know that they know, and so on and so forth *ad infinitum*, or they must be fallibilists. There is no satisfactory answer for the certification of their knowledge that "P" is a complete knowledge of P, because they must constantly be appealing certification of their knowledge of P to a knowledge of their knowledge. But their knowledge claims about their knowing the mind of God has no ground aside from their own insistences, which is no justification, whether religious or philosophical. To be sure, this would amount to a poor use of the concept of faith, because faith here would become an excuse for blind insistence. Therefore, any insistence on the absolutist's part that he has the truth, even though he may very well have the truth (he just cannot know it) is not faith, rather it is a bald-faced insistence that he knows the mind of God![51] This is, of course, anathema to the Christian concept of God and something that no religious practitioner (or tradition) faithful to P (however it is conceived) can lay claim to. Since neither of A's two possibilities are acceptable, we are left with disjunct B, where it is not the case that the Vatican thinks that it knows it has a complete knowledge of P. This, of course, means that the Vatican

---

[51] An appeal to religious experience does not solve this certification problem. This is not a question about whether one can experience or even come to know "the presence of God", but whether one can know *the mind of God*.

does not have the authority, internally or in inter-religious dialogue, to make absolute claims of "P" being the only legitimate path to P. B thus leads us to a seemingly contradictory position of a *fallibilist absolutism* that forces the faithful to an open and receptive inter-religious dialogue with others who purport to have access to P as well. To avoid the loss of meaning that results from disjunct A, a religious absolutist must be willing to accept a little bit of pluralistic humility.

What does this humility look like and what would this mean? It means accepting the two distinctively pluralistic criteria, the positive and the negative! This, therefore, necessitates at least the temporary acceptance of religious pluralism for the faithful absolutists.[52] Absolutists are constantly met with the necessity to be falliblists and therefore pluralists. If they refuse these obligations, then they are substituting their own conceptions ("P") for Gods (P).

Absolutist dogmas thus need to be reinterpreted with a religious pluralism in mind and this means that a shared vision of reality as a philosophical basis for this pluralism and the necessary ensuing dialogue needs to be found. Ratzinger writes that "[m]an cannot come to terms with being born blind, and remaining blind, where essential things are concerned."[53] If this is true, then it gives us all the more reason to seek out these truths as they exist in their various forms across the spectrum of religious traditions. Although he follows up this observation with the statement that "[t]he farewell to truth can never be final,"[54] we should not be deluded into thinking that this means we can ever trust faithfully that we have full understanding from one tradition alone, as he seems to think we do. Rather, what this seems to point us towards is the next best thing: a shared inter-religious dialogue on the religious experience involving religious leaders and practitioners, philosophers and theologians, lay persons and clergy. Any who enter this dialogue to convert others to some

---

[52] Note that this argument *does not* mean that a tradition's truths cannot be universally true (i.e., true everywhere, for all time), but only that these allegedly universal truths, therefore, cannot be faithfully thought to be *exhaustive* of all religious truth. Therefore, it is religiously incumbent on the absolutist who wishes to be faithful to her ultimate to engage in genuine inter-religious dialogue and therefore to downgrade her religious beliefs to being universally rather than absolutely true, thereby adhering to a pluralistic account of religious diversity. Or at least, as Cobb suggests, temporarily bracket them as such.
[53] Ratzinger, *Truth and Tolerance*, 165.
[54] *Ibid.*

"absolute truth" engage not only in deception, but also offer themselves up as "an exhibition of folly."[55]

While both Vatican II (relativist or not) and the absolutism of theologians like Ratzinger are firmly rooted in faith, they both seem to be philosophically unpalatable and, if the argument just made obtains, they are also theologically and philosophically untenable. This pushes us towards a middle, pluralistic path because, if one cannot be certain that one properly grasps P on one's own, and one wants to come as close to grasping P as possible, then one must be open to genuine inter-religious dialogue and learning alleged perspectives of P from other traditions. Genuine inter-religious dialogue and religious pluralism is, therefore, dead center in the Catholic tradition.

Pluralism is the *only* philosophical ground that can deal with religious ultimates as actual, unconditioned objects. I argue that it is also the only way a deep inter-religious dialogue can occur. Other grounds, such as absolutism, may be able to handle dialogue about beliefs and ideas that are not essential to the religious, but they will not be able to dialogue about *seemingly* contradictory ultimate realities. Only a deep religious pluralism can accommodate these seemingly contradictory ultimates. Therefore, it alone is able to get people to talk across traditions and learn from varying religious beliefs and ideas (including beliefs and ideas that are properly normative in their *own* traditions). This is because religious beliefs and ideas are typically understood vis-à-vis the religious ultimate identified in their respective traditions.

Does this argument then mean that absolutists cannot engage in inter-religious dialogue? To the contrary! What it calls for is the absolutist (to still be absolutist) to at least be capable of displaying the ability to temporarily *imagine* what it would be like to still maintain all of her tradition's beliefs, but with the provision that they are universally true rather than exhaustive of truth. Or, as Griffin writes: "[t]he crucial point is that we hold fast to the universal validity of our own norms without insisting that these norms are the *only* ones with universal validity."[56] To not display at least a modicum of humility such as this with regard to one's self-assurances (or tradition's assurance) as to the *completeness* of religious and spiritual truths of one's tradition is a mark of utter profanity. If these absolutists are committed to a conception of their religious beliefs as absolute, and their religious ultimate as an unconditional reality, then

---

[55] Alfred North Whitehead, *Process and Reality: An Essay in Cosmology* (orig. ed. 1929), Corrected edition, ed. David Ray Griffin and Donald W. Sherburne (New York: Free Press, 1978), *xiv*.

[56] Griffin, *Deep Religious Pluralism*, 63.

this leads them to be committed to dialogue. Therefore, they must also be committed to pluralism. Should they wish to stop anywhere along the way, they cannot do so without contradiction.

Conclusion

The pluralistic turn broadens the scope of what can or should be considered as possibly true to include what have been heretofore considered incommensurable traditions, or incommensurable truth-claims within different traditions, viewing them instead as holding potentially compossible worldviews, praxes, and soteriologies. One's understanding (or in Ratzinger's case, misunderstanding) of religious pluralism, however, will inevitably *effect* one's view of inter-religious dialogue and thus also one's engagement in such activity. Furthermore, one's engagement in such activity will inevitably influence one's understanding of the possibility (or at least the appropriateness) of there being a viable theology of religious pluralism. If one does not engage in inter-religious dialogue, has little or no contact with other traditions, or only tries to engage in polemics or evangelism one will inevitably isolate oneself from the understanding necessary to maintain and nurture the inroads to pluralism. If one does not see the pluralistic turn (much less religious pluralism) as a viable option, the point of inter-religious dialogue comes into question. But for those who do see pluralism as viable, they must understand that it is not something that will be attained via inter-religious dialogue alone. The two – inter-religious dialogue and religious pluralism – must form a hermeneutic circle wherein greater understanding and efficacy of one facilitates a greater understanding and efficacy of the other, each leading to an enriched understanding of oneself, the human condition, and the various means of diagnosing and addressing its challenges and realizing its opportunities. For the spiritual individual, this process should have no end of diminishing returns. Neither should it result in some meta-religion that consists of cherry-picked components of divergent traditions, as this would isolate unique aspects of various traditions from the lineages in which they derive meaning. Indeed, this is why we need to maintain individual traditions—because they have individually and esoterically developed rich, efficacious praxes that bring us closer to the religious ultimates (viz., creativity, God, and actual occasions). Instead of a meta-process-based religion, this interplay of dialogue and religious pluralism should yield constant and novel enrichment for its participants and for the traditions that the participants adhere to. This is not only an enrichment of one's own spirituality, but also of one's familiarity with religious truth. This is a truth, however, that no one tradition can reasonably claim a monopoly on, because it is a truth about the manifold challenges that face the human condition and the varied responses to the personal and impersonal ultimates in this world.

There are multiple religious ultimates in a Whiteheadian deep religious pluralism, but Whitehead reminds us that

> the accurate expression of the final generalities [or ultimates] is the goal of discussion and not its origin.... Metaphysical categories are not dogmatic statements of the obvious; they are tentative formulations of the ultimate generalities.[57]

To get a better picture of how we can better orient ourselves to these ontologically and religiously significant generalities, inter-religious dialogue becomes indispensable. The only tenable ground for a philosophical basis of this dialogue lies between the untenable positions of absolutism and relativism, and it is pluralism. The benefits and aims of inter-religious dialogue and religious pluralism are thus mutually supportive; the practice can test and strengthen the theory from numerous religious traditions, while the theory, in turn, provides a philosophical basis for the practice. The metaphysical pluralism of ontological cum religious generalities thus serves as a philosophical basis for more than just deep religious pluralism, but for deep inter-religious dialogue as well. Together, the theory of deep religious pluralism and the practice of inter-religious dialogue can strengthen religious worldviews and serve to assist the faithful in the attainment of their spiritual goals.

---

[57] Whitehead, *Process and Reality*, 8.

Matthew Lopresti, Ph.D., is Visiting Assistant Professor of Philosophy and Humanities at Hawai'i Pacific University. He has lectured in philosophy at numerous universities in the United States and served as Lecturer of Buddhist Philosophy for the Antioch Buddhist Studies Program in Bodh Gaya, India and Pre-Doctoral Fellow with the Department of Philosophy at West Virginia University. He has published articles and a book review in philosophy of religion, process thought, existentialism, and South Asian philosophy. His most recent being "*Sanātana Dharma* as a Whiteheadian Religious Pluralism?" *Process Studies* 36.1 (Spring/Summer 2007): 108-120 and corrigenda in *Process Studies* 36.2. In August 2008 he is defending his dissertation titled "Religious Pluralism in Analytic, Process, and South Asian Philosophies of Religion" with the Department of Philosophy at the University of Hawai'i at Mānoa.

'THE CONTRASTED OPPOSITES' IN NISHIDA AND WHITEHEAD

HIROMASA MASE

It was Nishida, the founder of the Kyoto School and a contemporary of Whitehead, that Buddhism needed an authentic understanding of transcendence. Nishida put stress on the need of an idea of transcendence in the Buddhist context. Whitehead, in contrast, put emphasis on the need of an idea of immanence in the Christian context.

Whitehead was critical toward the traditional theism, because its interest was mainly in God's transcendence, which necessarily meant the separation of God from the world. In his *Religion in the Making*, Whitehead dealt with a comparative study of Buddhism and Christianity. In the Buddhist thought, he was impressed by the idea of immanence and was convinced that the renewal of Christianity should be made by the sincere dialogue with Buddhism. By this he meant that Christianity needed a proper understanding of an idea of immanence in the concept of the Christian God.

In contrast, however, Nishida felt the need of an idea of transcendence in case of Buddhism. The reason is that Japanese tend to identify the transcendent (God) with the universe (the world) in their spirituality. No doubt, this is pantheism and Nishida was critical toward the traditional Buddhist understanding of the transcendent.

He was anchored his spiritual home in Zen Buddhism. In youth, as his diaries show, he dedicated himself to Zen practice and attained Zen enlightenment. He studied in Germany and when he returned to Japan he became a lecturer of Western philosophy. In his lectures he dealt with Brentano, Husserl, Bergson, and James, popular at the time, and later chiefly with German philosophy from Kant to Heidegger through Fichte, Hegel and Dilthey. He paid particular attention to the mystics such as Eckhart, Nicholas Cusa, and Boeme. These currents from the West enriched him intellectually, but did not succumb to Western modes of thought.

His early philosophy of 'pure experience' drew from the source of Zen Buddhism, which was in its essence 'direct experience'. Later the Zen Buddhist element came out more clearly. His mature major work is *Fundamental Problems of Philosophy* (1933), but already in his essay on "The Self-Identity of Absolute Contradictories" (1930), Nishida found his definitive standpoint, that is, 'the logic of topos of nothingness', which led him to the religious problem discussed in his *Last Writings: Nothingness and the Religious Worldview* (1945).

The self-identity of contradictories is, as he says in his last essay, "the root of man's religious urgency" and has its goal in absolute negation. In the argument of this essay, the metaphysics of Mahayana Buddhism is normative. He quotes saying of Zen masters, especially Rinzai (~867) and Dogen (1200~1253)), the heads of the two leading schools. Zen Buddhism exhaustively investigates the self itself. Thus Nishida quotes Dogen's famous saying about the self. "To study the way of Buddha is to study the self, and to study the self is to forget the self. To forget the self is to be enlightened by all things, that is, Dharmas, laws of the universe. Nishida quotes this in his last essay as expressing the necessity of self-negation so that a true self can be attained.

In the study of the self, Nishida distinguishes between the superficial self and the ground of the self. His language avoids objectifying presentation of God while making it clear that his philosophy is neither atheistic nor pantheistic. "God appears to the religious self as an event of one's own soul," says Nishida. "It is not a matter of God being conceivable or not conceivable in merely intellectual terms. What can be conceived or not conceived is not God". In seeking the logic of the religious event, Nishida becomes the first Buddhist philosopher to introduce the notion of the *kenosis* or self-emptying of God.

> I hold that when we express God, or the absolute, in logical terms, we must speak in this way. Because God, or the absolute, stand to itself in the form of a contradictory entity—namely as its own absolute self-negation.... Because it is absolute nothingness, it is absolute being. It is because of this that we can speak of the divine omniscience and omnipotence.... The true absolute One expresses itself in the form of the infinite Many. God exists in this world through self-negation.... A God merely transcendent and self-sufficient would not be a true God. God must always, in St. Paul's words, empty himself.[1]

---

[1] As noted above all quotations in this text come from:
Nishida, Kitaro [1930]: "The Self-Identity of Absolute Contradictories".
—. [1933]: *Fundamental Problems of Philosophy.*

The point he has made clear is that God, or the absolute, gives himself to the world through his self-negation or self-emptying. This is what Nishida understands in Christianity as the fundamental teaching about God, namely self-immanence of the transcendent. Then he turns to Buddhism and explores into the concept of the transcendent in Buddhism.

He finds in Buddhism the thought of immanence, but not that of transcendence. Therefore he begins to say that Buddhism should seek for the thought of transcendence, namely the thought of self-transcendence of the immanent. Nishida strongly felt the need of this thought in Buddhism, so that the Buddhist conception of the absolute could be complete.

Toward the end of his *Last Writings: Nothingness and the Religious Worldview*, Nishida begins to use the word 'panentheism'. He says, "my understanding of God, or the absolute, is *Panentheismus*". (He used the German word in his writing as an emphasis).

Nishida saw in Christianity a dynamism of the conception of the transcendent in the way that the transcendent should become the immanent through its self-negation, or self-emptying. So, he now strongly proposes to Buddhism to have the conception that the immanent should become the transcendent through its self-negation. Then he thinks that the Buddhist understanding of the absolute would be complete.

Nishida's logic of panentheism is, in his Japanese word, *soku-hi* (is not), or absolute self-negation. It goes like this:

> Buddha *soku-hi* (is not) Buddha. All life *soku-hi* (is not) all life.
> Therefore, Buddha is Buddha for the sake of all life. All life is all life for the sake of Buddha.

Buddha and all life are 'the contrasted opposites'. Buddha and all life 'stand over against each other, expressing the final metaphysical truth' that 'opposed elements stand to each other in mutual requirement'.

In contrast, Whitehead proposed the need of understanding that the transcendent should become the immanent in its self-emptying in the Christian context. He proposed it in his theory of dipolarity of God. In the final chapter of his *Process and Reality*, he deals with immanence of God. And he implies in it his fundamental criticism toward the traditional theism, because God has always been conceptualized as 'ganz Andere', or the absolute Other, or the transcendent One. There is nothing wrong in it,

—. [1945]: *Last Writings: Nothingness and the Religious Worldview.*
Whitehead, A.N. [1926]: *Religion in the Making.*
—. [1929]: Process and Reality.

but there is something wanting. Whitehead says that there is another side to the nature of God which cannot be omitted.

Considering the primary action of God on the world, we understand that God is, in Whitehead's words, "the principle of concretion", which is the primordial side of the nature of God. But God is, says Whitehead, "as well as being primordial, is also consequent". To quote from *Process and Reality*:

> But God, as well as being primordial, is also consequent. He is the beginning and the end. He is not the beginning in the sense of being in the past of all members. He is presupposed actuality of conceptual operation, in unison of becoming with every other creative act. Thus, by reason of the relativity of all things, there is a reaction of the world on God. The completion of God's nature into a fullness of physical feeling is derived from the objectification of the world in God.... God's conceptual nature is unchanged, by reason of its final completeness. But his derivative nature is consequent upon the creative advance of the world.... Thus, analogously to all actual entities, the nature of God is dipolar. He has a primordial nature and a consequent nature.

Concerning self-immanence of the transcendent God, Whitehead describes it in an image—the image under which it is best conceived. That is "the image of a tender care that nothing be lost". Another image which is also required to understand it is "that of an infinite patience". God's saving work is always to be done with patience. That is why Whitehead says: "We conceive of the patience of God, tenderly saving the turmoil of the intermediate world by the completion of his own nature".

No doubt, Whitehead sees these images in the Galilean origin of Christianity. And his final comment on the consequent side of God is, in his words, that "God is the great companion—the fellow sufferer who understands".

Thus, I understand that Whitehead's idea of God is panentheistic in that God has a primordial nature and a consequent nature, eternal and everlasting, transcendent and immanent, actually deficient and fully actual, and so on.

For us, Japanese, it is hard to understand that God is transcendent and that the Christian God is an absolutely transcendent One. However the same God having become an immanent God by denying or emptying himself to the world as "the great companion, the fellow-sufferer who understands", then the Japanese will certainly understand who and what God is. Japanese words for companion (*dohansha*) and fellow-sufferer (*kyokusha*) are very dear to the Japanese hearts. Faced with a terrible earthquake, they would not deny God, if God should also suffer with them.

In case of Whitehead, he is also justifying himself to crave for permanence, or to desire for existence, in his panentheistic idea of God. His Process and Reality ends with this justification.

> We find here the final application of the doctrine of objective immortality. Throughout the perishing occasions in the life of each temporal Creature, the inward source of distaste or things, redeemer or of goddess of mischief, is the transformation of Itself, everlasting in the Being of God. In this way, the insistent craving is justified—the insistent craving that zest for existence be refreshed by the ever-present, unfading importance of our immediate actions, which perish and yet live for evermore.

Finally, my conviction is that Nishida's theory of absolute self-negation and Whitehead's theory of dipolarity of God share with each other a very important idea of 'the contrasted opposite' and therefore the idea of 'the contrasted opposite' can be used as the basis of a fruitful Buddhist-Christian dialogue in the present time and for the future as well.

Hiromasa Mase is Professor and ex-Dean of Tohoku University of Community Service and Science in Sakata-shi, Yamagata-ken, Japan. Until 2001 he was a professor in the Faculty of Letters at Keio University in Tokyo, where he is now professor emeritus. He is a member of the Board of Directors of The Japan Society for Process Studies. He is the author of numerous books and articles on the Philosophy of Religion.

BUDDHIST 'ŚUNYATA' AND CHRISTIAN 'KENOSIS': AN ATTEMPT OF COMPARISON ON THE GROUND OF WHITEHEAD'S METAPHYSICS

BOGDAN OGRODNIK

> In the Hwa Yen terminology, what Whitehead has stressed is exactly the simultaneous-mutual-containment aspect of reality.
> The difference is that the style and the approach with which Hwa Yen philosophers express themselves are more poetic and devotional than philosophical.[1]
> —Garma C.C. Chang

> Whitehead philosophy is evidently and necessary theistic and particularly ready for receiving Christian revelation.[2]
> —Lewis S. Ford

In the paper I compare two notions, *kenosis* and *śunjata*, that come from Christianity and Buddhism respectively. The reason for making this choice is philosophical in nature. Prof. Stefan Swieżawski (leading Polish metaphysician) once said that the dialogue between religions would force the philosophers to revive metaphysics. Both *kenosis* and *śunjata* point at the deepest level of reality experienced by a human being. Many Christian

---

[1] Garma C.C. Chang, *The Buddhist Teaching of Totality. The Philosophy of Hwa Yen Budhism*, (London, George Allen, Unwin 1971), p. 124.

[2] Lewis S. Ford, *Tomasz z Akwinu i współczesne prądy filozoficzne*, (transl. into English B.O.), „Znak. Idee" nr 5, Kraków 1988, p.54.

philosophers and theologians like Hans Waldenfels[3], Donald W. Mitchell[4], Thomas Merton[5], Rajmundo Panikkar[6] and Buddhist philosophers like Masao Abe[7], Keiji Nishitani[8], Daisetsu T. Suzuki[9] studied notions *kenosis* and *śunjata* as crucial ones from the point of view of dialogue between Buddhism and Christianity. At the same time this research possesses great importance for metaphysics in general.

Nowadays, Whitehead's metaphysics is treated as an important frame of reference by some Christian theologies and by Buddhist philosophers. Thus the comparison between the two title conceptions is made on the ground of process metaphysics. It should support the (hypo)thesis that inter-religious dialogue is possible if and only if it is illuminated by the experience of the deepest level of reality and takes place by means of any suitable metaphysics.

In his little but impressive book "Religion in the Making" Whitehead pointed at Christian and Buddhist doctrines and experiences as a source of intuition which was important to build a new metaphysics. He claimed:

> Buddhism is the most colossal example in history of applied metaphysics. Christianity took the opposite road. It has always been a religion seeking a metaphysic, in contrast to Buddhism which is a metaphysic generating a religion.[10]

Whitehead's thesis is simple: a bridge between rational religions[11] can be built by metaphysics which is faithful to its vocation, namely: to

---

[3] Hans Waldenfels, *Absolute Nothingness. Foundations for a Buddhist-Christian Dialogue*, (New York: Paulist Press 1980).

[4] Donald W. Mitchell, *Spirituality and emptiness. The Dynamics of Spiritual Life in Buddhism and Christianity*, (New Jersey: Paulist Press 1991).

[5] Thomas Merton, *Zen and the Birds of Appetite*, (New York: New Directions 1968).

[6] Raimundo Panikkar, *The Intrareligious Dialogue*, (New York : Paulist Press 1978).

[7] Masao Abe, *Zen and Western Thought*, (Honolulu: University of Hawaii Press 1985).

[8] Keiji Nishitani, *Religion and Nothingness*, (Berkeley: University of California Press 1982).

[9] Daisetz Teitaro Suzuki, *Wisdom in emptiness*, in Merton, *Zen...*

[10] Alfred North Whitehead, *Religion in the Making,* (New York: Fordham University Press 1996), p. 49.

[11] Whitehead pointed at Buddhism and Christianity as religions which partly fulfill his definition of a rational religion.

research of reality in context of all type of human experiences.[12] Thus metaphysics has to interpret religion experiences by means of one general scheme of categories.

> Thus rational religion must have recourse to metaphysics for a scrutiny of its terms. At the same time it contributes its own independent evidence, which metaphysics must take account of in framing its description.[13]

Many of Whitehead's disciples went this road and examined Whitehead's metaphysics as a philosophical ground both Buddha's teaching and Jesus Christ's Gospel like N. Hartshorn, John B. Cobb. Nowadays situation is much more complicated because both rational religions and metaphysics should also face up to the modern scientific vision of reality.

> Both (religions—B.O.) have suffered from the rise of the third tradition, which is science, because neither of them had retained the requisite flexibility of adaptation. Thus the real, practical problems of religion have never been adequately studied in the only way in which such problems can be studied, namely, in the school of experience.[14]

---

[12] It is worth mentioning the exact utterance of Pope Leo's XIII recommendation in his encyclical *Aeterni Patris* to develop contemporary philosophy. this document was very often interpreted in a narrow sense as a recommendation to renewing St. Thomas' metaphysics. However restitution of metaphysics must be a result of openness to every aspect of reality not only these ones which can be reconciled with Tradition. In this light, the following remark by Levis Ford is very accurate: that if St. Thomas lived today he would go in process philosophy. Lewis S. Ford op. cit.
„31. While, therefore, We hold that every word of wisdom, every useful thing by whomsoever discovered or planned, ought to be received with a willing and grateful mind, We exhort you, venerable brethren, in all earnestness to restore the golden wisdom of St. Thomas, and to spread it far and wide for the defense and beauty of the Catholic faith, for the good of society, and for the advantage of all the sciences. The wisdom of St. Thomas, We say; for if anything is taken up with too great subtlety by the Scholastic doctors, or too carelessly stated-if there be anything that ill agrees with the discoveries of a later age, or, in a word, improbable in whatever way-it does not enter Our mind to propose that for imitation to Our age." *Aeterni Patris*, Leo XIII. In:
http://www.vatican.va/holy_father/leo_xiii/encyclicals/documents/hf_lxiii_enc_04 081879_aeterni-patris_en.html
[13] Whitehead, *Religion...*, p. 77.
[14] Op. cit. p. 147.

It is almost a miracle that a new metaphysical system was born in the twentieth century, the system which belongs to the greatest European tradition and avoids many pathologies as scientism, minimalism, reductionism, etc. A debate devoted to adequacy of Whitehead's metaphysics accelerates today. It is a meaningful fact that among leaders of the examination are many theologians, Buddhist philosophers and scholars come from different branches of science and the humanities.

At the beginning I reconstruct the famous Christology hymn which comes from St. Paul's Letter to Philippians w. 2.5 – 2.11:

> Let the same mind be in you that was in Christ Jesus, who, though he was in the form of God, did not regard equality with God as something to be exploited, but emptied himself, taking the form of a slave, being born in human likeness. And being found in human form, he humbled himself and became obedient to the point of death – even death on a cross. Therefore God also highly exalted him and gave him the name that is above every name, so that at the name of Jesus every knee should bend, in heaven and on earth and under the earth, and every tongue should confess that Jesus Christ is Lord, to the glory of God the Father. [15]

The kenotic moment consists in decision of self-denying, self-empting of all those things which interfere with becoming of a man. The most important thing of this kind is equality to God. God's incarnation needs to humanize of God's nature. Humbling of Jesus is at the same time his exalting. While Jesus' humbling is a result of his decision, Jesus' exalting is performed on the will of God the Father.

As one knows the St. Paul's intention of citing the above hymn was to build an analogy between Jesus Christ and every Christian. The aim of each Christian is to be saved through the love (*agape*). Christian love and serving others as its fruit possesses analogous *kenotic* moment to this one which was necessary condition of God's incarnation. It consists in the will of abandoning everything which interferes with Christian love. The most important obstacle is man's egoism as love (*eros*) of oneself. The well-being of ego is the only point of reference for all deeds, their basic motive and their aim. Than "equality of men" means that every man has the same natural law to fulfill his love of oneself.

By means of the analogy St. Paul shows that Christian equality should be based on the new commandment: unconditional love to the others: God, man or even – as was showed by St. Francis – love to all beings. But the

---

[15] *The New Revised Standard Version (Anglicized Edition),* 1995 by the Division of Christian Education of the *National Council of the Churches of Christ in the United States of America.*

necessary condition of actualization of this new state of existence is cutting off an ego in above sense of this word. An old man, whose essence was closed in himself must die and the new one, whose essence is constituted by reference in a special way to other beings can be born. Then as St. Paul said: "I have been crucified with Christ and I no longer live, but Christ lives in me". In this place Buddhist philosopher Keiji Nishitani asks Western theologians "Who is saying these words?" This question has a character of a Christian koan.[16]

From philosophical point of view *kenosis* of Jesus becoming a man and *kenosis* of a man resulting in transformation of his essence towards divinity have fundamental meaning for metaphysics.

Following questions arise:
1. What should be a human nature if such a transformation can be possible?
2. Is a human nature so exceptional among other beings or rather the nature of all beings is such that this transformation is possible?

As theologians claim, Christ's kenosis is not something accidental but derives from his nature. If so I would like to put the following metaphysical hypothesis: nature of man has *kenotic* character and this is a necessary condition of emergence of his relational nature. Then man's nature is an exemplification of Whitehead's metaphysical thesis about relational nature of each actual being.

If *agape* belongs to the man's nature and it demands unconditional openness to Thou, then it agrees with *kenotic* character of the nature. In other words relational nature of a man is metaphysical ground for Christian love.

Now I try to present the basic Buddhist category – śunjata. As one knows this is an extremely difficult task, but this description will concentrate only on a few aspects which are important for the purpose of the paper. In general one can distinguish in conception of Śunjata its soteriological dimension and a metaphysical one. When a mind has awoken it is empty in the sense that there is nothing which can be described as its permanent property. Then each thing can reflect in it without any deformation. One can see things as they are. Such a Mind is unconditioned and creative. This experience is a starting point of Buddhist philosophical doctrines because it was Buddha's experience, who – as Buddhists believe - realized himself fully as a man. So this experience is the aim of Buddhist practice. It is very important to understand this

---

[16] Hans Waldenfels SJ, *Odkrywać Boga dzisiaj*, (Krakow: Wydaw. WAM 1997), p. 73.

experience as a transformation but not as a simple change from one mental state to another or emerging of some new qualities. The Mind is often described by means of metaphor of space. It is undetermined and it permeates through everything and each thing finds its proper place in it. The Awakening or the Enlightenment as a transformation is in fact returning to the very nature of a man. Having awoken the Mind experiences itself and all beings, as empty in nature but at the same time interconnected with others. It feels and recognizes a real presence of other sentient beings. This state of affairs   is a metaphysical ground for compassion – *karuna* but also wisdom – *pradźnia*. One can say that compassion is based on co-feeling.

I would like to formulate the following analogy: *kenosis* is a metaphysical foundation of *agape* **the same as** *śunjata* is a metaphysical ground of *karuna*.

Now it will be showed very briefly a few theses of Buddhist metaphysics which were working out during hundreds of years when the efforts were being made to rationalize the basic experience of reality.[17]

1.   Interdependent becoming of each thing is determined by things which have become earlier. This aspect of reality is presented by the metaphor of Indra's net of jewels or Fazang's hall of mirrors.

2.   Becoming things emerge from dynamic and indefinite *śunjata* so the world possesses an indeterministic character, too.

3.   Momentariness of being means that arising and vanishing of being is not separated by duration of being but happens at once. Our world is made up with such instantaneous dynamic atoms.

4.   Buddhist philosophy claims that such an atom is a gathering or accumulation of simple elements, so called skandhas. Such being hasn't got any constant essence but it has its own individuality and character.

5.   The atom of reality is a sentient being. Organicity is a primary characteristic of the experienced reality. Sentient beings constitute all things which we know from our everyday life. The whole Universe is filled up with myriad

---

[17] This summary draws on Garma C.C. Chang: The Buddhist Teaching of Totality...

sentient beings striving to liberate from suffering, where liberating consists in recognizing of their true nature.[18]

At the last part of the paper I will try to show a possible comparison between contents of basic religion experiences (or rather their conceptualizations) coming from Christianity and Buddhism by means of a few notions of Whitehead's metaphysics.

1.   According Whitehead's metaphysics the deepest level of reality is substantial activity of realization or pure activity. This metaphysical factor is totally indefinite, dynamic and it is a source of creativity of Nature.

2.   The smallest unit of the universe is so called actual entity, which has many other names: drop of experience, actual occasion, quantum of process, micro-process or organism. The last name indicates that organic type of analysis of reality dominates in Whitehead's metaphysics. Actual entity or organism is momentary and determines the unit of space-time.

3.   Becoming of each organism depends on all organisms which belong to the past of a given organism. In other words what a becoming organism *is*, depends on a way of presence of past organisms in the becoming one. What Whitehead called feeling is a connection between organisms and it has constitutive character for them. In a way, an organism is built from feelings of other organisms. One can briefly say that "esse" equals "sentire".

4.   The similarities between Buddhist metaphysics and occidental metaphysics made by Whitehead are striking. The differences between them come from the presence of category of God in Whitehead system and its absence in Buddhist way of conceptualization of reality. In his idea of primary nature of God as an unconscious but mental source

---

[18] It is worth mentioning that atomicity is considered in Buddhist philosophy in the context of divisibility of time. Instantaneous beings determine atoms of time (ksana) and are connected by karma principle and in fact all past events are present in a some way in a just becoming entity. It means that past events are spatially undetermined. Greek atomism is totally opposite to the above conception: spatially determined atoms are eternal and unchanging. Both conceptions need "space" for atoms and give its similar name: *kenon* as vacuum and *śunjata* as emptiness. But Greek *kenon* is mechanical in nature because it is an ontological condition for atoms movement, and a place where lifeless atoms can change their configurations. Buddhist *śunjata* is like an alive matrix from which momentary and sentient beings emerge.

of every determination Whitehead followed the Eastern model of final reality. And in his idea of derivative nature of God as an everlasting, dynamic and conscious one Whitehead followed the Western model of final reality.

5. All organisms, all sentient being are looking for the way to realizing and achieving the Divine order, which in Christianity is called Kingdom of Heaven and in the Buddhism is called Nirvana.

Finally I would like to sketch a starting point of philosophical anthropology based on Whitehead's metaphysics and take into account above reconstructions of category of *kenosis* and *śunjata* and their first derivatives. It seems obvious that the process anthropology leads to radically new vision of a man. A man is constituted by his feelings of God and myriad of organisms, especially feelings of other people. This constitution runs moment by moment and at each moment a man should achieve his own satisfaction. The satisfaction consists in creative answer to the question about "expectation" of the Universe i.e. God and the world. Such an answer is possible if a man participates both in the foundation of reality i.e. in the Pure Activity and in the divine order or its realization as the Kingdom of Heaven. So a man's nature must be transparent, or empty.

In the end of the paper it could be interesting to cite two general Whitehead's thoughts about co-existence of these religions, which fulfill Whitehead's criteria of rational religion in the highest degree, i.e. Buddhism and Christianity.

> But even today, the two Catholic religions of civilization are Christianity and Buddhism, and if we are to judge by the comparison of their position now with what it has been both of them are in decay. They have lost their ancient hold upon the world.[19]
>
> The decay of Christianity and Buddhism, as determinative influences in modern thought, is partly due to the fact that each religion has unduly sheltered itself from the other. The self - sufficient pedantry of learning and the confidence of ignorant zealots have combined to shut up each religion in its own forms of thought. Instead of looking to each other for deeper meanings, they have remained self-satisfied and unfertilized.[20]

The question is whether we find the common ground for meeting all parts of our knowledge which are crucial for understanding of experienced reality and come from rational religions, science and metaphysics.

---

[19] Whitehead, *Religion...*, p. 46.
[20] Op. cit. p. p. 147.

Bogdan Ogrodnik, Ph.D., works at the Institute of Philosophy of the University of Silesia, Poland. He is also the chairman of the Whitehead Metaphysical Society in Katowice, Poland.

THE PURPOSE OF HUMAN EXISTENCE AND THE MEANING OF IMMORTALITY IN DAOISM

ROMUALDAS DULSKIS

Introduction

The pluralism of religious ideas is a challenge for today's religious person. It raises numerous questions about the authenticity of one's own religion. Nonetheless, at the same time, this pluralism also offers a chance to view the mystery of God's work in human history with fresh eyes and comprehend one's own Christian identity more deeply. The Catholic Church has the deepest respect for other religious traditions and seeks to engage in sincere dialogue with their followers[1].

Today some questions should be raised. Was not it necessary to have Christianity for a comprehensive understanding of Daoism and Daoism for understanding the full breadth and depth of Christianity? Does not enclosing oneself within the narrowly understood Christian tradition actually mean enclosing oneself in the European-Western method of thought? Meanwhile, is not an open and well-meaning reflection on the experiences and teachings of other world religions, even when it involves criticism at the same time, actually the opening of oneself to the entire plentitude of the gifts of grace from God, the Creator and Savior?

In China's history, Daoism was always in opposition to the prevailing Confucianism. To take a more important governmental position in ancient China, it was necessary to acquire a special education. Learning was based on the Confucian doctrine and it included studies in politics, theology, etiquette and music. By completing these studies, a person attained solid information for implementing duties ethically and on the laws of the country and rules of behavior. Furthermore, an individual was taught for a lifetime, to observe humaneness, righteousness, dutifulness and respect for

---

[1] Cf. John Paul II. Post-Synodal Apostolic Exhortation *Ecclesia in Asia*, New Delhi 1999. § 6.

elders. However, Laozi stressed that such teachings do not provide answers to the essential questions in life. Laozi did not deny culture but attempted to instill a dimension of deeper insight to it. He was dissatisfied with the achievements of civilization that were deficient in perception regarding the meaning of human existence and its final purpose[2]. Therefore, he taught that, only through a passion for becoming acquainted with Dao, a person could understand the origin of the universe, its primary unity and harmony and the Daoist meaning of "non-action" (*wu wei*) – matters which meant the acquisition of true wisdom. Only due to Dao, a person can cultivate the inner peace that assists in overcoming all selfish desires.

The sage or wise person – the *shengren* – is the highest Daoist ideal for a human being[3]. This individual is often understood to be the opposite of the Confucian sage. However, these opposites do not negate each other; instead, one fulfills the other. Although it often seems that Daoist sages are negating the Confucian ethic, actually Daoism endeavors to enrich it by strongly emphasizing the metaphysical dimension of human existence. On the basis of Dao as a universal principle, Daoism seeks to present the crucial milestones in life, thereby indicating the purpose of human life while paradoxically asserting that a true sage lives "purposelessly"[4].

Mysterious mirror – returning to the source

Because Dao is the beginning of the universe and humanity, the true nature of a human being is a reflection of Dao. It is pure and simple, unrepressed by superficial information and undisturbed by fatal passions. Human nature at its purest depth is as clear as a mysterious mirror,[5] and peace, quiet, simplicity and emptiness are the true characteristics of human nature. When acted upon by the surrounding world, a human being loses the features of his/her own nature, becomes self-serving, seeks an education of doubtful value and succumbs to earthly yearnings, passions and purposeless whims. Thus, human nature becomes polluted. A person, who has distanced him/herself from one's own true essence and the eternal

---

[2] Cf. J. Ching, *Konfuzianismus und Christentum*, Mainz 1989, pp. 52-53.
[3] "The perfected human being in Taoism can be any individual, man or woman, from any social stratum – in fact Taoist literature often presents simpleminded wood-gatherers or fishermen as true sages. In the *Dao de jing*, however, the sage is ideally the ruler." L. Kohn, *Early Chinese Mysticism. Philosophy and Soteriology in the Taoist Tradition*, (Princeton: University Press, 1992), p. 50.
[4] Laozi 20.
[5] Cf. Laozi 10, transl. by D. C. Lau.

truths of Dao, becomes blind to goodness. "Not to know the eternal is to act blindly and court disaster"[6]. Therefore, it is necessary for a person to cleanse the mysterious mirror of his/her own soul, so that no stains remain on it, and return to the primordial quality of life delving into peace and emptiness. This is how one can return to one's own essence, to one's own nature. Such a return to a primordial quality helps an individual to understand the laws of eternity. Having understood them, a person becomes resistant to temptations since negative yearnings weaken.

"Returning to the source is serenity;
it is to realize one's destiny.
To realize one's destiny is to know the eternal.
To know the eternal is to be enlightened"[7].

By cleansing oneself and contemplating in solitude, a person pursues the most significant kind of recognition. "One can know the world without going outside. One can see the Way of heaven without looking out the window. [...] Therefore the wise know without going about, understand without seeing"[8]. Such knowing cannot be achieved by ordinary studies, because the object of the research is nature and its phenomena. Thus academic studies alleging to provide valuable knowledge are not capable of revealing Dao. Yet, by failing to become acquainted with Dao, a person lacks the essential component regarding his/her own existence. Since the uppermost value is Dao, Dao is provided with the priority above all else. This is the reason why Laozi spoke out against education, fearing that acquired knowledge might be considered the highest value. The purported skepticism of Daoists towards education can be understood explicitly within the context of Confucian education. It is not a refusal of knowledge or knowing but an objective to consolidate all of one's powers for the essential and most important issues of life. This is why Laozi invites us to turn towards one's own "mysterious mirror", in other words, to contemplate Dao with a heart cleansed of egoism and all sorts of debris[9].

A return to the primordial state begins by submerging into a state of peace and quiet. A sage experiences being misunderstood and ignored by others, because peace and quiet are in sharp contrast to a culture of entertainment. In spite of this, the sage realizes the value of his/her own choice and does not change it. The sage believes that faithfully holding

---

[6] Laozi 16, transl. by Sanderson Beck.
[7] Laozi 16, transl. by Sanderson Beck.
[8] Laozi 47, transl. by Sanderson Beck.
[9] Cf. Zhang Yi, *Komentarai*, in: *Laozi*, Vilnius: Vaga 2005, p. 218.

fast to the selected Way of Dao is far more important than achieving recognition and popularity by subordinating one's principles. Peace and quiet serve to mature the spiritual forces within a person. Thus, Laozi notes, a peaceful person is stronger than the anxious one is. "Stillness overcomes heat. The serene and calm are guides for all"[10]. Those who achieve perfect serenity acquire the power to redirect others onto the Way of Dao.

Characteristics and Pursuits of the Sage (Shengren)

By delving into Dao, the wise person adopts Dao's natural simplicity. Therefore, a sage selects a life devoid of battle as much as possible. The sage does not wish to fight; he/she does not consider the self as the only intelligent and righteous one. The sage does not desperately hold on to his/her own opinion but remains open to accept the views of others. By evading many meaningless conflicts, the sage consolidates forces for more important matters and wins the most important victory in life. Laozi claims that Dao and virtue assist those who seek them. "He who conforms to the way is gladly accepted by the way; he who conforms to virtue is gladly accepted by virtue"[11].

The sphere of quiet and peace form the conditions for a person to delve into a state of emptiness. Dao is a vacuum; nonetheless, specifically for this reason, it is the source of everything. All arises from it and all adheres to it. Thereby the emptiness of Dao is not empty; conversely it is the emptiness of fullness. Laozi illustrates this lesson of his with vital, earthly examples: The wagon wheel only accomplishes its function due to the space at its center[12]. It is only possible to pour water into a bowl, because it is concave. The empty spaces within a home make it possible to reside therein. Explicitly it is emptiness that makes such things beneficial and functional. Thereby the quest of delving into emptiness actually means a quest of delving into Dao and living the life of Dao.

Laozi compares the sage with a fish that delights in the depths of waters and never tries to rise to the surface[13]. Special significance is given to the symbolism of water. Water is the symbol of the weak that overcomes the strong. "Nothing in the world is softer and weaker than water. Yet nothing is better at attacking the hard and strong. [...] The weak

---

[10] Laozi 45, transl. by Sanderson Beck.
[11] Laozi 23, transl. by D. C. Lau.
[12] Cf. H-G. Moeller, *Daoism Explained. From the Dream of the Butterfly to the Fishnet Allegory,* (Chicago: Open Court, 2004), pp. 27-36.
[13] Laozi 36.

overcomes the strong; the soft overcomes the hard"[14]. Water is beneficial and necessary for all because it provides moisture and drink and it softens the earth hardened by drought. Water calms; it does not race or compete with anything. Water is similar to Dao. The image of the valley[15] teaches to select modesty, tolerance and humility.

Laozi, when opposing Confucianism, emphasized the difference between inferior and superior virtues. An inferior virtue is a declaratory demonstration of virtuousness, accenting dutifulness, politeness and superficially comprehended humaneness. Such virtues are notable for their artificiality, forcing oneself and external morality. The person with such a virtue is seemingly virtuous but is actually far from true virtuousness. To the contrary, the superior virtue has its roots deep in the heart of a person and it is natural and spontaneous[16].

Laozi taught that dogmas – in other words, the stiff, dead, formal "truths" – should not be grasped. Albeit dogmas contain positivism, nonetheless, they are more likely in actuality to cloud truth and goodness than to reveal them. The Daoist sage is inclined to disregard the rules of external life, strict orderliness, formal laws and Confucian ceremonies. In their stead, he/she seeks to consolidate forces so that the entire heart can be devoted to Dao and the superior virtue.

The sage refutes any endeavor for luxury, and enjoyment of some surplus of material goods is unacceptable to such a person. Therefore, this person does not constantly attempt to own more things, does not fret about losing something and does not thirst for new things. The sage seeks to satisfy "the belly and not the eyes"[17]. Here the belly indicates the natural and humble needs of a human being and the eyes – the excesses and amusements. Being moderate is a necessary feature of the wise person. External glitter and a desire to appear ahead of others do not appeal to the sage. This person chooses that it would be better to be like a stone – simple and modest albeit strong and reliable. "They do not wish to show themselves elegant-looking as jade, but (prefer) to be coarse-looking as an (ordinary) stone"[18].

---

[14] Laozi 78, transl. by Sanderson Beck. Cf. Zhang Yi, op. cit., p. 229.

[15] Laozi 6 and 15.

[16] Laozi spoke about three categories of human beings: the wise human, the average human and the fool. The wise person, once hearing about Dao, begins to live according to the laws of Dao. The person of average intelligence doubts Dao. The fool ridicules the teaching of Dao. Cf. Laozi 41.

[17] Laozi 12, transl. by James Legge.

[18] Laozi 39, transl. by James Legge. Cf. S. Eskildsen, *Asceticism in Early Taoist Religion*, (New York: State University of New York Press 1998).

The sage is as free, insistent, strong and unpredictable as the sea and the wind[19]. Being strong means, first of all, to be resolute and brave. However, that also means overcoming oneself and one's weaknesses. "Those who overcome others require force. Those who overcome themselves need strength"[20]. However, paradoxically, the description of strength in Chapter 52 in *Laozi* reads, "to stay with the gentle is strength"[21]. Thus, the sage is distinguishable not only by simplicity, openness, modesty and humility but also by a certain gentleness and frailty. According to Laozi, assertion and strength must be intelligently matched with gentleness and humility. This is necessary when wanting to reach a mature personality. The entirety of the characteristics of a sage are even reflected in his/her gait. The sage walks carefully as if stepping on thin ice in a river. Nonetheless, the sage is always as alert as a soldier.

In this context of strength-weakness, Laozi also submits the image of an infant. An infant is distinct for his/her inborn pleasant manner, an undisturbed soul in balance, sincerity and naturalness. Many of the baser passions of adults are foreign to an infant. However, on the other hand, the infant is also a symbol of a person who does not waste his/her vital energy on negative pursuits. Thus, infancy not only means innocence but it also focuses strong energy on positive deeds. Laozi calls attention to the fact that infants often cry loudly but do not become hoarse. Furthermore the muscles of infants are feeble "but their grip is firm"[22]. Not only does the sage resemble an infant but, when interacting with the sage, others feel they have approached infancy. A task for every person is to attempt a return to infancy[23].

Even upon receiving honorable recognition, the wise person remains ordinary, humbly realizing that "humility is the basis for nobility, and the low is the basis for the high"[24]. Characteristic of a sage is the ability to remain common in the face of great success and to reject a high status in the community. As Laozi expresses this, "know glory and keep to humility"[25]. The sage considers it more important to retain internal powers than to achieve external successes. The reason is that internal forces determine the fruitfulness of external activities, not the other way round.

---

[19] Cf. Laozi 20.
[20] Laozi 33, transl. by Sanderson Beck.
[21] Laozi 52, transl. by Sanderson Beck.
[22] Laozi 55, transl. by Sanderson Beck.
[23] Cf. Zhang Yi, op. cit., pp. 221-222.
[24] Laozi 39, transl. by Sanderson Beck.
[25] Laozi 28, transl. by Sanderson Beck.

Wise people try to be kind to those who are good and those who are not. "They are good to people who are good. They are also good to people who are not good. This is the power of goodness"[26]. The wise person understands that goodness has the power to draw others to behave in goodness.

Although Dao is distinct and clear, it often seems sullen, hazy and mysterious to people. The same as with Dao, many people cannot understand the sage who follows Dao and delves into Dao peace. Such a person appears mysterious to many a person. Similarly a great and powerful virtue can appear poor and weak to the person who does not understand because it contains features of commonness and gentleness[27]. The virtuousness of a sage reaches such subtleties that most people do not understand such a person and consider such a person simple-minded and strange. The sincerity, caring, mercy, goodwill, respect and generosity of such a person appear unpractical and naive to others in the surroundings.

> "The people of the world make merry as though at a holiday feast or a spring carnival. I alone am inactive and desireless, like a new-born baby who cannot yet smile, unattached, as though homeless.
> The people of the world possess more than enough. I alone seem to have lost all. I must be a fool, so indiscriminate and nebulous.
> Most people seem knowledgeable and bright. I alone am simple and dull"[28].

The true basis of the value of a person lies within his/her own nature. Therefore praise belittles a person's dignity equally as much as contempt does. Laozi encouraged not paying attention, neither to admiration nor contempt, but faithfully going the Way of Dao.

Resemblance to Dao and "Straw Dogs"

Laozi asserted, on the basis of his observations of nature, that nature is not biased. Nature offers no undeserved benevolence to anyone and hates no one. The impartiality of nature was described by Laozi in his famous comparison with "straw dogs."

> "Nature is not humane. It treats all things like straw dogs. The wise are not humane. They regard people like straw dogs"[29].

---

[26] Laozi 49, transl. by Sanderson Beck.
[27] Laozi 41.
[28] Laozi 20, transl. by Sanderson Beck. Cf. W. Bauer, *Geschichte der chinesischen Philosophie*, München 2001, pp. 76-78.

The impartiality of nature reflects Dao's lack of bias; thus it is an example for the wise. A sage also seeks impartiality and remains free of influences from any groups of people. In ancient China, stuffed straw dogs were used for rites and then thrown away as unneeded. In this regard, the text by Laozi does not teach contempt but merely teaches a certain indifference. A sage must not be indifferent to people as such but must learn calmly to accept the changes in human life, such as death. Just as Dao is devoid of form, so a person must not be bound to his/her present-day "form". All things and phenomena in the world are connected with the law of change. Laozi noticed that the development of a being, thing or phenomenon usually reaches a certain limit whereupon its change begins a transference into another quality and another shape. Therefore a person must also be open to the reality of this life and ready to accept the approaching transformations in his/her life. Once a person has become familiar with the eternal law of cyclical movement in the universe, he/she seemingly regains sight due to an understanding of the inevitability, naturalness and goodness of changes in human life.

No selfishness of any sort can be perceived in the existence of the sky and earth. "Heaven is eternal, and the earth is very old. They can be eternal and long lasting because they do not exist for themselves"[30]. Exactly in the same way, the sage does not raise any selfish goals in his/her own life. In this sense, it can be said that such a person lives without purpose, "seeming aimless, drifting as the sea"[31]. The same as Dao, there are seemingly indiscernible wombs giving birth to all, just as a sage gives rise to valuable insights, ideas and actions from his/her own silence, peace and emptiness. Furthermore the characteristic feature of such birthing is, "to give birth without taking possession"[32].

The Daoist view on the evolvement of society and the ruling of a country differs essentially from the Confucian perspective. Regarding national rule, Confucians emphasize the importance of knowing rules on ethics, correctness of behavior and the significance of customs. According to Daoists, the foundation for the evolvement of a society, as much as that of the country lies in an individual's decision to live in accordance with the principles of Dao. Well-being for a country and a community cannot be reached merely due to societal ethics and external rules. A country can

---

[29] Laozi 5, transl. by Sanderson Beck.
[30] Laozi 7, transl. by Sanderson Beck.
[31] Laozi 20, transl. by Sanderson Beck. Cf. G. Wohlfart, *Der Philosophische Daoismus. Philosophische Untersuchungen zu Grundbegriffen und komparative Studien mit besonderer Berücksichtigung des Laozi*, Köln 2001, pp. 27-54.
[32] Laozi 10, transl. by Sanderson Beck.

only prosper when its rulers and its common citizens direct all their being towards Dao. Merely the decision to live by the laws of Dao can mature true and concrete, ethical attitudes in society. Concrete ethical attitudes are capable of overcoming the egoism and selfishness of citizens thereby severing the roots of evil in the society.

By following Dao, the wise sovereign rules by *non-action*. Then the citizens of a country are not suppressed by governmental authority, because the sovereign "does not utter words lightly"[33] and "says few words"[34]. In other words, such a sovereign does not pass unnecessary orders and does not threaten punishments for no good reason. The power and secret of success of the rule by such a sovereign lie in the naturalness and commonness of the manner for ruling. Such a sovereign leads the country while remaining faithful to the principle, "to lead without dominating"[35]. This kind of ruling does not cause confusion and tension, and its successes are long-term because they are reached in a calm and natural manner. Conversely, the leader who prefers to act thoughtlessly and hastily can cause misfortune, as much to him/herself as to others. Desiring fame, such a sovereign rules strictly and utilizes brutal penalties. The sovereign who rules by "action" which causes anxiety, fear and tension in the nation resembles a raging storm and an unexpected torrent of rain. However, neither the storm nor the downpour lasts for long; the same way, the work done by the fiery sovereign will not survive for long.

Once a person knows Dao – there is knowledge of the essence of all beings in the world. An internal light fills the person who holds fast to Dao, and that person radiates into the environment. Such a person steps onto the way of immortality. The internal maturity of this person transfers naturally into the surroundings. Once one has learned to discipline and cultivate oneself, personal attitudes on life are easily noticed by others. Children in a Daoist family form naturally and mature as conscious and responsible individuals. Therefore the formation of the family as much as society is a spontaneous and naturally developing process[36].

---

[33] Laozi 17, transl. by D. C. Lau.
[34] Laozi 23, transl. by Sanderson Beck.
[35] Laozi 10, transl. by Sanderson Beck.
[36] Cf. Kersten Reich, Yuqing Wei, *Beziehungen als Lebensform. Philosophie und Pädagogik im alten China,* Münster / New York / München / Berlin 1997, p. 181-203.

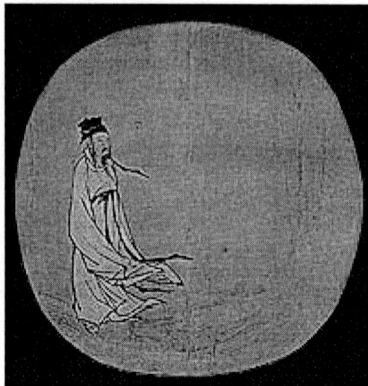

Daoist Immortal Lu Dongbin Crossing Lake Dongting. Mid-13 Century. Boston's Museum of Fine Arts.

Conclusion: Immortality

The processes in the evolvement of human history permitted the development of various cultures and religions in spheres more or less closed from the surrounding world for lengthy periods, for centuries. Intercultural contacts were never as intensive over history as they are today. That is why the postmodern person has the duty and opportunity to contemplate the advantages of an intercultural and inter-religious dialogue and make use of these advantages. A meeting of religions should be judged today as an essentially positive and advanced matter. This permits a more comprehensive review of the phenomenon of religion and evaluation of the strongest and weakest aspects of one or another system of religion. Inter-religious dialogue assists in highlighting the most mature elements in the doctrine of every religion. Thus an assumption can be made that the deepest essence of Daoist teaching unfolds specifically in a Christian context. It is significant that in his message to the participants in the international conference commemorating the fourth centenary of the arrival in Beijing of the great missionary and scientist Matteo Ricci, S.I., Pope John Paul II noticed: "Historically, in ways that are certainly different but not in opposition to one another, China and the Catholic Church are two of the most ancient "institutions" in existence and operating on the world scene: both, though in different domains – one in the political and social, the other in the religious and spiritual – encompass more than a thousand million sons and daughters.[...] I hope and pray that the path opened by Father Matteo Ricci between East and West, between

Christianity and Chinese culture, will give rise to new instances of dialogue and reciprocal human and spiritual enrichment"[37].

In the perspective of Daoist doctrine, it would seem that certain aspects of Christian teaching become more highlighted. Upon analyzing the truths and religious practices of both religions, we can consider the issue of the salvation of humanity in a new light. The Christian endeavor for eternal life is similar, from the phenomenological perspective, to the Daoist doctrine of immortality. Daoism pays exceptional attention to immortality[38]. There are many tales about sages purportedly reaching immortality. A variety of rituals and magical practices are used hoping that, by their help, immortality can be achieved. Added to that, in today's popular culture, e. g. movies, the theme of Daoist immortality often emerges in various forms. Nonetheless, along with these superficial treatments of immortality, we are seeing a very serious doctrine, worthy of our attention, about immortality which accents the human's ever-increasing resemblance to Dao and delving into Dao. The goal of this doctrine is essentially to touch a person's life and raise it to another, more qualitative plane. Here it becomes possible to perceive the connection with Christian teaching about the necessity to form one's earthly life in accordance with the mandates of the Gospel.

The pursuit of a full-fledged familiarity with Dao and formation of one's life according to the laws of Dao is not an easy way. Regardless, there are times when analyzing a text by Laozi, an impression can form that the life of a sage may not require great efforts and that the life of a sage is a peaceful and harmonious devotion to the wisdom of Dao as revealed by nature. Nevertheless, upon a more in-depth view, it becomes clearer that Laozi invites the highest pursuits, involving all personal powers and encompassing all of life. The delving into Dao and familiarity with Dao are global objectives enveloping all human existence, which harmonize and transform. Opening the self to the eternal laws of Dao signifies the opening of the self to the immortal Dao. Concurrence with this is concurrence with immortality.

---

[37] John Paul II, *Message to the Participants in the International Conference Commemorating the Fourth Centenary of the Arrival in Beijing of Father Matteo Ricci*, Vatican 2001, § 6-7.

[38] Cf. J. Blofeld, *Der Taoismus oder die Suche nach Unsterblichkeit*, Köln 1986.

Romualdas Dulskis is a Roman Catholic priest and Professor at the Catholic Theology Faculty in Vytautas Magnus University, in Kaunas, Lithuania.

He is a member of the Curatorium of European Society for Catholic Theology. Professional Interests: Ecumenism, Spirituality, Inter-religious Dialogue and Theology of Vocation. He is the author of several books and many academic articles.

THE TRUTH PROPAGATED BY MAHATMA GANDHI AS A BASE OF STRONG DIALOGUE BETWEEN RELIGIONS

MARIOLA PARUZEL

"When God asks us [...] who we are, this means – how we act, he will not ask for the name of our religion. For God a deed is everything and faith without a deed is nothing."
—Mahatma Gandhi

Introduction

Dialogue is a conversation, which means that it is a process of exchanging interesting information between different people. However, it is also full of emotional content and when among these emotions hostility appears- the dialogue disappears. "Dialogue is the main and necessary part of every human ethical thought, regardless of who those people are. It can be seen as an exchange, and thanks to the existence of speech, as a communication between human beings, it is indeed a collective search"[1] – as John Paul II said. In literature it is being emphasized, that the dialogue can exist on the conditions of existence of principles of equality, dignity, love patience and understanding of the fact that another person can possess a worldview different than ours. The aim of dialogue is to become closer to each other, to establish peace in the world, to enrich our own ideas, to understand another religion, to solve problems, to destroy prejudices and "to build the unity", as John Paul II used to say. Dialogue is characterized by two intentions: the agathological and the axiological. Many authors believe that the existence of the international dialogue is an effect of the existence of many religions which are hostile towards one another. However, we should notice that it doesn't have to be the truth. Since when

---

[1] John Paul II, „Orędzie na XVI Światowy Dzień Pokoju", Roma 8 XII 1982 in: Byron L. Serwin, Harold Kasimow, *Jan Paweł II i dialog międzyreligijny* (Kraków: Wyd. WAM, 2001), p. 46.

we throw aside the burden of history we will be given a chance of standing next to each other and create a profound dialogue. The next generations who won't experience prejudices against the believers in other religions, have of course greater possibility of achieving this aim. This should be our aim. We should endeavor to implement the ideal of the inter-religious dialogue into our lives and to pass this idea to our children, who hopefully will never experience religious hostility.

In order to understand the idea of inter-religious dialogue and the attempt to implement it into our personal lives, it is worth to learn from those whose lives were testimonies of dialogue. Aside from John Paul II, whom I mentioned before, the proof of the possibility of the inter-religious dialogue was also shown to us by the simple life of a modest man, often called Mahatma, which in Sanskrit means "Great soul". He considered himself Hindu, Christian, Muslim, Jew and Buddhist. He was classified as an adherent of neohinduism, alongside such famous people as Ram Mohan Roy, Keshab Chandra Sen, Śri Ramakrishna Paramahasa, Vivekananda, Sarvepalli Randhakrishnan. According to the Gandhi's will I will not use the word "gandhism". Let's take a closer look at this extraordinary man.

Bapu Ethics

The base of the international dialogue was the ethic of the "Father of Nations". Ija Lazari-Pawłowska distinguishes three most important claims of Gandhi's ethics, those are: ahimsa, which means kindness; equality, which means egalitarian justice; and perfectionism, which is closely related to ascethism.

According to Gandhi, the motives determine the value of a deed. The claim of ahimsa, called the claim of kindness, was close to his practice and concerned all the living beings, regardless of their faith. It consisted of the demands of opposition to violence, kindness for the opponent and struggle without violence. This rule was already known in India in the antiquity. It is connected to the protection of life of every creature, but not at all costs. Gandhi explained, that if his friend was incurably ill, he wouldn't see a reason against allowing him to pass away earlier. It would even be his duty to take his friend's life. Bapu claimed that cruelty, called himsa, should appear in every action. Ahimsa relates not only to killing but also to the minimization of the suffering of others and offering them kindness, help and solidarity. Although as Ghandi admitted, that it is sometimes impossible to survive without hurting animals, he never accepted hurting another man. He claimed that harmony between people is possible, and that it is conditioned by non-violent action. It is closely related to the opposition to the evil, which signifies an active involvement in the human relations. It is a struggle liberated from violence. It is a moral responsibility. In relation to an enemy, Gandhi commended to reject hatred and to try to love them. In fact, his struggle was against the evil, not against men. When writing letters to Englishmen in defense of his nation, he used to entitle them "Dear Friends". It was because his goal was to reconcile with enemies, not to defeat them.

Ija Lazari-Pawłowska emphasizes that though the idea of non-violent struggle was not a new one, Gandhi was a man who turned it into a mass movement. He wanted a fight which renounces any kind of hatred and which is a voluntary one to be the only way of fight. As Bapu explained: "violence is a deprivation of the possibility of taking an action by creating physical obstacles which are for some reasons impossible to breach"[2]. It also includes a threat, lie, slander, deceit, unkindness and hatred. The only difference is that, as he would say, "hatred is the most subtle form of violence"[3].

Gandhi tried to show in his life, that "by turning to force we are not going to save anything – nor ourselves, nor our dharma, nor the Empire"[4]. Gandhi's methods consisted of talks, letters, petitions, demonstrations, strikes, marches, rallies, boycott of elections, refusal to observe certain regulations and exhorting people not to pay taxes. He called his actions satyagraha, which means "persistence in truth". Gandhi often went on hunger strikes to convert other people to the Truth. Despite the fact that his actions were seen as a way of extorting concessions, they were usually successful, because of the compassion and liking people had for him more than because of any change in their beliefs. Gandhi also used persuasion, e.g. he made people realize the truth about the injustices, and tried to raise their awareness. He arose feelings of compassion and of guilt. Moreover, he avoided all kinds of prejudices. When somebody spoke ill about the English, he suggested that nobody is perfect so people should love Englishmen as they are.

Furthermore, Gandhi believed that we are all equal. He struggled for India without castes and for the world without any form of discrimination. He supported the idea of resigning one's property in order to help the poor, which resulted in the creation of bhudan and gramdan movement after

[2] Ija Lazai-Pawłowska, *Etyka Gandhiego* (Warszawa: Wyd. PWN, 1965), p. 52.
[3] *Ibid.,* 54.
[4] Mahatma Gandhi, The speech about resolution connected with congress's credo, delivered 28 XII 1920, in: Mahatma Gandhi, *The collected works of Mahatma Gandhi* (The Publications Division Ministry of Information and Broadcasting Government of India, volume19), p.165.

Gandhi's death. The most important principles propagated by Gandhi concerned poverty and temperance in regard to eating and sexual life. The members of an ashram had to observe the principles of the Truth, ahimsa, chastity (bramaczaria), control of the eating habits, not stealing, not possessing, physical labour, economic self-sufficiency, fight against untouchability, tolerance. Gandhi's main goal was the Truth and to find the truth we have to fulfill an important condition - "to see the universal and all-pervading spirit of Truth face to face one must be able to love the meanest of creation as oneself"[5].

Gandhi on different religions

"The true faith can be smelt around just like the smell of a rose. It is easier to see than the beauty of colorful flowers"[6] – as he used to say. "Father of the Nation" claimed that there is one God and many gods at the same time. On the contrary, he also said that "Truth is God" and that he regards "God as the highest incarnation of Truth"[7]. He was convinced that different religions lead to the same goal. He believed that religions are being taught by people who are imperfect, which is the reason of the contradictions between them. Behind these contradictions there is the revealed Truth. Therefore, we should respect the adherents of other religions in the same way as we respect the believers in our own faith. Such attitude means that instead of trying to convert others to our religions, we should let them perfect themselves. For Gandhi "religion is a deeply personal matter. It is a matter of heart"[8].

Furthermore, we have to be aware of the imperfections of our own religion and seek the Truth. Therefore we should constantly reinterpret the religion in order to perfect it. Bapu emphasized the necessity of friendly relations between religions as a road leading to the Truth. Mahatma Gandhi struggled to convince people of different faiths that ahimsa is more precious than tolerance[9], because applying it allows as to respect different religions just as we respect our own faith. Only through ahimsa the real inter-religious dialogue is possible, since every religion took a different way heading for the same goal. Every religion possesses some

---

[5] Mahatma Gandhi, *Autobiografia* (Warszawa: Wyd. Książka i Wiedza, 1958), p. 577.
[6] Mahatma Gandhi, *Young India*, 23.4.1931 in: Ija Lazari-Pawłowska, *Gandhi* (Warszawa: Wyd. Wiedza Powszechna, 1967), p. 181.
[7] Mahatma Gandhi, *Autobiografia*, p. 10.
[8] Mahatma Gandhi, *Young India*, p. 181.
[9] Notice that his characteristic makes the dialog stronger and deeper.

imperfections, so they can learn from each other through the dialogue. According to Gandhi contacts with other religions will bring not only respect, but also the understanding of the imperfections, which in effect will help to make them better. He claimed that it is crucial to achieve a certain level of morality, to which the type of worship is insignificant, as "morality is the essence of religion"[10]. He stated that "You believe in God in the same way as I do. God can not be so cruel and unjust to distinguish people for the better and the worse ones. God of Truth and Justice could not have done so"[11]. He manifested solidarity with Muslims by publicly quoting the *Qur'an*. He thought that it would allow Hindus to find in *Qur'an* contents close to their own beliefs and to unite with Muslims. He told his compatriots that the "true faith" does not apply untouchability. To all the people he said that "the victory belongs to those who follow the road of truth and faith"[12]. He wrote that "we have to use this power that can be gained only by unity and truth. It means than our slavery will finish when people will be united in their demands and ready to endure the whole suffering that may afflict them"[13]. As we can see, the slavery still lasts but according to Gandhi's beliefs, it is can still be overcome.

The most wonderful thing is that there is no discrepancy between Gandhi's words and his deeds. That's why Stanley Wolpert calls him a "religious genius and innovator"[14]. Bapu asked about the principles he obeys, used to say that one should look at his deeds because there lies the whole knowledge about his principles. Gandhi fought against hunger, poverty, lack of education and sanitation, discrimination of women, ill treatment of children and untouchability. The effects of his actions were often instant. Thanks to him the spinning wheels called "gospel of hope" were introduced, as well as weaving mills for the jobless and many schools and sanitary facilities were launched. He did not wait for India's independence inactively but worked every day, also through his writings (he wrote articles, essays, manifestos, letters, speeches, diaries). Ija Lazari-

---

[10] Mahatma Gandhi, *Autobiografia*, p. 9.

[11] Mahatma Gandhi, *CWMG*, (The Publications Division Ministry of Information and Broadcasting Government of India, volume 3), p. 287.

[12] Mahatma Gandhi, "What Has Satyagraha Achieved?", *Indian Opinion*, 3 VI 1911, in: Mahatma Gandhi, *CWMG* (The Publications Division Ministry of Information and Broadcasting Government of India), p. 104.

[13] Mahatma Gandhi, "When Women Are Manly, Will Men Be Effeminate?", *Indian Opinion*, 23 II 1907, in: Mahatma Gandhi, *CWMG* (The Publications Division Ministry of Information and Broadcasting Government of India, volume 6), p. 335.

[14] Stanley Wolpert, *Gandhi* (Warszawa: Państwowy Instytut Wydawniczy, 2003), p. 364.

Pawłowska said that "Gandhi enraptured crowds"[15]. He was able to do it thanks to his faith in God and man.

In 1908 Gandhi wrote to Hindus from prison: "suffering is our only cure. Victory is certain"[16]. Unfortunately, in 1947 his enthusiasm fell and Gandhi experienced a crisis in his faith in the idea of kindness. When India Gained independence a period of poverty and fights full of hatred began. Jawaharlal Nehru mentions this period as a very hard one for Gandhi. During everyday massacres in Calcutta, Gandhi went to people on foot and called for peace, In New Delhi he went on a hunger strike which lasted until the end of fights. Though for some time he lost the faith in peace which was achieved by himself, he did not resign from ahimsa, but he announced "his own bankruptcy".

All of these ideas of Gandhi allow us to understand the essence of the inter-religious dialogue and the ways of implementing it into our lives. Knowing what Gandhi thought of religion, it is worth asking why the Truth he talked about did not spread over every continent and did not cease the existence of religious hostility by bringing us closer to the everyday dialogue between religions? In 1947 Gandhi himself understood that people used to listen to him, because the had no alternative, but when they could start to use their guns – they became the easiest way of "dialogue" for them. He understood that he was never able to change their attitude about the inter-religious dialogue and what he had done was to damp the fire of hatred in people's hearts. Trying to answer this question we must consider not only the philosophical approach but also thy psychological one.

Conditions of a dialogue

In order to fully understand what inter-religious dialogue is it is necessary to look at the psychological mechanism existing behind human communication. I am going to focus only on some of the issues related to this topic, for further details I recommend professional literature[17]. Using the psychologists' language we would say that the aim of dialogue is to

---

[15] Ija Lazari-Pawłowska, *Gandhi* (Warszawa: Wyd. Wiedza Powszechna, 1967), p. 25.

[16] Mahatma Gandhi, *Indian Opinion* (24 X 1908) , in: Mahatma Gandhi , *CWMG* (The Publications Division Ministry of Information and Broadcasting Government of India, volume9), p. 104.

[17] For example: Gerd Mietzel, *Wprowadzenie do psychologii* (Gdańsk: GWP, 2003); Jan Strelau, *Psychologia* (Gdańsk: GWP, 1999, volume 3); C. Neil Macrae, Charles Stangor, Miles Hewstone, *Stereotypy i uprzedzenia* (Gdańsk: GWP, 1999).

establish an interpersonal relation, which Michael Argyle defines as regular meetings of some people and expectation that such meetings will be continued in the future. According to Michael Argyle and Monika Henderson, interpersonal relations posses such features as- activity of the participants, their goals, norms, interpersonal abilities, ideas, convictions as well as social power and social roles. Interpersonal communication consists in performing common actions and achieving satisfactory goals in accordance to the norms. In order to come into an interpersonal relation it is necessary to posses such features as the abilities to avoid conflicts, negotiate, respect, listen and to use emotional intelligence.

The main foundation here is the possession of mature personality which can result in a profound religious faith. Gordon Allport defines religious feeling as a "general attitude which allows individuals to relate themselves to the wholeness of Being"[18] or as "a disposition which develops on the basis of an experience of favorable reaction and of reacting in the same way to the problems and norms which an individual treats as the most important ones in their lives and which are meaningful to the whole of constant and central facts and factors of a dynamic life"[19] and a mature religious feeling is a disposition that consists in habitual reaction to things important to a man and to the central and constant rules of the world's nature. Gordon Allport claimed that there are no religious geniuses who could perfectly perform the duties of their religion.

It is know that Gandhi was also not a perfect man, especially in the relation to his family he behaved unsuitably and his sons bore a grudge against him because of his constant control and his sacrificing of their lives to his cause. Bapu himself felt that he is an imperfect being, although a one that heads towards ahimsa. He stated that not only sages and saints should aim at ahimsa, but also a common man has enough strength to achieve it. He said about himself: "I'm a weak mortal, like all of us and [...] I never had anything extraordinary in myself [...] I Assert that I'm a common human being, which makes mistakes like anybody else. However, I admit that I am humble enough to confess my faults and to change the wrong road. I admit that I have a strong faith in God and in His

---

[18] Gordon Allport, *Osobowość i religia* (Warszawa: Instytut Wydawniczy PAX, 1988), p. 77.
[19] Gordon Allport, *The individual and his religion* in: Zdzisław Chlewiński (eds.), *Psychologia religii*, (Lublin: Wyd. Towarzystwa Naukowego KUL, 1982), p.64.

Goodness and inexhaustible passion for the truth and love. But aren't these features present inside all of us?"[20]

The maturity of a religion lies in a reflection and, according to Gordon Allport, it is characterized by six features. These features are: good diversity, which lets us to seen not only advantages but also disadvantages of a religion; dynamic religious feeling, mature in the matter of autonomy of its motives (which means that we are not guided by or wishes, impulses, fear or fanaticism); religion's own impulsion and dynamics; consequences of the directives, which lie in the stability of moral consequences; comprehensiveness (religion concerns every part of our lives); integration, which is a harmonic wholeness; and the last one, heuristic, which means that the faith is a working hypothesis in which the doubts are acceptable and the answers are not stable. Certainly, it is an interesting conception, since it takes religion as an unfinished matter. Only this kind of religion gives individuals laws and obligations, gives the understanding of life and encompasses the totality of existence. In such a grasp of the problem religion is favorable to tolerance, because it claims that there is one truth, only the names given to it are different.

The second condition of a dialogue is the possession of some abilities that allow us to avoid the rule of first impression and stereotypes and allow us to conduct open talks and continuing contacts in the future. It is essential to know the mistakes that we are likely to commit. An example of a mistake is a so called basic mistake in attribution, which lies in the fact that we underestimate the influence of a situation on other people's behavior while overestimating the role of internal impacts. For example, when a person of a different faith hurts us we tend to look for the causes of such behavior in themselves, in their features, views etc. instead of searching them inside the particular situation. It is also worth knowing that we have the automatic tendency to distinguish people who are "my" from those who are "other", which was proved by Muzafer Scherif (1953). Furthermore, we tend do favour our own group, which was shown by Henri Tajfel (1970). We also look at different religions as very homogeneous while we tend to notice greater differentiation within our own religion (Brigham, 1985). Gandhi himself wrote in his *Autobiography* that when he had his first contact with Christianity he thought that it is "a religion which makes man eat meat, drink vodka and change the way of dressing, doesn't deserve to be called a religion"[21]. However, through the

---

[20] Mahatma Gandhi, "From Far-Off America", *Young India*, 6 V 1926, in: Mahatma Gandhi, *CWMG* (The Publications Division Ministry of Information and Broadcasting Government of India, volume 30), p. 226.

[21] Mahatma Gandhi, *Autobiografia*, p. 51.

studying of the Bible and talking to Christians he overcame these stereotypes.

This clearly shows that the best way of solving problems is to increase one's experiences by contacting with the "other" group. It allows us to get to know it better and to throw away our prior notions. A collective experience lets us destroy stereotypes in their cognitive, emotional and behavioral (which lies in putting a stop to discrimination) aspects. It does not mean that an experience can appease all the inter-religious conflicts and create a dialogue. The sole experience is not enough if it is not combined with a proper level of a "meeting". Only under specific circumstances the tension between groups can be eased. These circumstances are, e.g. contacting with other person as with an equal, aiming at such things that cannot be achieved without the other group keeping in mind that only achieving them can ease conflicts. If they are not achieved the conflict worsens. Therefore, it is important to pursue goals which are possible to achieve, not the idealized ones, which even if they are possible to achieve, are of long duration. It is also essential to look for similarities which make us closer to each other. This is exactly what Gandhi was doing. Although he was not a psychologist, he had the ability to show the religions of the world as a quest for one Truth. It is worth noting that the inter-religious dialogue doesn't consists only in "meeting" and "talk" but also the actions which are their consequence. Our deeds have to confirm our words. Gandhi put his convictions into practice and said that his deeds show what his views are. Though, looking from the universal perspective he was not a perfect man – from the human perspective we may say that he was the best of us. That's how a man becomes an example to follow.

Summary

Ija Lazari-Pawłowska points out that the originality of Gandhi's philosophy doesn't lie in its contents but in the whole context of the situation and its scope. Gandhi showed us that one man can fight against the religious hostility. It is worth asking why he didn't manage to do something more about the inter-religious dialogue. First and foremost, he could not change the mentality of people which was shaped by their former experiences. The change of attitude cannot be made by anybody else but each single individual. Behind the hostility we could often see an authoritarian personality (Theodor Adorno 1950), which develops from the first years in human life. An individual can't forget about harms done to them by other people and sees fight as the only way of living. Of course, Gandhi was aware of it, e.g. when a man asked him what he should do when his son was killed. Gandhi told him to adopt a boy of different religion who had lost his father.

Although Gandhi gave a lot to people believing in different religions, the main problem still lies in a single man and his rigid views, habitual feelings and actions. As Abraham Joshua Heschel said, we have to accept that "the diversity of religions is God's will"[22] and we have to constantly broaden our awareness of the mechanisms by which we are trapped. The best example of such attitude is showed by the rock band U2 who propagates Gandhi's ideals. In one of their songs Bono sings: "Jesus, Jew, Muhammad, it's true... All sons of Abraham. Father Abraham, speak to your sons. Tell them, No more!". A Polish designer Piotr Młodożeniec created a symbol connected to these ideas, which is recognizable to most of us- the famous CoeXist with the Muslim crescent symbol representing the "C;" the Jewish Star of David, the "X;" and the Christian cross, the "T".

Mariola Paruzel is a student of philosophy at the Faculty of Social Science and at the same time she is studying psychology at the University of Silesia in Poland. She had also studied psychology in Madrid within the confines of the Erasmus Programme. She is a member of three scientific circles: the Scientific Circle of Philosophers, the Scientific Circle on Psychotherapy and Psychological Training and the Scientific Circle on Psychology of Life Quality MERITUM. She wrote about a dozen articles for *Racjonalista, Gnosis, Episteme, Ponad*-to.

---

[22] Abraham Joshua Heschel, "No Religion Is an Island" in: Harold Kasimow, Byron L. Serwin, *No Religion I san Island: Abraham Joshua Heschel and Interreligious Dialogue* (New York: Oris Books, Maryknoll, 1991), p. 14.

THE DIALOGUE AS A PRECONDITION FOR THE FREEDOM OF BELIEF AND AS PREREQUISTITE FOR THE CHRISTIAN INCULTURATION: THE EXPERIENCE OF THE BULGARIAN ORTHODOX PRIESTS AFTER 1989

PETAR KANEV

The thesis that the inter-religious dialogue is a precondition for the freedom of belief and in the same time is also a prerequisite for the religious enculturation is connected with a specific theoretical interpretation of the analyses of the empirical data (and data bases) of 3 (separate/different) projects:

1. *"Priests and the Orthodox Church Community as Factors for the Transition Societies' Social Integration. Cultural Traditions and Potential of the Civil Society in Bulgaria"* in cooperation with Munich University and FOROST for implementation, transliteration, and the scientific proceeding of overall 200 biographic interviews with East orthodox priests from all over Bulgaria with the help of oral history methods. (2003-2005)

The project includes about 200 biographic interviews with the 10 % of the total number of the acting priests in Bulgaria, who for now, according unofficial data are a little bit over 2000, by quotas: different bishoprics, towns and villages, age, education.

2. *"The Social Role of the East Orthodox Priest in Bulgaria and in Eastern Europe – Parishes, Social Practices, Free Access Discussions of Spiritual Issues"* - Department of History and Theory of Culture, Faculty of Philosophy, Sofia University "St. Kliment Ohridski" (2005)

3. Project "The *Bulgarian Ethnic Model– Myth or Reality within the Common European Problem of the Tolerance between*

Christians and Muslims" – Bulgarian Ministry of Education's Fund for scientific research in close cooperation with the Institute for research in philosophy in BAS, project's field work. (2006-2010)

In the context of the philosophical and religious discourse and by the means / with the help of an in-depth study, the goal of this project is to explain concrete issues through the prism of several basic problems – are the people who declare themselves as Christians or Muslims religious at all? Does really the religious syncretism in domestic forms of Orthodox Islam and Orthodox Christianity assume predisposition to religious fanatism? What are the actual latent conflicts between Christians and Muslims? Can they escalate? Does the Bulgarian ethnic model exist?

The present project's focus is also the philosophical aspect of the question of understanding the inter-religious dialogue between orthodox Christians and Muslims. The use of cultural-and-anthropological and philosophical analysis could also help the deciphering of the double meaning of the religious dialogue as a precondition for the freedom of belief and in the same time is also a prerequisite for the religious enculturation.

The empirical data of those 3 projects is growing up to a large data base of interviews, biographical material and reports in the field of cultural and social anthropology. The biographical interviews with priests and religious people are at the core of the three researches. Predisposing the respondents to normal conversation however enables them to share in details their views and to say even more than what they originally intended. The biographical interview is liberal, meaning that: the interviewed person is not asked any direct questions; it is a dialogue between the interviewer and the interviewed persons, as the interviewer is directing the conversation to specific subjects.

The interviews taken alone are essentially a practice of dialogue. Additional oral inquiry of the priest actually leads to intercourse of different interpretations and translations of common values, metaphysical, ontological and religious ideas, semantic relations and ethical and cosmological worldviews. The interviewers completed this inquiry with their own impressions and observations for the condition of the church and their impressions for the life of the parish, as well as for the entire atmosphere in the eparchy, in the town or village, in the district, vicarage and bishoprics. Systematizing the scattered information is connected with the question how to analyze the empirical data base of those 3 researches – in what kind of theoretical point of view, in which method. This question was carried out in specific interdisciplinary outlook. My own studies are connected with the understanding that the Christianity could be analyzed as a specific paradigm, a specific religious and ethical-metaphysical paradigm. This thesis takes up the problem about the dialogue as a sustainability and renewal of the traditional Christian patterns and propensities in the present European context.

But how could we understand the Christianity as a paradigm? The specific methodological considerations brought up by Hans Küng, about the adoption of Thomas Kuhn's paradigm theory for analysis of the Christian world view (Weltansicht) and value adjustments, are well known. For better understanding of the biographical interviews with the Bulgarian orthodox priests I prefer to analyze the Christian paradigms not only in historical point of view (the changes of the Christian paradigms in the last 2000 years), but mostly the inner character of the paradigm as a specific worldview, as a dynamical process of understanding, translating and interpreting the Christian sensibility in an permanent dialogue with the others. Küng's theoretical model for better understanding of Christianity as an evolution of different Christian paradigms, „constellations"and a "macro paradigm" (*Theology for the Third Millennium, 1988; Yes to a Global Ethic, 1996*) could be interpreted also in the context of the late theoretical works of Thomas Kuhn, which analyze the meaning of his concept of paradigm (*Postscript 1969, Second Thoughts of Paradigm*). Hans Küng's theoretical model for analysis of the Christian world view and value adjustments as a different Christian paradigms could be translated also in its anthropological dimensions in the context of the depth psychology of the Unconscious, interpreted in the field of Christos Yanaras Eastern Orthodox adoption of Lacan's views about the human personality (*prosopon* in Yanaras's philosophy), which could be developed only through active conversation with the Others and with the Transcendental Otherness.

In our study of the inter-religious dialogue in Bulgaria both of these separate lines for understanding the dialogue as a precondition for the Christian enculturation and for the being of the religious type of paradigms in general are complementary to an another one in regard of the contents, as well as in the used methods – uniting those leads to one meaningful and methodological interdisciplinary approach, enriched with the oral history elements. Our analysis shows that there is no real religious tolerance without inter-religious dialogue. That's why the dialogue is a precondition for the freedom of belief. On the other hand the inter-religious dialogue as a real communication is always connected with the Christian mission. Only the dialogue leads to spontaneous processes of Christian enculturation during the conversation with the others. That's why the dialogue is also a prerequisite of the Christian enculturation.

The type of this presentation is hardly conducive to a full description of our theses and theoretical methods for analyses of the interviews. That is why I will only mark the main aspects of the method and the conception of our study. The religious paradigms are very different from all other kinds of paradigms (scientific, cultural, etc.). They are connected with borders of the common sense and the borders of the being – the birth, the death, the superreality. The Christian paradigms are in the same time ethical and metaphysical, which means that the ethos in the Christianity has metaphysical dimensions and also the metaphysics have ethical sense. In Christian paradigms the ethics is actually metaphysics and the metaphysics is actually an ethics.

The Christian ethical-metaphysical paradigms could be recognized in four components, analogical to the Kuhn's concept of the paradigm as a disciplinary matrix: symbolic generalizations, metaphysical presumptions, values and exemplars. It's easy to recognize these four components of the Christian sensibility and worldview during the analysis of the biographical interviews with religious people and orthodox priest in Bulgaria. The symbolic generalizations in the apostolical Christian paradigm could be understood also as a system of living symbols of the faith in the context of Carl G. Jung's concept of the living symbols, which are not emblems, allegories or metaphors, but self-dependent forms of living collective psychological reality. In this case the systems of the living symbols of the traditional Christian paradigm are fully expressed in the Nikkeian symbol of the Christian faith. The metaphysical presumptions of the Christian paradigms are connected with the idea of the absolute, creative and transcendental personality of the living God – the salvation and the Savior, the eternal live, the Holy Trinity, the Logos and the love, the kingdom of Heaven, the free will and the human personality as *imago dei*. The common values of the Christianity are connected with the humanity as a love of mankind, compassion, sympathy and love of God (*the absolute transcendental personality, the cosmogonical creator of all, the spring of life, the unknown other*) and the communication and the love for the others, for the other persons, for the fellow man. The exemplars of the Christian paradigms reveal themselves fully in the Christomimesis, which can be found in the orthodox interpretation of the Christian religion worldview also in the patristic, in the martyrology, in the cherigma, in the orthodox theology. But the main exemplar for every Christian remains Jesus Christ, the live of Christ, the words of Christ, the action of Jesus the Savior. For the real religious Christian the vocation of the man is to be

Christ, to live his live as a following and imitation of the live of the Savior. This outlook shows up the paradigm not only outside as an object, but also inside as a dynamic process of interpretations and translation during the inter-religious dialogue.

These four elements hold the ideal forms of the Christian paradigm in the interviews that we have studied. In all respects the religious dialogue with the other human beings is always a translation – in the concrete case of the Bulgarian orthodox sensibility it's a translation of the four elements of the traditional Christian worldview on the language of the respondent in seeking and spontaneous creation of a collective language to understand and share the believes in a common semantic system – in a common paradigm of the community. Consequently the real fulfillment of the paradigm is always in the dialogue – in the interpretations and in the enculturation that the dialogue presumes; in its dynamical hermeneutic and interpretative character. The dialogue with the fellow man could be seen also as a dialogue with the transcendental otherness of its personality – the image of God in the human being. This theoretical point of view for the character of the religious paradigms, similar to the Christos Yanaras's philosophy of human person, proposes a new model for understanding the specific meaning of the Christian paradigms in the light of Kuhn's idea that the paradigm could never be static and complete, but is always subjected to dynamic debates and spontaneous translations during communication within the community that upholds it.   By this point of view the signification of the dialogue for dynamic of the apostolical Christian paradigm is definite as adequately enculturation, which depends on one hand on its understandability and approachability in the actual European socio-cultural world, and on the other hand on its own specific Christian sensibility and matter.

Another specificity of the proposed method for analysis of the interviews with the Bulgarian priests and ordinary believers brings to the fore that the Christian ethical and metaphysical paradigms are revealed, not only in the theological and institutional interpretations of the church elites, but also in egalitarian everyday-life Christianity and in the Christian ethical adjustments on deeply intimate psychological level. This method are to clarify the studied problem of the religious dialogue as a relation between the Bulgarian traditional orthodox Christianity and other types of religious and quasi-religious believes (such as Islam, atheism, occultism, parapsychology), between the Church and the non-clerical people, between the traditional believes of the Church and the secular paradigms of the Modernity in the field of the actual globalization processes. Therefore the study brings out also the problem about the modifications of the secular paradigms of the Modernity, connecting with the processes of "religious revivals" in the recent years. In conclusion the study outlines also some tendencies and perspectives, related with the newest communicational and technological revolution as an opportunity for forthcoming adequate conservatism and innovation of the traditional Christian enculturation, which could become a shape of maximally wider debate and dialogue on the egalitarian European level.

How and why does the dialogue guaranty the freedom of belief is not as simple as it seems. The analysis of the tolerance of the Bulgarian priest depending on the data base of the biographical interviews shows two different kinds of tolerance – one virtual – based on prejudices, and one real – based on real communication and dialogue with the others.

The analyses of our data bases show 5 types of orthodox believers and priests – the active ones, who are looking alone by themselves for conversation with persons with different faith or with secular believes, are about 13 % of the interviews; the second type of orthodox believers are those who are open for every conversation and dialogue with the others, but as a passive site, they do not look for active communication by themselves – about 35% of the interviews; pent and closed in theirs own orthodox communion believers, always ready for conversation with the others not as inter-religious dialogue, but mostly as a monologue in front of the audience (*this type of orthodox believers are often tolerant to the Muslims, Lutheran, evangelist, "classical" protestant, but are not tolerant to the roman catholic, Pentecostal and charismatic cults and sects, Buddhism, occultism, religious and quasi-religious movements from the far East*) – about 45% of the interviews; unsociable, uncommunicative, marginalized, inert orthodox priests and believers – they are paranoid, suspicious, upset and intolerant, in most cases they are also orthodox fundamentalists, even fanatics – about 10 % from the interviews, "orthodox businessmen" – tolerant for all that can be traded and turned into money – about 7 %.

The marginalization of the priests and common believers is connected with the marginalization of the Bulgarian society as a whole. It is a large-scaled process in the futureless regions, and it is connected also with the poverty and social stagnation. It leads to incommunicativeness and intolerance, and it's dangerous for the freedom of belief, and also ruins the real Christian metaphysical-and- ethical enculturation of the post-atheist secular society. The loss of the inter-religious dialogue in this case leads also to the disintegration of the orthodox translation of the traditional Christian paradigm, to tearing apart of the connection between its four basic elements, and mostly between the Eucharistic orthodox liturgical communion, and the Christomimesis as a basic exemplar of the Christian metaphysical and ethic paradigm.

In opposite, the inter-religious dialogue leads to the positive Christian ethical and metaphysical enculturation. But the dialogue as a neo-Christian mission has one more and different dimension – it strengthens the freedom of belief, it leads to living dynamical faith and "dismantles" the static virtual prejudices of the fanatism, it leads to competition and emulation in "doing good". There are many exemplars for this in the interviews with Christians and Muslims in the Rhodopes. The Muslims who are in active inter-religious dialogue with the orthodox Christian became much better Muslims, and Christians who are in active inter-religious dialogue with the Muslims became much better Christians. And the good Muslim is much closer to the values of Christianity than the orthodox fanatics, the old priest Erolski in the village of Hvoina in the Rhodope Mountains, has told us.

Petar Kanev, Ph.D., works at Religious Studies Section in Institute for Philosophical Researches Bulgarian Academy of Science.

DISCURSIVE CONSTRUCTION OF THE SUBJECT AND INTER-RELIGIOUS DIALOGUE FROM THE PERSPECTIVE OF PROCESS THEOLOGY

MIROSŁAW PATALON

Introduction

This article[1] is centered around the question of subject identity in the religious aspect. It seems that this topic is vitally important in view of the fact that today no longer is a person shaped exclusively by separate and monolithic communities, even if he or she is rooted in a uniform and homogenous setting. Common access to the Internet and other media, along with the ability to travel, facilitate contact with cultural diversity, including religious diversity. It seems justified, therefore, to consider the dynamics of religious views of an individual in this new social reality. This issue is even more important if one accepts the assumption that social structures continue to be inspired by religious paradigms. The (self) formation of a subject is a basic problem not only in pedagogy and sociology but also in philosophy and theology. Is an individual subjected to absolute socialization within imposed and existing social structures or does he or she participate in the process of relatively free self-development? Are we determined by nature or called to achieve human maturity? Who or what specifies standards of that maturity? Is the world of values given to us or are we supposed to work it out? These are some possible questions that follow from the main problem stated above. In the ontic aspect, the question also concerns religious education and the content mediated in this process: is it permanent or subject to change? That, in

[1] This paper has been written as part of the project *Discursive construction of the subject in selected areas of contemporary culture*, carried out in 2007-2010 in the Institute of Pedagogy of the University of Gdańsk, funded by the Polish Ministry of Science and Higher Education (grant no. 10702632/3637).

turn, leads to the question regarding the openness of teachers of religion to a theological discourse shaped by traditions other than their own. The problem outlined above inspired me to conduct research whose results are presented in the last part of this paper. However, let us first discuss the theoretical framework on which the research was based[2].

Theoretical assumptions

Process philosophy, as well as the related theological and pedagogical reflection, is strongly connected to American pragmatism, represented by Charles S. Peirce, William James, George Herbert Mead, Charles Horton Cooley and – above all – John Dewey. According to these philosophers, knowledge should always be oriented towards the real world characterized by diversity and changeability (using Dewey's terms, reality is subject to continual 'reorganization' and is never 'finished' in its development). Abstract and holistic models are useless fancy; what matters is everyday life and solutions to real problems (the ethical and political dimensions of philosophy). It is also noteworthy that pragmaticians refer to the naturalistic assumption that a human being is a part of the broader world of nature but – contrary to Spencerian evolutionism – they strongly oppose social determinism. Culture does not have a spiritual or metaphysical source but is a form of an active and responsible adjustment to actual conditions of life. Consequently, it is not established ontically nor grounded in a transcendental pattern, which in the pedagogical context considered here means that the subject is being continually constructed. Reality is a dynamic collection of interactions between its participants; it is open (processual) by character and every aspect of the world consists of continual becoming. A human being is a unique participant of these processes: on the one hand, conditioned naturally and culturally, and on the other hand, free to change the encountered reality through his or her active involvement[3]. Pragmaticians criticized dualism of reality and abandoned the rigid differentiations between the soul and body, consciousness and being, thinking and acting, organism and environment, individual and society. Rather, people are in the constant process of mutual adjustment to one another and to the environment. The essence of

---

[2] See Mirosław Patalon, *Pedagogika ekumenizmu. Procesualność jako paradygmat interkonfesyjnej i interreligijnej hermeneutyki w ujęciu Johna B. Cobba*, (Gdańsk: Wydawnictwo Uniwersytetu Gdańskiego, 2007).

[3] See William James, *Pragmatism. A new name for some old ways of thinking*, (Cambridge, Mass: Harvard University Press, 1978).

socialization is a harmony of continuation and creativity; any innovations cannot be hostile towards tradition.

The pragmatists view truth in a distinctive way: it always refers to the practice of everyday life (a statement is true if it works) and, as such, is not a closed or static notion. Truth is not to be discovered but to be experienced; the experiencing subject should not be raised above the experienced object but should be immersed in it (thus the borderline between the subject and object of experience is blurred). Consequently, knowledge constantly escapes possession and rather than being conceived of statically as a commodity it must be approached dynamically as a process dependent on the entire context of time, place, etc. This principle refers to both gnoseology and axiology: values are constructed through a person's concrete involvement, which means that some disappear and others emerge. Social values are established democratically; that is why education should above all develop human activity and responsibility. Educational processes are not limited to a specific area or time and all established educational institutions must as much as possible reflect the currently experienced world[4]. Because of the changeability and diversity of reality, learning is based on the principle of novelty viewed as a virtue and, consequently, on pluralism which leads to that novelty. A school, therefore, is a place in which knowledge is not merely transmitted but created through the exchange of experiences of the participants (teachers, students, authors of course books, etc.). Being in a rut kills the spirit of development while an educational success consists of awakening the students' courage to experiment with and change the reality they experience.

Despite his emphasis on diversity in education, Dewey carefully avoided the two extremes of individualism and collectivism. An individual is always a part of a larger social organism; that is why it is important to be aware of common pursuits and achieve a relative uniformity in perceiving the world[5]. Democracy is therefore primarily a form of exchange of experiences and it is in this sense that it is vitally important for the development of both individuals and entire societies. The life of an individual must not be considered apart from the life of the social organism but, at the same time, it is individuals that affect the character of the society. This mutual and constant influence is a result of communicative processes, that is interactions between all participants of a

---

[4] See John Dewey, *Democracy and education. An introduction to the philosophy of education*, (New York: The Macmillan Company, 1929).

[5] John Dewey, *Logic. The Theory of Inquiry*, (New York: H. Holt and Company, 1938), pp. 66-67.

community. This democratic ideal of education is founded on the conviction that the occurrence of desirable changes is directly proportional to the intensity of exchange of experiences between the participants of social life. The evolution of thought is therefore founded on the freedom of individuals and social groups as well as on shared activity. Cooperation and dialogical coexistence of participants of the social life is the absolute foundation for the development of culture and social organization.

Likewise, Charles H. Cooley – because of the assumption concerning the organicity of social life – maintained that notions and phenomena that appear to be mutually exclusive (e.g. freedom and necessity, the individual and the group, the spirit and the matter, science and art) must not be separated as antinomies but viewed in a complementary way as collective and distributive aspects of one reality[6]. That is why we should oppose any particularism and artificial isolation of specific aspects (e.g. biological, economic, psychological, etc.) as if they functioned independently of one another. For everything is a part of a single process of life in its entirety. From this perspective, both isolated collectivism and individualism must be viewed as destructive extremes; through communication processes an individual exists within a group and a group exists in an individual (mutual interpenetration[7]). However, this does not mean that opposites blur in some homogeneous structure. The author of the theory of symbolic interactionism, George Herbert Mead, also overcomes dualism (of the body and soul, instincts and consciousness, etc.) through the category of act and social act, in which inner experience is always a part of a broader whole[8]. Within that whole, conscious processes of action and reaction build up human personality while life becomes meaningful through act (social interaction). According to Mead, the self has social origins: an individual may only experience himself or herself through the mediation of the other.

The basic tenets of pragmatism were recognized and developed by Richard Rorty, who related the idea of democracy not so much to emancipation but to tolerance and openness to cultural difference. However, he did not insist that a juxtaposition of differences must always result in a synthesis; at the same time, this does not mean that some

---

[6] Charles Horton Cooley, *Human Nature and Social Order*, (New York: Schocken Books, 1964), pp. 36-37.
[7] See Talcott Parsons, *Stability and Social Change*, (Boston: Little, Brown, 1971), pp. 5-6.
[8] See: George Herbert Mead, *Mind, self & society from the standpoint of a social behaviorist*, (Chicago: The University of Chicago Press, 1934).

borders are not to be crossed[9]. The tension between objectivism and subjectivism in Rorty's thought is manifested in the idea of solidarity and voluntary agreement, based on the fundamental principle of a person's loyalty towards other people. This is some sort of a third way (between dogmatic conservatism and heartless liberalism) which allows for a critical attitude towards the encountered values only from the inside of a social system, i.e. when the values established democratically have been sufficiently internalized. In other words, an individual is only capable of a responsible (i.e. non-revolutionary) implementation of innovations if he or she is bound to the local community through socialization processes resulting in a similarity and partnership of values and experiences. At the same time, Rorty, though recognizing the relative and casual nature of these similarities, argues not only for a local but also global responsibility; otherwise, misunderstood freedom will lead to acculturation, uprooting, alienation, and ultimately to social disintegration. Rorty's neopragmatism does not permit challenging the social consensus at the lower levels of education though it protects the freedom of the university; the freedom of democracy is therefore an educational goal[10].

Democratic coexistence of cultures and ideas must then be based on the ethics of consultation and compromise, i.e. competing statements should be in the state of balance rather than fight. We should prevent a social domination of a single option creating a false sense of objectivity. Free and open encounters of various philosophical, theological, and ethical ideas should lead to repeated choices of best solutions for the respective social groups. This means that no truth should aspire to being established as absolute; rather, what we deal with are continual transformations of particular truths resulting from their interaction. A relative sense of stability comes only from accumulated social and individual experience. In order to overcome this awareness, Rorty suggests an ironic attitude which helps us retain a necessary distance when faced with no ultimate answers to human questions. A free and distanced person may belong to various social groups, experiment with different lifestyles, and experience a number of value systems. Only then can one develop by making conscious choices, though at the cost of being aware of one's casualness. It may be expected that mature societies in the future will derive their sense only from this world and the reality will no longer have to be rooted in

---

[9] Richard Rorty, *Cosmopolitanism Without Emancipation. A Respond to Lyotard*, [in:] Scott Lash, Jonathan Friedman (ed.), *Modernity and Identity*, (Oxford, UK, Cambridge, USA: Blackwell, 1992), p. 61.

[10] See: Richard Rorty, *Contingency, irony, and solidarity*, (Cambridge-New York: Cambridge University Press, 1989).

transcendence of any kind. This is exemplified even today by citizens of Western democracies. This does not mean, however, rejecting the irrational aspect altogether but perceiving it in esthetic terms as complementary to the rational aspect (the union of art and science), thanks to which the postulated utopia will not slip into nihilism.

Even though neopragmaticians (not only Rorty but also Hilary Putnam, Donald Davidson and John B. Cobb) are critical of metaphysical realism (in Cobb's case, of theological dogmatism), they do not advocate relativism. On the contrary, they stress the necessity to retain discursive analyses of great contemporary problems. Putnam calls Rotry a cultural relativist, accusing him of identifying truth with norms of a specific cultural community, which means that all statements have particular meanings only to their authors. Thus it becomes impossible to construct some holistic – though not absolute –system; entities are separated by impenetrable barriers (no continuity and relationship); repetition (e.g. quoting) is impossible because the respective statements only work in their original contexts. As a result, social isolationism grows deeper and any kind of discourse becomes immaterial as knowledge is either totally private or confined to the already existing cultural or religious circles (because of this, Putnam also criticizes Michel Foucault); propositions cannot be compared because relativism assumes no cultural commensurability which would make it possible[11].

Cultural relativism views particular cultures as closed monads; by accepting symbolic untranslatability it sanctions social separationism. Consequently, under some conditions it is potentially dangerous because it builds up a tension between the particular monads that cannot be reduced. Ethnocentrism viewed in this way is opposed by both Putnam and Rorty, as well as Cobb. Unlike Putnam, Rorty is looking for opportunities to build bridges between the isolated islands-monads, trusting that there is a way out of the extremes of individualism and collectivism. He believes there must be some third way between absolutism and cultural imperialism on the one hand and relativism on the other hand. In the opinion of both Cobb and Putnam, it is based on the capacity of the human reason to operate in several systems of notions and on the existence of some transcendent framework of reference, enabling successful exchange of ideas and experiences between cultures. This is provided by rationality immersed in the experience of life. Rationality, which goes beyond accepting the function of a mere observer, is both entitled and compelled to declare a certain state of affairs. Life itself establishes canons of truth

---

[11] H. Putnam, *Realism and Reason. Philosophical Papers*, vol. 3, (Cambridge-New York: Cambridge University Press, 1983), p. 195.

and falsehood, being the most important human commodity and creating an area of exchange between individuals, this enabling the sustained existence and development of a society. As a result of this approach, Cobb rejects the extremes of both religious pluralism (cultural relativism) and exclusivism (the fiction of the so-called 'divine point of view'). Rationality conceived of in this way is not the capacity to discover truths or achieve common consensus (which Hans Küng seems to suggest in his pursuit of global ethics) but the ability to act in order to maximize the likelihood of causing the desired results within the community (which includes their relational and contextual character). Cobb's pedagogy of ecumenism, then, is based on a community of experience which *de facto* enables further reconstruction of the socio-cultural matter. In this sense, neither scientific nor theological rationality exists beyond the context of concrete experience; truth about God (transcendence) in separation from life is an illusion.[12]

A human being, along with the culture he or she creates, is neither separated from nature nor placed above it as God's representative who subdues the earth. Rather, he or she is settled in nature and connected with

---

[12] Obviously, the processual thought discussed here is not only related to neopragmatic philosophy; it is also referred to by e.g. Gilles Deleuze's poststructural philosophy of difference (particularly addressing *Process and Reality*), demonstrating the coexistence of casualness and chaos with order and identity. The process of perpetual differentiation of beings (termed by Alfred N. Whitehead the very principle of process) is the basis of their identity; what we have here is a phenomenon of coherence amidst disintegration, the unity of reality and its concurrent diversity, though Deleuze is more radical than Whitehead and Cobb in asserting the irrationality and indeterminism of the chaotically differentiating world. At any rate, they share the rejection of substantialism as the starting point for the reflection on identity and the assumption that logos governs the world – instead, Deleuze points to chance and process philosophers to the relation between the world and God, which after all is a kind of unpredictable game (at best, we can speak of probability). Reality, therefore, is always transitional (processual), which means that there is no timeless and absolute truth. Even scientific truth – much like being – is still emerging, so it has no right to monopolize the description of reality. Deleuze stresses the creative character of differentiating but his idea goes beyond the holistically balanced and organic system God-world-creativity, lacing an integrating synthesis or ordering factor. See: Krzysztof Kościuszko, *Chaos i wiedza. Przyrodoznawczo-epistemologiczny aspekt filozofii różnicy Deleuze'a*, (Olsztyn: Wydaw. Uniwersytetu Warmińsko-Mazurskiego, 2000), p. 118; G. Deleuze, *Negotiations, 1972-1990*, (New York: Columbia University Press, 1995), s. 159-160.

it; nature and culture are unified[13]. Because of this, the sense and fulfillment of human life is not the exclusive result of analyses of the mind (soul) or experiences of the material body – as independently operating spheres of experience – but comes from dialogical creating new possibilities, which in process theology is compared to the dance of life; the meaningfulness of reality consists of its participants' creative acts. In the process of the constant development of an organism the key element is not the desire of the individuals to survive (evolution) but the interactions between them; the dance of life does not incorporate steps planned ahead but develops unpredictably, fancifully, surprisingly, and yet surely! Creative relationships built up the meaning and sense of existence of beings and conversely: singleness, isolationism and solitude lead to nihilism. Dance, typical of all pairs and rooted in nature, in this light becomes the hermeneutic key to unlock the meaningfulness of life at large. All knowledge is transitory; one should rather speak of attempts to "capture" reality and multiple perceptions thereof. Changes do not occur according to a simple principle of causality: some may be predicted, others not. Neither are they designed and controlled from the outside; rather, the world is in a constant process of self-creation.

However, it must be stressed that in process philosophy God is not viewed as a person separate from the world, as a sovereign Lord manipulating reality using a hierarchy of intermediate beings. Such a cosmology (*notabene* based on Platonic ontology) in fact reinforces the dualism of reality which in Cobb's opinion is still upheld in the post-Cartesian rationalistic culture of the West. The distance between "this world" and the world of divine ideas of thoughts suggests that nature (including a human being) is oriented towards a specific purpose, namely to overcome the earthly temporariness and transience and find fulfillment in an ideal God. According to both Whitehead and Cobb the world will never be finished in the process of self-creation, therefore every stage of its development – as well as the development of every being – is fully valuable. This is crucial for education because it eliminates the hierarchical arrangement of stages in learning. As we learn, we know not more (the value of our knowledge "today" is greater than of our knowledge "yesterday") but differently. Beings no longer strive for higher and more perfect knowledge (until the level of complete knowledge, typical of God) but for harmony. This holarchic (i.e. holistically balanced) system in the process of changes and relations abandons the goal of

[13] John B. Cobb, *Thinking with Whitehead about Nature*, [in:] J. Polanowski, D. Sherburne (ed.), *Whitehead's Philosophy. Points of Connection*, (Albany: State University of New York Press, 2004), pp. 175-196.

subduing the earth to the human mind, stressing the pursuit of fulfillment instead. In this sense, education consists of a person's finding his or her place in creative relationships with other subjects of nature; it is a constant process, which follows from the dynamic character of these relationships. Because of this, every culture and every human being at every stage of existence will be concerned about education[14].

Report from empirical research

Phenomenographic research described below was conducted in June and July 2007 in a group of teachers of religion in Gdańsk, Poland. Among the respondents there were 20 teachers of the Roman Catholic religion and 15 teachers of other religions (including Christian denominations: Polish National Catholic, Greek Catholic, Lutheran, Baptist, Pentecostal, Adventist churches, as well as other religions: Islam, Buddhism and Judaism), all teaching in gymnasiums (Polish middle schools with students aged 13-16). Interviews were held in schools in which religion is taught or in educational facilities run by parishes. Roman Catholic respondents were selected randomly while the group of teachers of other religions – because of their minority status – practically included the whole population. In the phenomenographic procedure, the following categories of meanings assigned by teachers to the examined phenomena were isolated (fragments of selected responses are quoted in parentheses):

Phenomenogram

A. Roman Catholic teachers

What inspires you to think about God? Where do you look for inspiration of this kind?

1. Participation in the liturgical life of the Church (*Lenten or Advent retreats are important moments for this sort of reflection; adoration of the Holiest Sacrament; the Holy Mass is source of my greatest experience of God's nearness; to me, the real inspiration is the Holy Mass and the Eucharist*).

---

[14] See: Michael Kazanjian, *Learning Values Lifelong. From Inert Ideas to Wholes*, (Amsterdam-New York: Rodopi, 2002), p. 100.

2. Personal prayer and reading of the Scripture (*I draw knowledge from the Scripture; the first inspiration is always prayer, a personal encounter with God*).

3. The Internet and reading books (*I read a lot, including online materials; I try to consider literary texts, not necessarily religious ones; works and teaching of John Paul II and Benedict XVI*).

4. Life experiences, difficult situations (*as a mother, I can see other riches of God, I focus on other aspects and truths; difficult situations call for our reflection and taking a position with respect to God; an illness provides some inspiration of this kind*).

5. Other people, including students, and their experiences (*exchange of thoughts and experiences – one can confront one's own views with what others are going through; I look for inspiration in people, particularly in wise, seeking, and curious people; looking at another person, I seek God in him or her; the teaching process involves feedback, the inspiration comes from what we work out together in the religion class – in this way the image of God is enlarged*).

6. Contact with nature (*I do a lot of mountain hiking, which defines me to a significant extent*).

How do new inspirations change your understanding of God?

1. God remains the same but becomes closer (*God becomes more of this Father; books only complement the Scripture; I would not say that books change my understanding but they complement it; complementation is not the same as change*).

2. The image of oneself and the surrounding reality is changed (*understanding God is, as it were, a secondary issue: we will never know or understand him here on earth but through prayer, reading, and other people God reveals some things in me; I try to think less and do more – new inspirations change my approach to a number of things*).

3. The image of God is changed (*earlier I thought of him as a person who punishes; with time, God in the Church changed – first he was stern, now he loves as a real father; I can see God's acting in the world, which later leads to changed thinking about him*).

4. New inspirations reinforce the desire for seeking God even more (*new inspirations show that we still need something new, that we still discover God, it is not that I once believed and that's all but I have to keep learning; my image of God does not change fundamentally but the new experiences somehow expand my perspective; whatever we come up with*

as theologians – that will be totally different and irresponsible – is a puzzle which prevents intellectual and emotional stagnation).

How do you evaluate changes in your perception of God?

1. Change is desired development (*something is happening in the spiritual life; I started to develop; it is a process – I hope I will never be indolent, I would be afraid of stagnation, I hope I will never be in a rut; a static image of God does not necessarily prove internal development; this shows that God lives in us and we in him – if there were no changes this would mean that he is dead, he does not exist).*

2. Changes are a result of a natural psychophysical development of a human being until the "mature" image of God is established (*this happens in stages, because a person develops; a grown up person establishes himself or herself in their faith in God and does not usually change, it is difficult to change for a person who really believes if this whole process takes place properly).*

3. Changes are dangerous (*there are sometimes situations in which a person is lost in his or her perception of God; I am a little worried because of the evil and confusion brought about by those postmodern books like* The Da Vinci Code)

B. Teachers of other confessions and religions:

What inspires you to think about God? Where do you look for inspiration of this kind?

1. Personal prayer and reading of the Scripture and religious texts (*the notion of God is formed very early and is read out directly from the Torah, which is the source; the writings of Church Fathers).*

2. The awareness of what God has done (*he sacrificed his own Son in order to save me, the Gospel of grace – beyond these, I do not usually look for inspiration; to me, the first thing is that He gave his life for me – that is why I do not look for inspiration, I already have it).*

3. The transience of life, the uncertainly of the future (*inspiration to spiritual, religious life comes the fact that life passes by; when I feel bad [the inspiration is] the fear of death, sometimes [it is] the fear of the future, and sometimes the fear that there is nothing out there; the thought that my time on earth will end one day).*

4. Contact with other religions and cultures (*visiting places connected with religious cult, not only protestant ones, what we teach at religion*

classes is the idea of multiculturalism, the fact that we are surrounded by people from various cultures and religions – this is also inspiring in my work).

5. Other people, including students, and their experiences (*I find it inspiring to see that God works, that something changed another person – that is when I want more – reaching out to people inspires me to look for ideas and opportunities; I look for them in real life events, when I see that this or that person needs God).*

6. Life experiences, difficult situations (*from the perspective of a forty-year-old, I can see some things in retrospect – this is the source of my inspirations; my everyday life – I have a family with three kids, which means facing challenges and struggles every way, especially facing my own weakness).*

How do new inspirations change your understanding of God?

1. God remains the same but becomes closer in the sense of conforming to the biblical message (*reading books and the Scripture somehow reinforces my conviction that this is the way things are; they do not seem to change my understanding of God in a significant way … it is not that He changes but is confirmed with every event I experience; they draw us closer to God or we are more established in the conviction that what we do, the path we have taken, is the soundest; obviously, within certain limits – this must always be in agreement with God's Word).*

2. The image of oneself and the surrounding reality is changed (*they change not so much the perception of God but the awareness of my own role in this world; seeking God has strongly changed my self-image: I started to see that I am not different from other people, I am not better than them).*

3. The image of God is changed (*I can see that God is not confined to some simple framework, that God is very, very diversified, and that people may think in various ways, totally different from mine; I do not see the total God and he is still dynamic, knowing him is operating in a dynamic sphere).*

4. God is a mystery, he is unknowable (*man has a limited understanding of everything, and of God in particular; Judaism gives no reasons to change our perception or understanding because it has no doctrine – we know that we do not know what the intentions of the Almighty are).*

How do you evaluate changes in your perception of God?

1. Change is desired development (*I can see that they found God in a different way, which expands my thinking about God; God's presence in life grows*).

2. Changes are a result of a natural psychophysical development of a human being until the "mature" image of God is established (*at the age of twenty one or twenty two this conviction is established and then, at least in my case, it is usually quite stable; I would say that the image of God matures as I grow older*).

3. Changes are dangerous (*when someone, as a result of his or her experience, starts to blame God, as it were, and views him as unhelpful ... I try to correct this change in the perception of God; just as God does not change, so the Church does not change either*).

Conclusion

It may be stated in general terms that the interviewed teachers of religion working with 13-16 year-olds in Gdańsk are aware of the changes taking place in the world. A number of them, however, see those changes as a threat to the religious identity conceived of in static terms because they assume it to be based on some established standards derived from the transcendent. Consequently, they are not open to inter-religious dialogue which could introduce new elements into the discursive structure, dynamizing the process of creating new meanings and developing the theological identity of the subject. Some respondents openly declare that in their case this process has been finished, others are only open to changes within the paradigms operating in their own traditions. Only a small group of the interviewed teachers looks for new inspirations to think about God, and only single individuals within that group in their search turn to other religions. This is true of both the Roman Catholic confession, dominant in Poland, as well as of the minority confessions and religions. It would certainly be interesting to compare this study with one focused on the openness to theological difference of students, representative of the young generation of Poles, living in the reality of the multicultural European Union. It may be suspected that the results of that study would be somewhat different.

Mirosław Patalon, Ph.D., is a professor of religious education at University of Gdansk, Poland where he is also a vice-dean of the Social Sciences Faculty. From 1989 to 2003 he was a pastor of Baptist churches in Wroclaw and Gdansk. He is the author of several books and articles on the philosophy of religion and the theory of education.

CONFESSIONS 2008

MINORU INADA

Introduction

The Nicene Creed, or "Credo" in short, survived for a long periods in days when people believed the Roman Catholic was the only authority.

However, in sixteenth century, a suspicion arose against authentic belief, questioning what the true belief is. Thinking peoples studied seriously their inner call for the true belief and proposed a new style of church system. In 1529, Martin Luther wrote "*Der grosse Katechismus*". And in 1530, Philip Melanchthon, a key leader of Lutheran Reformation, released "*Confessio Augustana*" by request from the Holy Roman Emperor Charles V.

After that, Christendom centering on the Roman Catholic Church quaked by the protestant reformation movement for over a century. Reformed church leaders tried to put their beliefs in their own languages and forms. French Confession, Scots Confession, Belgic Confession, on and on to the Westminster Confession of Faith in 1648.

These Confessions are formulated for the purpose of declaring the reformation movement is not heresies against the Roman Catholic Church. Before expressing disagreement with the Authority, they wanted to clarify that they stay within the Bible. Accordingly, content of those Confessions did not differ from the Bible stories. The Creation, Ten Commandments, Life of Jesus Christ and so on were reconfirmed. For example, Westminster Larger Catechism states the Creation as: The work of creation is that wherein God did in the beginning, by the word of his power, make of nothing the world, and all things therein, for himself, within the space of six days, and all very good.

Today, we cannot take statements of the Bible at their face value. They seem too much symbolized from scientific view point. As we live in an era of big-bang cosmology, we cannot but hesitate in admitting the truth of the Creation story. Don't we feel contradiction when we chant Credo or Confession in the church neglecting the scientific knowledge?

A new-type Confession complying with the modern scientific knowledge must be established. Stories of the Bible are to be understood as metaphors and parables. Literal approach may cause misunderstanding.

Existence of God

In 1781, Immanuel Kant wrote a book named *"Critique on Pure Reason"*, where he said that no one can really know whether there is or is not a God[1]. However, in 1788, he wrote another book named *"Critique on Practical Reason"*, where he said that supposition of God existence is very much required to know the effectiveness of moral principles.[2] De jure he cannot affirm the existence of God, but de facto he want to admit it. This is of course nothing more than a requisition, not a proof.

The above schematic shows my understanding of Kantian transcendental idealism, where filtering mind corresponds to Buddhist Manas-vijnana, the uncontrollable subconscious mind.

The agnosticism implies neither "Yes" nor "No". Kantian thought is remarked that it pushed the argument of God's existence to the brink of atheism and also restrained it there.

Beyond the epistemology — more human-centric

In 1844, in the era of unease about God's existence, Kierkegaard wrote *The Concept of Dread*. In that book he said "The mere fact that one has the possibility and freedom to do something, even the most terrifying of possibilities, triggers immense feelings of dread"[3]. This is the greatest anxiety, or the anxiety of existence charged to human beings. From our first father Adam to our selves, everybody may feel such an anxiety. This is the meaning of the Original Sin. To be freed from this feeling might be one of the reasons why people require Gods, religions or faiths.

Salvation is the main theme of world major religions. But it cannot be instantly understood when we are only told about Original Sin, Corruption, or Karman in Buddhism. Some body would say "Why should I be blamed for the disobedience which some strange body had committed before the Flood?" Kierkegaard gave us an answer to this qestion that we have anxiety of existence.

---

[1] Immanuel Kant, *Kritik der reinen Vernunft*, 1781, (Japanese translation).
[2] Immanuel Kant, *Kritik der praktischen Vernunft*, 1788, (Japanese translation).
[3] Søren Kierkegaard, *Begrebet Angest*, 1844, (Japanese translation).

In 1885, Friedrich Nietzsche wrote a book named *Thus spoke Zarathustra*. He declared "God is dead" and foretold that we develop ourselves towards the Übermensch, Superman[4]. The Übermensch is a man who requires no God, relies only on himself and assumes everything to himself. Or the Übermensch is a man who can carry on living with no contradiction or absurdity, or to the contrary, a man who can admit every contradiction and absurdity. This is one of the ways that can break through the sense of stagnation of the era.

But will the idea of Übermensch really work? Human beings endowed with insufficient talent might possibly not be able to reach both extremities, overcoming absurdity nor wholly accept it.

Rearrangement of metaphysics — A Proposal given by mathematicians

Transcendental idealism, which makes strict distinction between noumenon and phenomenon, was a challenge to the metaphysical philosophy represented by dogmatic and scholastic philosophy. Then, what is made to be knowable, and what is not?

Kant proposed that we have two types of reasons, one is empirical reason and the other is pure reason. Kant also set up transcendental idealism that supposes we cannot perceive noumena (things-in-themselves) but only phenomena (appearances of things), where both noumena and phenomena are confined to this physical world. The empirical reason builds various ideas and notions out of our experiences. However, it can do nothing about things when recognition targets do not come into perception field of our sensory organs. In other words, metaphysical beings are substantially unknowable to our empirical reason.

Then the pure reason comes in and tries to make a picture of a metaphysical object with hearing thousand words on it but without seeing it. The pure reason may sometimes paint a beautiful picture but sometimes paints ugly one which Kant named antinomy. The pure reason may even give opposing and incompatible dual answers to a single metaphysical question. Abstract ideas on existence of God or spatio-temporal limits of universe are the example of such antinomies. However, every time when metaphysical notions are spotlighted, the pure reason is called for, though its answers are neither definite nor clear.

Has the pure reason to fall silent, because of its uncertainty? No, it need not always go silent. The pure reason can work cooperatively with

---

[4] Friedrich Nietzsche, *Also sprach Zarathustra*, 1885, (Japanese translation).

the empirical reason to make answers more certain. Let us make a case for closer examination. The word "bravery" is an abstract idea and belongs to metaphysical world. To explain the word "bravery" to a man who has never seen brave actions will be a difficult work. But if the man had once seen a brave action, he could understand the word easier. What is more, if he had many times seen brave actions, he might be able to explain the word "bravery" to some other men. This case shows that the word "Bravery" is defined as a common property of a set of empirical information collected from brave actions, where the works of collection, classification and allocation are cooperatively done by the empirical reason. In case there is not any empirical information, the pure reason will solely work and make some notion in its own way, which will have, however, no guaranteed results. On the contrary, if sufficient empirical information was provided, the pure reason will work properly and make a beautiful picture. Here we should remember that word-definition or notion-building is deeply related with the set theory.

In 1918, Bertrand Russell wrote a book named *Introduction to Mathematical Philosophy* after collectively wrote *Principia Mathematica* with Whitehead in 1913. In this book he invented a way to define natural numbers based on set theory. For example, natural number "1" is defined as a common characteristic of a set of "singles". Natural number "2", that of "pairs"[5]. Before Russell, Peano axioms were known to be the definition of natural numbers in the way as; ... "0" is a natural number. For every natural number "n", S (n) is a natural number; where S (n) is a successor function or S (a) = a + 1.... .Peano axioms were in fact not an accurate way of definition. The important point of Russell's definition was that definition of any natural number did not require any help from other natural numbers. It coincides with the Whitehead's requirement "It is the ideal of speculative philosophy that its fundamental notions shall not seem capable of abstraction from each other"[6].

Nobody can answer to the question "Let me see the real existence of the natural number 1, if you say that it exists." But, fortunately it is also true that nobody denies its existence as a notion. This is because we can

---

[5] Bertrand Russell, *Introduction to Mathematical Philosophy*, 1918, (Japanese translation): The word 'Natural number "1" is defined as a common characteristic of a set of "singles"' is a simplified expression. In fact, he gave three words; 'One class is said to be "similar" to another when there is a one-one relation of which the one class is the domain, while the other is the converse domain.'; 'The number of a class is the class of all those classes that are similar to it.', and 'A number is anything which is the number of some class'.

[6] Alfred North Whitehead, *Process and Reality*, 1929, (Japanese translation).

see many examples of singles in this empirical world and we can perceive what the common characteristic of a set of singles means. In the same way as the natural number "1" is defined, the word "Bravery" can also be defined as the common characteristic of a set of tangible "brave actions".

But it is not the same case for defining the notion of "God". The notion of "God" could take the same form of definition as a common characteristic of a set of thoughts or feelings for some divine being that people cherish in their minds. But, thoughts and feelings can not be seen in the empirical world.

If God made His behaviors visible to us, we could easily get physical perception of God. Visible behaviors here mean mysterious experiences or miracles. However, divine behaviors cannot be verified because they cannot be shared with other persons. With any tangible means God will not show his existence to men on the street.

To define some notion by abstraction from other notion may violate the above mentioned Whiteheadian requirement and may cause an error. It has a chance to produce notions that are not based on the real existence at all.

Confession, again

We are going to make a picture named "Faith" based on retold stories and feelings on divine beings. Or, in case we were not endowed with talent of painting, we would try to learn about great painters and understand what their pictures mean. Admitting the God existence is unknowable to us in this real world, I would like to review the problem from the point of belief.

Nicene Creed was a grand-design to make the boundary between Christendom and heretical institutions. On this grand-design church leaders piled up complicated and intricate dogmas to answer questions arose from the laymen. However, providing consistent stories agreeable both to churchmen and to laymen would have been a hard work. Answers will induce other questions that demand further answers, and efforts to explain everything may cause a mistake.

Wise men say "lie is expedient." Both providers and recipients, answers for difficult questions should be given not by exact words but by metaphors. Answers will be found not in letters but in implied meanings.

For example, whatever noteworthy medical views were developed for Jesus' resurrection, people's faith seems not so much promoted. To this issue, Simone Weil said: "Resurrection, it is the Jesus' pardon to those who killed him"[7]. Much more substantial answer will be obtained by asking the meaning of the Resurrection instead of asking its medical possibility. In the similar meaning Buddhist's Samsara – Re-birth will serve as the consolation to the bereaved family.

To have a faith means to consent to a story that there is an ultimate Reality beyond all people, and the Reality wants to save everybody and fulfils everybody's wish for good wills. John Hick said: "The salvific transformation from natural self-centredness to a new orientation centred in God, the Transcendent, the Ultimate, the Real"[8]. Prayers for personal wishes will vanish in smoke. Straightforward words of "Help me out of this trouble" changes into "Thy will be done, in earth as it is in heaven" as we know in the Lord's Prayer.

John Hick introduced fair words of Julian of Norwich. She said: "All shall be well, and all shall be well, and all manner of thing shall be well"[9]. Her words indicate an ultimate acceptance of the God work. She lived in the 14th century England, when people suffered from pestilential turmoil. It is said however for Julian that suffering was not a punishment of God but a chance to have closer approach to God, which however was not the common understanding. I am wondering if she had been a Nietzsche's Übermensch.

Annihilating self-centeredness and believing in the ultimate Real comes up to the submission or zaraNa to Him. Here, the original meaning of zaraNa is said to be a refuge or shield, which we can find in the phrase "For thou, LORD, wilt bless the righteous; with favor wilt thou compass him as with a shield" in Psalter 5.12. It is the benefit of faith; one can say that he has a shield, as the last resort to save him when he came up against the massive wall.

Taking the faith for such zaraNa, we understand that the supplementary items around religions are no more than folktales based on individual culture, tradition and ethnicity. There is no need to believe that the world is made up in seven days but remember the wise men's word, "lie is expedient".

When we compare world various religions, we should not be too much absorbed in their differences. Removing folktales or anecdotes from them, only substantial part, namely deliverance from miseries, salvation or Shinto's purification, will remain. At that very moment the Rumi's word 'the lamps are different, but the Light is the same: it comes from Beyond.' will be attained.

---

[7] Simone Weil, *La Connaissance surnaturelle*, 1950, (Japanese translation).

[8] John Hick, *An Autobiography*, 2002, (Japanese translation).

[9] Julian of Norwich, *Revelations of Divine Love*, 1392.

I believe that metaphorical understanding of Holy Scriptures is one of the most effective ways to overcome differences between different religions and to make inter-religious understanding.

Discussions

1. Which way to choose?
Literal understanding of Holy Scriptures leads to Fundamentalism.
Metaphorical understanding of Holy Scriptures leads to Mysticism.
Kantian transcendental understanding of the world leads to Agnosticism.
Whiteheadian metaphysical understanding of the world leads to .....
Other ways of understanding .....

I would like to take metaphorical understanding, also seek the way of Whiteheadian understanding.

2. Pope Benedict XVI's words: "Kantian critique is 'self-limitation' of reason".
What it is able to say critically about Jesus is, so to speak, an expression of practical reason and consequently it can take its rightful place within the university. Behind this thinking lies the modern self-limitation of reason, classically expressed in Kant's "Critiques", but in the meantime further radicalized by the impact of the natural sciences.
Sept. 12, 2006, Regensburg lecture, cited from ZENIT
http://www.zenit.org/index.php?l=english

3. Examples of abstracted notions from each other
Is Purgatory abstracted from Heaven and Hell? Is it like a natural number '2' is given as the average of numbers '1' and '3'?

Metaphysics is a branch of philosophy that deals with empirically unknowable things. However, to tell about something unknowable possibly induces fabricated stories. Because of this suspicion or unreliability, metaphysics got left behind in the marvelous trend of scientific and technological development. When we aim to rehabilitate and reconstruct metaphysics, we must make efforts to recover its reliability. Below cited Whitehead's words denote the condition to substantiate the effectiveness of our efforts.

'Coherence,' as here employed, means that the fundamental ideas, in terms of which the scheme is developed, presuppose each other so that in isolation they are meaningless. This requirement does not mean that they are definable in terms of each other; it means that what is indefinable in one such notion cannot be abstracted from its relevance to the other notions. It is the ideal of speculative philosophy that its fundamental notions shall not seem capable of abstraction from each other. (*Process and Reality*)

Fundamental notions shall not be built as abstractions from other notions. Definition of natural numbers by Bertrand Russell is a successful example of the notion building that required no help from other notions. On the contrary, Peano axioms constitute no definition but only show a procedure to make a series of natural numbers with an indefinite starting point and an indefinite increment. Whereas Russell defines natural number "3" as a common characteristic of a set of "triples", Peano gives a natural number "3" (notion 'c') by making an addition (notion 'd') of natural number "1" (notion 'a') to a natural number "2" (notion 'b').

How about a religious notion "purgatory"? It is said to be the condition, process, or place of purification or temporary punishment in which the souls of those who die in a state of grace are made ready for heaven. But, it seems to me a compound of notions 'minor crimes', 'redemption', 'purification' and 'mediation' amidst a sharp contrast between 'heaven' and 'hell'. None of these notions are satisfactory defined. We'd better call it a competent example of fabricated stories.

Metaphysics' aim is to generalize, to collective interpret, or to constructive understand learnings from individual experiences. Generalized knowledge serves how to understand the meanings of similar experiences or to foretell the results of similar situations. If interpretation of an experience was confined to its own case, today's development of sciences and technologies was far from the actual status. Collective interpretation leads to constructive understanding of the world or the universe. It will not, however, permit arbitrary interpretation or notion building standing on a fanciful basis.

Minoru Inada is the chairman of Keio Study Group on Philosophy of Religions, an affiliate of Keio University, Japan.

WHAT NEW INSIGHT GIVES US WILBER'S INTEGRAL PHILOSOPHY/PSYCHOLOGY IN UNDERSTANDING THE WORLD?

PRZEMYSŁAW KOBERDA AND URSZULA STODOLSKA-KOBERDA

Introduction

It has been at least 150 years since Charles Darwin, initially in a scientific journal (1858) and then in a monograph (1859), described his conception of evolutionary variability across species. These and subsequent studies have made a great impact – comparable with the Copernican revolution – on the further development of knowledge about the descent of man and relations in the world we live in. It was the first time when the biological rules were applied to the man, which had enormous philosophical consequences. The thesis of having a common ancestor with anthropoid apes has started a revolution in outlook, and the modern perception of humankind as a part of nature and as a changing object of nature's processes is the result of it.

Nowadays the evolutionary theory, although in a much altered form in comparison to the original one, has become the basis for modern biology. However, it seems that the logic of the evolutionary development may have a much larger context. A number of psychological research studies convincingly show the depth of the human psyche development.[1] Similar conclusions have been reached in the fields of cultural anthropology[2] and

---

[1] Main field of evolutionary psychology with authors as Abraham Maslow, Jean Piaget, Lawrence Kohlberg, Carol Gilligan, Robert Kegan, Suzanne Cook-Greuter, among others.

[2] Jean Gebser, *The ever-present origin* (Athens: Ohio University Press, 1985; original work published 1949). Gebser describes five "structures of consciousness" as: archaic, magic, mythic, mental and integral.

sociology. These observations, together with the modern inflationary model of the cosmos, form the basis for more precise knowledge of the evolution of the Universe, the part of which is humankind and its development. Consequently, we get a basis for creating new, more relevant and more advanced philosophical theories.

Undoubtedly, one of the most noteworthy among them is an Integral AQAL model, also known as Integral philosophy/psychology, created by Ken Wilber, a modern American thinker and writer. Experts on his works appreciate his attempt to combine the achievements of modern scientific knowledge with metaphysics and the eternal search of the essence of human spirituality, which is present in every culture but in the eastern philosophies in particular.

Evolution

The widest meaning of the term "evolution" refers to the evolution of the universe – the domain of the cosmological research. On the present knowledge level the most probable is the Big Bang theory, assuming that some 13-14 milliards of years ago "our" part of the universe came into existence out of some cosmic oddity.

In the early phase of the birth of our world enormous amounts of energy turned into a very primitive form of matter which, as a result of further transformations, created the first simple elements with nuclear build – hydrogen and helium. The proceeding evolution of matter resulted in the creation of atoms with multi-layered electrons. Subsequently this enabled the creation of a whole range of variations of their combinations in the form of chemical compounds with more and more complex structure.

A vital moment in the process was first the creation of protein molecules and then cell membranes separating the interior from the environment and DNA as a replication matrix, which together initiated an evolutionary sequence of the development of life forms. On the basis of more and more advanced *structure* in which the central and coordinating element is the nervous system more and more advanced *functions* appeared, ranging from membrane excitability, simple sensory sensations and reflexes, through primitive reptilian emotionality, intuitive imagination appearing among mammals and operations on symbols among primates.

On the human level biology created a new quality which is *thinking*. Thinking is a basis for treating oneself as something separate from the environment and it lays foundations for ego. At the same time thanks to thinking man develops *consciousness* which, when understood in this way, presumably becomes the main axial element of the further evolution process. [fig. 1]

Fig. 1. Stages of Universe evolution

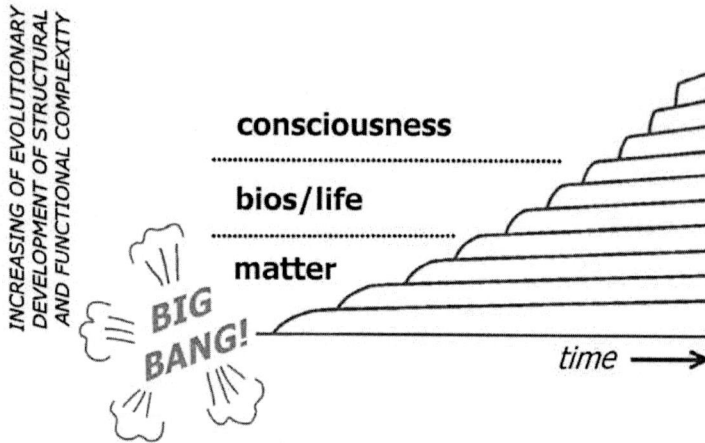

Spiral Dynamics (SD) of human consciousness evolution:

Spiral Dynamics argues that consciousness understood as a human nature is not fixed: humans are able, when forced by life conditions, to adapt to their environment by constructing new, more complex, conceptual models of the world that allow them to handle the new problems. Each new model includes and transcends all previous models.

Dr Clare W. Graves, professor of Union College in New York, and one of the author of Spiral Dynamics of human consciousness development idea explains:

I am not saying in this conception of adult behavior that one style of being, one form of human existence is inevitably and in all circumstances superior to or better than another form of human existence, another style of being. What I am saying is that when one form of being is more congruent with the realities of existence, then it is the better form of living for those realities. And what I am saying is that when one form of existence ceases to be functional for the realities of existence then some other form, either higher or lower in the hierarchy, is the better form of living. I do suggest, however, and this I deeply believe is so, that for the overall welfare of total man's existence in this world, over the long run of time, higher levels are better than lower levels and that the prime good of any society's governing figures should be to promote human movement up the levels of human existence.[3]

Tab. 4. Developmental levels of human consciousness according to Graves, Beck and Cowan[4]

THE LIVING STRATA IN OUR PSYCHO-CULTURAL ARCHEOLOGY				
Level	Color Code	Popular Name	Thinking	Cultural manifestations and personal displays
8	Turquoise	WholeView	Holistic	collective individualism; cosmic spirituality; earth changes
7	Yellow	FlexFlow	Ecological	natural systems; self-principle; multiple realities; knowledge
6	Green	HumanBond	Consensus	egalitarian; feelings; authentic; sharing; caring; community
5	Orange	StriveDrive	Strategic	materialistic; consumerism; success; image; status; growth
4	Blue	TruthForce	Authority	meaning; discipline; traditions; morality; rules; lives for later

[3] Clare W. Graves, "Levels of Existence: An Open System Theory of Values" *Journal of Humanistic Psychology* (November 1970), 34.
[4] Don Beck & Cristopher Cowan, *Spiral dynamics: Mastering values, leadership and change* (Oxford, UK: Blackwell, 1996), 41; also: www.spiraldynamics.net

3	Red	PowerGods	Egocentric	gratification; glitz; conquest; action; impulsive; lives for now
2	Purple	KinSpirits	Animistic	rites; rituals; taboos; super-stitions; tribes; folk ways & lore
1	Beige	SurvivalSense	Instinctive	food; water; procreation; warmth; protection; stays alive

Don Beck, younger college of Clare W. Graves and co-author of Spiral Dynamics idea describes it in words:

> Cultures, as well as countries, are formed by the emergence of value systems (social stages) in the response to life conditions. Such complex adaptive intelligences form the glue that bonds a group together, defines who they are as a people, and reflects the place on the planet they inhabit. These cultural waves, much like the Russian dolls (a doll embedded within a doll embedded within a doll) have formed, over time, into unique mixtures and blends of instructional and survival codes, myths of origin, artistic forms, life styles, and senses of community. While they are all legitimate expressions of the human experience, they are not 'equal' in their capacities to deal with complex problems in society.

> Yet, the detectable social stages within cultures are not Calvinistic scripts that lock us into choices against our will. Nor are they inevitable steps on a predetermined staircase, or magically appearing like crop circle structures in our collective psyche. And, cultures should not be seen as rigid types, having permanent traits. Instead, they are core adaptive intelligences that ebb and flow, progress and regress, with the capacity to lay on new levels of complexity (value systems) when conditions warrant. Much like an onion, they form layers on layers on layers. There is no final state, no ultimate destination, no utopian paradise. Each stage is but a prelude to the next, then the next, then the next.

> Each emerging social stage or cultural wave contains a more expansive horizon, a more complex organizing principle, with newly calibrated priorities, mindsets, and specific bottom-lines. All of the previously acquired social stages remain in the composite value system to determine the unique texture of a given culture, country, or society. In Ken Wilber's language, each new social stage 'transcends but includes' all of those

which have come before. Societies with the capacity to change, swing between "I:Me:Mine" and "We:Us:Our poles". Tilts in one direction create the need to self-correct, thus causing a shift toward the opposite pole. Me decades become us epochs as we constantly spiral up, or spiral down in response to life conditions. Some social stages stress diversity generators that reward individual initiatives and value human rights. Other social stages impose conformity regulators and reward cooperative, collective actions. Societies will zigzag between these two poles, thus embracing different models at each tilt.

Once a new social stage appears in a culture, it will spread its instructional codes and life priority messages throughout that culture's surface-level expressions: religion, economic and political arrangements, psychological and anthropological theories, and views of human nature, our future destiny, globalization, and even architectural patterns and sports preferences.[5]

Wilber's Integral model AQAL

Spiral Dynamics is only one but important component of Wilber's Integral model. The Integral model recognizes that there are at least four dimensions (perspectives, quadrants, aspects) to every occasion: the interior and exterior of the individual and the collective. Thus, a four-quadrant map of reality is created with the Left-Hand quadrants representing the interior aspects of the individual and collective while the Right-Hand quadrants represent the exterior aspects. Each quadrant uses its own injunctive examinations of reality to elucidate its partial truth.[6] [fig. 2]

The Integral model acknowledges the exterior and interior dimensions of individuals and groups. It includes a diverse and integrated array of methodologies for working with the material, measurable components of development as well as the interior, subjective dimensions of individuals and groups. None of these domains are "better" than any other; each one reflects an aspect of reality that contributes an *essential yet partial* piece to any development consideration.

Global history of civilization speaks a lot of these four areas of change. Wilber compiled this *co-evolution* or *tetra-evolution*. He explains how systemic changes progressed from foraging, to horticulture, to agrarian, to

---

[5] Don Beck & Cristopher Cowan, *Spiral dynamics: Mastering values, leadership and change* (Oxford, UK: Blackwell, 1996), 78-79.
[6] Wilber Ken, *Integral psychology: Consciousness, spirit, psychology, therapy.* (Boston: Shambhala, 2000), 112.

industrialization, to the informational age of the 21st century, can correspond with changes in individual's worldviews, from archaic, to magic, to mythic, to rational, to pluralistic, to integral, and onward. Personal changes that also emerged through this shared history include changes in our ways of knowing (from symbols, to concepts, to concrete operational, to formal operational, to visionlogic) and our values (from survival needs, to self care, to care for the group, to cross-cultural care, to care for all beings). As described by Wilber, evolution emerges in these four spheres of "I," "We," "It" and "Its". [fig. 3].

Fig. 2. Four perspectives of human psyche development (also pattern for all realities) according to Wilber

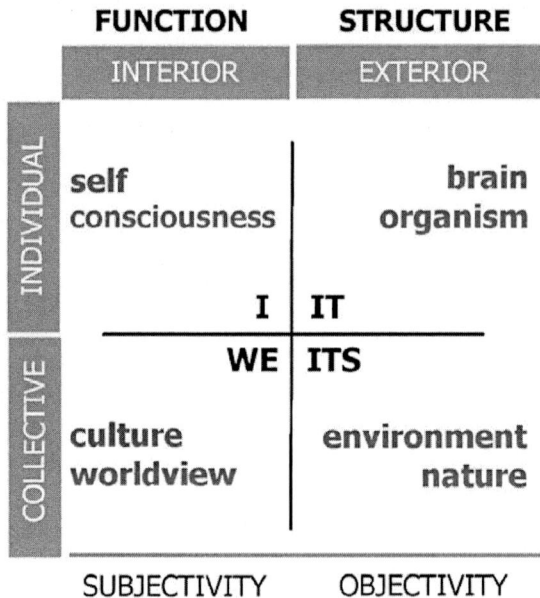

	FUNCTION	**STRUCTURE**
	INTERIOR	EXTERIOR
INDIVIDUAL	self consciousness	brain organism
	I	IT
COLLECTIVE	WE	ITS
	culture worldview	environment nature
	SUBJECTIVITY	OBJECTIVITY

The interior aspects of humanity that infuse our lives with meaning: dignity, aspiration, concern, sadness, exuberance, spiritual belief, and so on, are difficult to measure or quantify and thus tend to be excluded from scientific/rational way of thinking, characteristic for majority in current times.

Fig. 3. Evolutionary development in each of four perspectives (tetra-evolution) according to Wilber (with authors modifications)

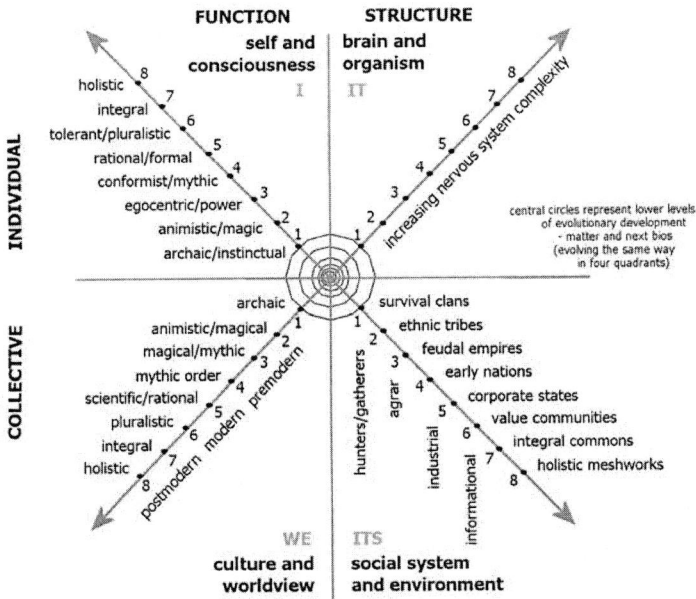

FUNCTION   STRUCTURE
self and   brain and
consciousness   organism
I   IT

INDIVIDUAL

holistic 8
integral 7
tolerant/pluralistic 6
rational/formal 5
conformist/mythic 4
egocentric/power 3
animistic/magic 2
archaic/instinctual 1

increasing nervous system complexity

central circles represent lower levels
of evolutionary development
- matter and next bios
(evolving the same way
in four quadrants)

COLLECTIVE

archaic 1
animistic/magical 2
magical/mythic 3
mythic order 4
scientific/rational 5
pluralistic 6
integral 7
holistic 8

premodern modern postmodern

survival clans 1
ethnic tribes 2
feudal empires 3
early nations 4
corporate states 5
value communities 6
integral commons 7
holistic meshworks 8

hunters/gatherers   agrar   industrial   informational

WE   ITS
culture and   social system
worldview   and environment

Conclusion

As Wilber puts it:

It is truly an extraordinary time—for the first time in history, all of the most important insights from all the world's cultures, spiritual traditions, arts, and sciences are available to just about anybody with an internet connection. Still wading in the shallow end the information age, even now we can be said to be experiencing somewhat of "an embarrassment of riches," surrounded as we are by a stupefying quantity of data, spilling forth from as many perspectives and fields of inquiry as we can possibly imagine. It can be easy to feel overwhelmed by this ocean of information, as many in fact do—after all, without an adequate map to make sense of all the billions of shouting voices in the world and throughout history, how can we possibly navigate ourselves through the world, or even to make sense of our own lives?

Fortunately, just such a map is finally beginning to emerge. The Integral map is the very first of its kind that is able to successfully synthesize all of the maddening complexity of the world, to identify the patterns that connect all of the seemingly disparate attempts to understand ourselves and our world, and to put all of the pieces of the universe together into a single jigsaw effigy of the human condition.[7]

"What is truth?", "what is goodness?", "what is beauty?". That has to be taken into consideration, that Integral framework provides a general orientation from which models or perspectives can be compared and synthesized, to better answer this timeless questions. Is Integral model pretends to be next step toward level of understanding the world we are living, as far as a spiritual and religious aspects of our existence?

Our life in the 21th century demands searching for modern and more efficient ways of communication. The Integral AQAL model is probably the simplest model that can handle all of the truly essential elements of all the aspects of world development. Thus it could offer a vital input for philosophical basis of inter-religious dialog.

Przemysław Koberda, MD is a physician and member of Polish Psychological Society, co-founder of Forum of Integral Development Society, Gdansk, Poland

Urszula Stodolska-Koberda, MD, PhD is an ophthalmologist, chief of Pediatric Ophthalmology Department in University Hospital in Gdansk, Poland; author of several scientific publications in the field of ophthalmology.

---

[7] Wilber Ken, *Sex, ecology, spirituality: The spirit of evolution* (Boston: Shambhala, 1995), 467.

ON MYSTIC EXPERIENCES OF SAINT HILDEGARD OF BINGEN

MAGDALENA OTLEWSKA

The word "mystique" previously belonged to the religious language. It meant "mystery". It was taken to philosophy in ancient times. Plato wrote about small and great mystery according to philosophy. He was an example of the connection between philosophy and personal religious life. The term mystique was moved into Christian writings thanks to the theological school of Alexandria. The term was used by Clemens of Alexandria and Origen. Pseudo-Dionysius the Aeropagite titled his work basing on direct knowledge of God: *Mystic Theology*. J. Misiurek[1] wrote, that the term mystique in theology seemed to have the connection with *mysterion*. In writings of Paul the Apostle the *mysterion* meant Jesus Christ. As well God's salutary plans, which came true in Jesus Christ.

The mystique can be described as a spiritual phenomenon which was known in different cultures and religions. It meant direct experience of divine transcendent reality. It can be divided into two kinds and levels. The first one is a sacramental cultic mystique which was meant for a greater group of people. The second – spiritual mystique – could be accessed by the chosen ones. The presumption of mystique is a secret relationship between a human being with a transcendent Divinity. Another presumption of mystique is this union not only in future life but also in mortal life. The relationship is realized completely in the mystic experience. This experience can be different each time. There are few kinds of it: it can be subjective *unio mystica*, the night of senses or ecstasy which meant the ascend of the soul and unity with God. There can be experiences which are more objective – for example visions on the character of revelations or prophecies. The last ones had been sensed by Hildegard of Bingen (1098-1179) – mystic and poet, prophet and

---

[1] Cf. Jerzy Misiurek, *Wielkie mistyczki Kościoła*, (Lublin: Redakcja Wydawnictw KUL, 1996), p. 9.

playwright, composer and scientist. Her century has rightly be called the greatest Christian Renaissance[2].

The experiences didn't have the character of a mystic union with God, they weren't ecstatic rapture, when one looses a contact with a surrounding world, but they were visions. She was a witness of the events which happened in the unnatural world. During these premonitions she got teachings from God. Later she was supposed to tell this teaching to other people. She herself called these experiences mystical and wrote about great God's secrets, which she saw and heard. She used the word mystic while writing about mystical shadow (*umbra*) or breath (*spiramen*)[3], which accompanied her visions.

Hildegard stressed the inspired origins of her works. She described herself as a feather which didn't have any weight and was carried by the wind[4]. The image of the relationship between God, the world and a human being can be seen through her visions. The structure of the material universe and a human microcosm is shown in her works with the whole moral, social and historical experience. Hildegard most often described the light sensation which were connected with the light form, a flame or aura. Only she could see them with her inner eyes. She wrote about living light, celestial brightness (*serena claritas*), or glitter (*splendor*)[5] which are shown in her paintings.

The similar character of the light have also her aural sensations, among them the most often are celestial (angelic) music and explanations of the seen images which were given by the voice from Heaven. In her visions it was the voice of God.

From my infancy up to the present time, I have always seen this light in my spirit and not with external eyes, nor with any thoughts of my heart nor with help from the senses. But my outward eyes remain open and the other corporeal senses retain their activity. The light which I see is not located but yet is more brilliant than the sun, nor can I examine its height, length, or breadth, and I name it the "cloud of the living light". And as sun, moon, and the stars are reflected in the water, so the writings, sayings, virtues,

---

[3] *Liber Divinorum Operum, Prologus* 27-28 [in :] S. Hildegardis abbatissae *Opera omnia, Patrologia Latina t. 197*, Turnhout 1980.
3,,Quatinus velut penna, que omni gravedine virium caret et que per ventum volat, ab ipso sustinear ." *Vita* I, 8 [w:] S. Hildegardis abbatissae, *Opera omnia, Patrologia Latina t. 197*, Turnhout 1997f.
[5] *Scivias, Prologus* [in:] PL 197, 387.

and works of men shine in it before me. Likewise I see, hear, and understand almost in a moment and I set down what I thus learn...[6]

It is appropriate to remember Hildegard with light imagery since that is how she describes her spiritual awakening.

When I was forty two years and seven months old, a burning light of tremendous brightness coming from heaven poured into my entire mind. Like a flame that does not burn but enkindles, it inflamed my entire heart and my entire breast, just like the sun that warms an object with it rays". What did this illumination do for Hildegard? "All of a sudden, I was able to taste of the understanding of the narration of books. I saw the Psalter clearly and the evangelists and other catholic books of the Old and New Testaments[7].

Hildegard was overcome by this experience of intuition, connection-making, and insight.

Hildegard's spiritual awakening is not without parallels in other cultures. Mircea Eliade in examining the phenomena of cosmic illuminations, draws some general conclusions: "It is important to stress that whatever the nature and intensity of an experience of the Light, it always evolves into a religious experience. All types of experience of the Light have this factor in common: they bring a man out of his worldly Universe or historical situation, and project him into a Universe different in quality, an entirely different world, transcendent and holy". The essence of the universe is now spiritual. The following results is fundamental to all these awakenings. "Whatever his previous ideological condition, a meeting with the Light produces a beak in the subjective existence, revealing to him the world of Spirit, of holiness and of freedom, in brief, existence as a divine creation, or the world sanctified by the presence of God"[8].

The Holy Spirit as a cosmic principle, as the inherent life of the universe, occurs in Hildegard's sequence *O ignis spiritus paracliti*. For instance , in the forth pair in sequence to the Holy Spirit, who is defined at the beginning as "life of life in every creature", *vita vitae omnis creature*, the Spirit is characterized first as an irresistible force that penetrates the universe from without; then, in the complementary half stanza, as a source of motion and fertility within natural world. When the pervasive power has

---

[6] *Epistola* 103, [in:] PL 197, 145-382 (Epistolae), ed. L. van Acker, pars I ep. I-XC, CCCM 91, Turnhout 1991.

[7] *Vita sc. Hildegardis* II,1,[in:] PL 197, 338-738.

[8] Mircea Eliade, *Traktat o historii religii*, (Łódź: Wydawnictwo OPUS, 1993), p. 262, (my own translation).

moved from the circumference of the cosmos right to its center, it becomes
the center-point from which new elemental life radiates.

> Most mighty course
> that penetrated all things
> in the heights and in the world
> and in the abysses-
> you harmonize and gather up all:
>
> From you clouds stream out,
> The pure air flies, the stones
> Have their moisture,
> Through you the waters dilate their brooks.
> And the earth floods with greenness[9].

Hildegard broadens our understanding and practice of psychology. For
her, psychology is not the mere coping with ego problems but the relating
of microcosm and macrocosm. She sees the human body and the human
psyche as creation in miniature. We are in the cosmos and the cosmos is in
us. "Now God has built the human form into the world structure, indeed
even into the cosmos," she declares, "just an artist would use a particular
pattern in her work"[10]. If this is so, then we are interdependent with all of
creation and it is from this law of interdependence that truly wise living
will be learned and practiced. This law of the universe Hildegard declares
in the following manner: "God has arranged all things in the world in
consideration of everything else"[11].

Hildegard offers a radical opportunity for global ecumenism because
she is so true to her own mystical roots and her own creative process. To
ground ourselves in tradition is the best and the most certain way to be
ecumenical in the fullest sense. Readers of Hildegard's illuminations will
see many examples of mandalas, those "maps of the cosmos", developed
in the East as well as in the medieval West to "liberate the consciousness"
and return us to a primeval consciousness which is fundamentally one of
unity. Clearly Hildegard's illuminations played the role with herself, a role
of reintegration and holistic relating, which is her intention in sharing them

---

[9] The text of the sequence is translated by Peter Dronke, [in:] Peter Dronke, *Poetic
individuality in the middle ages*, Oxford 1970, page 159. This is the latain version:
"O iter fortissimum, quod penetravit omnia, in altissimis et in terrenis et in
omnibus abyssis – tu omnes componis et colligis: De te nubes fluunt, ether volat,
lapides humorem habent, aquae rivulos educunt, et terra viriditatem sudat".
[10] *Scivias* II, 1, 2.
[11] *Liber Divinorum Operum* I ,3, 16.

with others, that they too may be healed. For Hildegard, her mandalas become a primary means by which the microcosm/ macrocosm, the human and the universe, are brought together again.

Tucci comments on: "In the space of the heart, magically transfigured into cosmic space, there takes place the rediscovery of our interior reality, of that immaculate principle which is out of our reach, but from which is derived – in its illusory and transcendent appearance – all that is in process of becoming"[12].

She helps us to broaden our understanding of ecumenism bringing together all the creativity of the human being in touch with the cosmos.

This is the drama Hildegard felt deeply and for her it is the primary focus of her mandalas and drawings: the drama of creation unfolding in the human "I have exalted humankind", she cites the Creator as saying with the Vocation of creation. Humankind alone is called to co-create. And she warns humanity "All nature is at disposal of humankind. We are to work with it. Without it we cannot survive"[13].

Humans become the musical instruments of God. The divine Spirit makes music through us.

Hildegard is not only a mystic; she is also a prophet and she sees herself and her work consciously and deliberately as prophetic. She herself described what the prophet was and in doing so described her own life. "Who are prophets? They are a royal people, who penetrate mystery and see with the spirit's eyes. In illuminating darkness they speak out"[14]. Hildegard spoke out. For no one was more in tune with symphony of the universe than she. No period in human history in the West was more awakened to the divine in nature than Hildegard's century. The simplest but not the least significant evidence of this discovery of nature was their perception the universe as an entity, the sacramental character of the universe. Hildegard is rich in expressing the internal holiness of being. For example, she writes:

> I, the fiery life of divine wisdom, I ignite the beauty of the plains, I sparkle the waters, I burn in the sun, and the moon, and the stars. There is no creation that does not have a radiance. Be it greenness or seed, blossom or beauty, it could not be creation without it. (…) The word is living, being,

---

[12] Matthew Fox, *Hildegard of Bingen: Cosmic Christ, Religion of Experience*, page 2, [in:] *http://www.sol.au/kor/5_02b.htm.*

[13] *Liber Divinorum Operum* I, 4, 14.

[14] *Vita* II, 2.

spirit, all verdant greening, all creativity. All creation awakened, called, by the resounding melody God's invocation of the word[15].

Hildegard led into rich world of symbolism. Eliade believes that the person "who understands a symbol not only opens himself to the objective world, but at the same time succeeds in emerging from his personal situation and reaching a comprehension of the universal". Paradox and personal experience, systematic imagination and diverse levels of meaning, cosmos and world patterns, are all expressed by symbol. Entering into Hildgegard's symbolism awakens the rich symbolic treasury of Christian history. Her century was peculiarly saturated with a symbolic consciousness, as Professor Chenu points out. "At stake is the discernment of the profound truth that lies hidden within the dense substance of things and is revealed by these means"[16]. We cannot understand Hildegard without understanding this symbolist mentality of her times. The same people read the Grail story and the homilies of St. Bernard, carved the capitals of Chartres and composed the bestiaries, allegorized Ovid and scrutinized the typological sense of Bible, or enriched their Christological analyses of the sacraments with naturalistic symbols of water, light, eating, marriage. What was at stake in all symbolizing was the mysterious kinship between the physical world and the realm of the sacred.

Magdalena Otlewska graduated from the University of Wrocław, Poland, Departament of Philosophy.

---

[15] *Liber Divinorum Operum* I, 1.
[16] See Matthew Fox OP, *Illuminations of Hildegard of Bingen* ,Bear & Company, Santa Fe, New Mexico 1985, page 47.

THE MEANING OF HEART IN CHRISTIAN AND INDIAN MYSTICS IN THE PHILOSOPHY OF BORIS VYSHESLAVTSEV

MARTA KUTY

In this essay I would like to make some brief remarks about the symbol of heart in the philosophy Boris Vysheslavtsev. His major accomplishments include elaboration of a 'philosophy of heart'[1]: his books *Serdtse v khristianskoi i indiiskoi mistike (The heart in Christian and Indian mysticism*, 1929), *Vechnoe v russkoj filosofii (The Eternal in Russian Philosophy)*[2] represent the first systematic attempt at an Orthodox interpretation of this problem.

The notion of „heart" occupies the central place in the mystics, religion and poetry of all the nations[3]. The idea of the heart (*smysl or self, ego*) is the irrational source of personality[4], the centrality of a person. The heart is a place of communication with God, and what is more, the heart is the home of the Divine, the origin of the personality. We know that for science and rationalism the *smysl* is not perceptible. When we mean to describe *smysl* we usually use metaphors and symbols, as for example the biblical term - „heart", which is mysterious, deep, accessible only to God. „The heart is deep" (Ps 64:6) – a very important text in Orthodox spirituality – means that the human person as a whole is the biggest mystery. The human heart is a secret. It is the puzzle and its solution should be added.[5] However, those terms are only approximate. In the

---

[1] It is necessary to note that the Russian „philosophy of heart" was developed by Theophanes the Recluse, Hryhorij Skoworoda, Fyodor Dostoevsky, Ivan Alexandrovich Ilyin, Semen Lyudvigovich Frank, Paul Alexandrovich Florensky, Nikolai Berdyaev, and Boris Vysheslavtsev.
[2] The article *The Meaning of the Heart in Religion* in his book *Vechnoe v russkoj filosofii.* (New York 1955).
[3] Boris Vysheslavtsev, *Vechnoe v russkoj filosofii* in his *Etika preobrazhennago Erosa* (Moskwa: Respublika, 1994), 271.
[4] Boris Vysheslavtsev, *Vechnoe v russkoj filosofii*, 285.
5 See books of Nikolai Berdyaev.

Bible we read that there is fullness of spirituality in the heart. In the Bible and in the common parlance of various peoples, the term "heart" conveys the fullness of the life of the spirit. There is not a case, that „the Greeks, being intellectuals by nature, substituted the biblical term *lev, levav* with *noùs* (mind, intellect)"[6]. Hence, classic definition of prayer is „the elevation of the mind to God."[7] In Vysheslavtsev's opines *cordatus homo* does not mean cordial person but rational person.[8] „According to Saint Thomas Aquinus, the New Testament precept of loving God with all one's heart meant *actus voluntatis qui hic significatur per cor.*"[9]

The Indian mystics placed the spirit of man, his real *ego*, in the heart. In fact, in Vysheslavtsev's opines, *ego* is the source of human activity, and the hearth of all human forces: spiritual, mental, and physical. „The heart is not only a physiological organ, but also an ontological origin beyond all rationality, in which the real autonomy of a person lies."[10] The heart is not the same as the emotional center of the psychologists. Vysheslavtsev writes it „consists in the fact that for it the mind, intellect or reason is never the final basis, the foundation of life; intellectual reflection about God is not authentic religious perception. The Church Fathers and the Russian staretzy give the following instruction for a genuine religious experience: 'one must stand with the mind in the heart'."[11]

His conception of heart and its role in the life of human beings is seen as a source of human spiritual life as a whole. It is „the absolute center", metaphysical center, „the center not only of consciousness but of the unconscious, not only of the soul but of the spirit, not only of the spirit but of the body, not only of the comprehensible but of the imcomprehensible; in one word, it is the absolute center."[12] The heart is all-embracing, a symbol of wholeness, integration, and totality, signifying a human person as an undivided unity. By the 'heart' Vysheslavtsev and traditional Christian and Indian Mystics mean not only our emotional nature, but the ontological super-rational principle in which our true selfhood consists. When the Hesychasts of the Christian East speak about „prayer of the

---

[6] Tomas Spidlik, *The Spirituality of the Christian East: A Systematic Handbook,* (Kraków: OO.Franciszków „Bratni Zew", 2005), 148.
[7] Tomas Spidlik, *Myśl rosyjska. Inna wizja człowieka*, (Warszawa: Księży Marianów, 2000), 340.
[8] Boris Vysheslavtsev, *Vechnoe v russkoj filosofii*, 204.
[9] Tomas Spidlik, *The Spirituality of the Christian East,* 148.
[10] Boris Vysheslavtsev, *The heart in Christian and Indian mysticism* in *Voprosy filosofii* 4 (1990), 69-70.
[11] Ibid., 69.
[12] Ibid., 68.

heart", they have in mind prayer of the whole person (spirit, soul, body). Macarius, who embodied the mystical hesychastic tradition, said:

> 1. The heart is first of all the central and controlling element in our physical structure: 'The heart directs and governs all the other organs of the body' (H.15:20). When the heart ceases to function, bodily death ensues.
> 2. The heart is likewise the place in which the intellect is situated: 'For there, in the heart, the mind (nous) abides as well as all the thoughts of the soul and all its hopes' (H.15:20). In Macarius' symbolic scheme, there is no dichotomy between head and heart: we think with our heart.
> 3. The heart includes what we today designate as 'the unconscious', whether personal or collective.
> 4. As moral center, the heart is the point where grace and sin are experienced: 'There is found the office of justice and of injustice. There is death and there is life' (H.15:32).
> 5. The heart is in this way also the point of self-transcendence where we encounter God. It is 'the palace of Christ', where he 'sets up his Kingdom' (H.15:33).[13]

Atman is a certain unifying factor of all creatures which live. Interpreted in this way, the heart is far more than a material organ in the body; the physical heart is an outward symbol of the boundless spiritual potentialities of the human creature, made in the image of God, called to attain his likeness.

The idea of the Self in "the heart" is certainly common in the Hindu thought. Indian mystics believed that heart is the locus of the self – Atman. The Brahmasutrabhasya IV.3 talks about a self in the heart:

> Which is the self ?' 'This infinite entity (Purusha) that is identified with the intellect and is in the midst of the organs, the (self-effulgent) light within the heart (intellect). Assuming the likeness (of the intellect), it moves between the two worlds; it thinks, as it were, and shakes, as it were. Being identified with dream, it transcends this world – the forms of death (ignorance etc.). (Brahmasutrabhasya IV. 3-7)[14]

Other references are in the Chandogya Upanishad III.14:

> This self (atman) of mine that lies deep within my heart - is smaller than a grain of rice or barley, smaller than a mustard seed, smaller even than a millet grain or a millet kernel; but it is larger than the earth, larger than the

---

[13] George A. Maloney (ed.), *Pseudo-Macarius: The Fifty Spiritual Homilies and the Great Letter*, (Paulist Press, New York 1992), XVI.
[14] Boris Vysheslavtsev, *Vechnoe v russkoj filosofii*, 275.

intermediate region, larger than the sky, larger even than all these worlds put together. This self (atman) of mine that lies deep within my heart - contains all actions, all desires, all smells, and all tastes; it has captured this whole world; it neither speaks nor pays any heed. (Chandogya Upanishad III.14)[15]

The philosopher Shankara says that Brahman "in the heart" is a form in which we are to meditate upon Brahman. We read:

The Purusha[16], the inner Self, of the size of a thumb, is ever seated in the heart of all living beings. (Kathopanishada VI.17)[17]
The person (purusha) not larger than a thumb, dwelling within, always dwelling in the heart of man, is perceiving by the heart, the thought, the mind, they who know it become immortal" (Svetasvataropan. III, 13) and „The self, smaller than small, greater than great, is hidden in the heart of a creature. A man who has left all grief behind, sees the majesty, the Lord, the passionless, by the grace of the creator (the Lord). (Svetasvataropan. III,20)[18]

According to Vysheslavtsev, Atman is brahman because atman as the essence of a being is the essence of Brahman in all things in the cosmos, and it is everywhere and in all things, it also lies within each individual's heart. Brahman in all things is the microcosm and the macrocosm. We can say that it is the mirror of the universe. Hindus call Brahman that dwells within all beings – the True Self. Atman is the true Self when one realizes the truth of its identity with Brahman. Thus the Upanishads state – "This Atman within my heart is that Brahman". We can say that the Self is the microcosm and the Brahman the macrocosm, and everything that exists can be found in either one, but the individual Self it is only a drop of water in the ocean.[19]

The heart is a place of union of God with man, a place of communication between people. S.L. Frank wrote about heart as a place of contact of two worlds and of intimate knowledge (*Real'nost' i chelovek*. Paris, 1956, p. 205). For heart has a two-fold significance in the spiritual life: it is both the centre of the human being and the point of meeting between a human being and God. It is both a place of self-knowledge, where we see ourselves as we truly are, and the place of self-transcendence, where we understand our nature as a temple of the Holy

---

[15] Ibid.
[16] „The first man"-Parusha was called Brahma.
[17] Boris Vysheslavtsev, *Vechnoe v russkoj filosofii*, 276.
[18] Ibid.
[19] Ibid., 278.

Trinity, where the image comes face to face with the Archetype. Heart is the point of meeting between human freedom and divine grace. If the heart is the center of a human person, we can establish relation with all that exists by the truth-loving and pure heart. In B. Vysheslavtsev's view, the heart makes a dialogue possible. He says that *smysl* in internal experience of man finds expression in statements which relate to the self – the body, the mind, and the soul. Man wanting to grasp the *smysl*, the *smysl* of the other man, must experience love which is the mediator and makes a dialogue possible. In such a love man can realize the image and likeness of God and can make the ideas of God-human real.

Vysheslavtsev was persuaded that he found a strong support from Pascal (Ch.12), and, indeed, the kinship of Pascal's thought with Orthodox tradition was pointed out more than once. His other Western forerunner was Max Scheler who "was actually the first philosopher to discover Pascal's idea about the „logic of the heart."[20] He constructed his own theory of values on the basis of this idea, a theory that was further developed by Hartmann and reflected in the psychology of Jung. Scheler showed that "values are arranged in a specific hierarchical order."[21] For Pascal, the idea of value is realized in the heart and feelings, but not in mathematical, logical (theoretical) reason. The heart has its own logic which is not the logic of mind. The heart has the proper order – spiritual order:

> The heart of man is microcosm of the world of values and it has its own logic just as the mind has its own logic. The heart's logic is not a chaos of blind feeling-states; the heart has its own laws and understanding of the order of things towards which the mind may be deaf and blind. The heart has its own judgment and is able to love or hate just as blindly or insightfully as the mind does.[22]

The heart transcends and cognizes God by love. Real love does not change, in the course of time or by external and internal changes in a man, because this feeling is directed towards these elementary signs, towards the *smysl,* which transgresses them:

> Love is that movement wherein every concrete individual object that possesses value achieves the highest value compatible with its nature and ideal vocation; or wherein it attains the ideal state of value intrinsic to its

---

[20] Ibid., 294.
[21] Ibid.,160.
[22] Max Scheler, *Selected Philosophical Essays*, (Evanston: Northwestern University Press, 1973), 116-117.

nature. (Hatred, on the other hand, is a movement in the opposite direction).[23]

The heart discovers and cognizes values in the ideal world. The free act of choice is deep-rooted in the logic of the heart and the logic of values. Man in his own heart and with his own sensitivity to values can realize them and determine what is real. Man has contact with values by feelings; only to feelings can values be manifested. Faith give birth to the emotional sphere. Thus the „pure" heart makes the dialogue possible and leads to the unity of people and the oneness of hearts. In Jeremiah 17:9-10 we can read:

> The heart is deceitful above all things
> and beyond cure.
> Who can understand it?
> I the LORD search the heart
> and examine the mind,
> to reward a man according to his conduct,
> according to what his deeds deserve.

The natural desire of the heart is to aspire to Beauty, Truth, and Good. And that trinity is the perfect foundation of the creation-loving community (*sobornosti*), in which man will be able to realize his personhood and the Divine Humanity. The heart is the „house of the Divine". Only in the heart a primary, religious experience is possible, without them there's no place to religion and true ethics. „The heart is a sanctuary at the center of which there is a little space wherein the Great Spirit dwells, and this is the Eye. This is the Eye of the Great Spirit by which He sees all things, and through which we see Him. If the heart is not pure, the Great Spirit cannot be seen." (Black Elk)[24]. According to the Russian philosopher Boris Vysheslavtsev, the Hindus or the Christians understand that the divine is beyond us and around us, they know that God dwells in their hearts. „The heart is a symbol of our personal unity, the center where physical and non-material, created and uncreated converge. It is the point of meeting: between body and soul; between unconscious and conscious; between human freedom and divine grace."[25]

---

[23] Max Scheler, *The Nature of Sympathy*, (Hamden, CT: Archon Books, 1970), 161.

[24] Michael Oren Fitzgerald, Judith Fitzgerald (eds.), *Indian Spirit: Revised and Enlarged*, (World Wisdom, 2006), 5.

[25] George A. Maloney (eds.), *Pseudo-Macarius:The Fifty Spiritual Homilies and the Great Letter,* XVI-XVII.

In Eastern spirituality, the heart is not an organ that is different from the intellect and will, but it is a symbol expressing the integrity and the wholeness of man. We cannot experience true knowledge through intellect only, and realize true morality of one's own free will. We cognize the Absolute truth by the entire person – with all of his or her faculties and cognitive instruments. In Russia intellectuals intentionally defended faith in heart, because it was a reaction against Hegel's philosophy, against Western rationalism in general. The spiritual ideal is *katastatis* (prayer). Spiritualists say that the only true prayer is the prayer from the heart.

In Vysheslavtsev's opines, the contemporary people have got a „heart villainess", they lost the „higher knowledge of the heart", the ability to distinguish between good and evil, they are value-free society.[26] He thinks that thinkers like Marx and Freud cannot participate in true sublimation because for them the sacrum, spiritual values are illusions.[27] The solution to such a problem of deafness and blindness is faith and love, which can be found in the „religion of love" – Christianity and Hinduism since they broaden and deepen the ethical judgment.[28]

Marta Kuty is a Ph.D. Candidate at the Institute of Philosophy of the University of Wrocław, Poland.

---

[26] Boris Vysheslavtsev, *Vechnoe v russkoj filosofii,* 213-214.
[27] Ibid., 220.
[28] Ibid., 214.